CHILD
FROM HOME

CHILD FROM HOME

MEMORIES OF A NORTH COUNTRY EVACUEE

JOHN T. WRIGHT

The
History
Press

First published 2009

The History Press
The Mill, Brimscombe Port
Stroud, Gloucestershire, GL5 2QG
www.thehistorypress.co.uk

British Library Cataloguing in Publication Data.
A catalogue record for this book is available from the British Library.

ISBN 978 0 7524 5229 6

Printed in Great Britain

Contents

Acknowledgements

The author extends his sincere thanks to all of those that have given so generously of their memories and time, which have proven invaluable in the compiling of this book. Whilst space prevents my listing all of them, I wish to acknowledge the particular contributions made by Catherine Brown (Kitty) of Pickering; Monica Tingle of Hartburn, Stockton-on-Tees; Eric Ward of Orpington; Stan Ward of Brotton; Alan Clark of York; Maud Eskriett of Haxby; Brian Mann of Haxby; Angela Hewins of Harbury; Irene Reynolds (Aunt Renee) and my cousins Jimmy Nolan and Keith Reynolds. Especial thanks go to my long-suffering wife, Enid.

I wish to dedicate this memoir to my wife and family, not forgetting my cousin Jimmy, who was more like a brother to me at that time.

Preface

Our deeds still travel with us from afar
and what we have been makes us what we are.
George Eliot (1819–1880)

As I entered the winter of my life I found myself reflecting on what had happened to me in my childhood, in what seems an age ago. In order to recall the old days I would need to penetrate the fog of the years and get inside the mind of the boy I once was. I would have to reassemble and set down my dim, swirling thoughts and vague half memories in some sort of chronological order. It seemed to me that it would be a great pity if my wartime experiences should be lost and gone forever.

Family stories passed down through the years can be inaccurate, with the true facts elusive and difficult to verify. Although there is now snow on the roof, I thought that I should make the effort while there was still a little fire in the grate. I felt that I had to get it written down before life's fast-moving currents pulled me under. Life is never a closed book; words can be powerful weapons that can help bring to life the thoughts and feelings of days long gone. To be a youngster living through a global war is an incomparable experience; a time of great emotional upheaval and change, and I felt it deserved to be recorded and preserved.

I have been fortunate enough in recent years to make contact with various people from my past, some of whom I had not seen or heard of for over sixty years. Their recollections of those distant times have been invaluable. Looking back can stir up mixed emotions – some painful and some pleasant. The pleasant and poignant memories tend to linger in our minds and seem eager to come out, but the sad and painful ones crouch in the deep recesses.

Questions arise: How permanent are the experiences and associations of childhood? How much bearing do they have on our later lives? To my mind, what happens in the first ten years of life can never be eradicated. We all carry the past within us; it is in our blood and our bones. So as not to hurt or upset relatives and descendants, I have changed the names of certain people.

War makes victims of us all. Some, like me, have lived through events that changed the world forever. Our daily lives were lived out within the turmoil of a world conflict; our small commonplace acts were carried out against a backdrop of world-shattering events and it is the little things that make the story whole. I have thoroughly enjoyed this journey into the past and hope it will be of some interest to others.

I feel that younger people should be aware of those dark years when the world went mad, in order to shape a better future and not make the same mistakes. I hope that my memoir will serve as a small tribute to those who died too soon.

I

Beginnings

'Come on sweetheart, up you go!' said my mother as – with George balanced in the crook of her left arm – she helped me up the wooden steps. Never having been on a steam train before, we were thrilled at the thought of the great adventure to come. As I reached the sill of the carriage I kept a tight grip on my wooden Tommy gun. It had a spring and a ratchet that made a loud rat-a-tat noise when the handle was turned. This much-treasured toy, made by Dad five months earlier, had been a present for my fourth birthday and I really loved it. My brother George, who was two, clung on to his ragged teddy bear – the authorities had stated that we were to take only one toy each. Mam gripped the vertical handle beside the door and pulled herself up into the maroon and cream railway carriage. The long, plush, upholstered seats of the third-class carriage had a slightly fusty smell.

Mam had another six toddlers to look after apart from us and, after getting us seated, she heaved the heavy brass-handled door shut. She pulled down the long leather strap to close the window and fitted the hole in it over the brass peg to keep it shut. She hoisted our meagre items of luggage onto the netting of the brass-railed rack, checking at the same time that she looked respectable in the long rectangular mirrors screwed to the wall. Shortly afterwards, a railway guard appeared wearing a shiny, black-nebbed cap, a brass-buttoned waistcoat and trousers of the same thick, heavy, black material. After slamming shut any doors that remained open, he blew loudly and shrilly on his whistle, waved a green flag above his head and clambered into the guard's van. The great beast snorted as its pistons squirted out clouds of steam and the glinting, well-oiled, steel rods began to force the huge wheels into motion. Very slowly we began to move and the great black train groaned as it heaved its fully laden carriages out of the station and we were off, blissfully unaware that we were never to see our house or our pet tortoise again.

Gradually the train settled into a clanking diddly-dee, diddly-da rhythm as it picked up speed. We gazed out at the ugly squalor of our sprawling industrial town. The old smoke-blackened buildings on the outskirts of Middlesbrough were far from pretty, and were certainly showing their age. We were on the North-Eastern Railway line – designed by the renowned railway engineer George Stephenson – one of the first in Britain. Ramshackle allotments lined the tracks.

A month earlier, on 3 September 1939 to be precise, war had been declared and, thankfully, none of our family had the slightest inkling of the dire consequences for us. On that sunny Sunday morning after Mam had turned the knob on our Ecko wireless set in its brown Bakelite casing, it took five minutes for the humming, glowing, glass valves to warm up sufficiently for it to operate. Bakelite was the only material that could be moulded at the time the set was made and it was called a wireless as it was powered by a heavy, electric accumulator – a kind of transparent, wet cell battery made of thick glass in which a row of vertical lead plates submerged in sulphuric acid could be seen. It had to be recharged (for a small fee) every two weeks or so.

Two days earlier the government had closed down all the regional broadcasting stations to ensure that everybody would have to listen to the new BBC Home Service. Dad was not with us as he had rejoined the army the previous year. While on leave, he had made a rectangular wooden box with a secure handle, which Mam used to carry the accumulator to Rogers' electrical shop on nearby Newport Road whenever it needed charging. The wireless and the accumulator were rented from there and a heavy, fully charged accumulator was brought home in its stead.

At 11.15 on that fine morning, the two of us had sat by the wireless with our mother and her teenaged sister. Renee was at our house more often than she was at her own; she was a great help to Mam and we loved being with her. We were dressed in our Sunday best having just come back from the service at St Cuthbert's Church where, in his sermon, the vicar had reminded the large congregation to listen to their wireless if they had one. In a solemn tone of voice, he had told them that, 'BBC broadcasts are being made at fifteen-minute intervals and an announcement of national importance will be made soon. Let us pray that the news will not be too bad. Hope springs eternal in the human breast. God bless you all!'

Mam held us very close as she sat riveted to the set and we eventually heard the reedy, tired-sounding voice of our seventy-year-old Prime Minister, Neville Chamberlain. Mam had once said to Renee, 'Some folk call him "the undertaker" because of his grim and severe appearance, but his old-fashioned black tailcoat and out-of-date wing collar don't help matters. Since last year's meeting with Hitler in Munich he has lost all credibility, but I'm sure he thought that he was doing his best for the country at the time.' He gravely ended his announcement to the nation with the words, '… consequently, this country is at war with Germany!'

We were too young to understand what it was all about and as Mam switched off the wireless she looked bewildered and stunned. The fact that war had finally arrived must have been a frightening and terribly uncertain prospect and there was no means of stopping or questioning it. The colour drained from her face and there were tears brimming in her eyes as she sat there in a daze and George and I didn't dare to break the silence or move a muscle. Even at that tender age, by some mysterious process, I had sensed the extreme gravity of the situation. It seems that at that moment, right across the nation, there was a communal holding of breath. Who knew what the future held? Everyone had been aware of the impending danger, but they had prayed that it wouldn't come to this. For Mam there was a feeling of numb disbelief and it became a matter of adjusting the brain to accept what the heart already knew.

Our mother was thirty years old and Dad, who was five years older than her, was serving with a Royal Artillery regiment on his second spell in the forces. Fourteen years earlier, as a young man, he had enlisted into the East Yorkshire Regiment and had seen stretches of service in India, Egypt and China. While in India he had taken a course at the British Military Hospital in Lucknow where he qualified as a nursing orderly, and in 1932, after seven years of service, he returned to civvy street.

In the latter years of the worldwide recession, my father was fortunate enough to obtain employment as a steelworker in a local foundry. He thought that, having seen much of the world and having 'done his bit', his army career was over, but it was not to be. His aunt lived just a few doors from the Bradford family home, and it had been on one of his visits to her that he met Granny Bradford's eldest daughter, Evelyn, for the first time. She was a shy, quiet and warm-hearted young woman with an open childlike innocence. He loved the way she moved and the soft cadence of her voice. When she smiled her whole face lit up and Dad was entranced and couldn't keep his eyes off her. She was small and slim with a good figure and shapely legs. She always tried to look smart and fashionable, even though Middlesbrough was a provincial backwater which always seemed about ten years behind the latest London styles. On their first date she had worn a cloche-hat; artificial pearls; a waistless and bustless, knee-length frock and low-heeled, buttoned, strap-over shoes.

They were rather shy and tentative with each other at first, both being afraid of rejection, but Dad persevered and set about winning her over. Fortunately for George, and me, Mam had returned his affection and they were soon a courting couple talking dreamily of their future together. There was a joy and spontaneity in each other's presence and Dad was totally smitten. Each set the other's heart a-flutter as they fell into that deep and intense love to which I owe my life. They became inseparable and were completely devoted to each other. Hating to be apart, each stored up the other's touch and smell until they were together again.

Early in 1934 they had walked hand-in-hand up the approach road of the newly built Tees (Newport) Bridge to join the cheering crowds that lined the route beneath colourful streamers and buntings. Large shields, bearing the royal crest, had been fixed on to every lamppost and the bandsmen of the 1st Battalion of the Durham Light Infantry kept the flag-waving onlookers entertained. When the royal party, accompanied by a retinue of civic dignitaries, arrived in a cavalcade of gleaming, black cars, they had watched as the Duke and Duchess of York completed the official opening. Mam thought that the Duchess looked stunning in her pale-coloured fur coat with its thick, fox fur collar, her white strap-over shoes and her white gloves. On 7 July of that year, Mam and Dad were married in St Cuthbert's Church – the year in which the driving licence, which cost five shillings (25p), became compulsory.

My brother George and I were born during Dad's six 'civilian years', in my case almost exactly nine months after the wedding. New blood from old blood! To Mam we were both little miracles – sublime gifts from heaven – and to her, childbirth was a powerful and mystical event. I was brought into the world by the local midwife in the front bedroom of a small rented house at number four Stanley Street. Our red-brick house was the second of a long row of two-up, two-down, Victorian terraced houses that faced each other across a grimy side street off Cannon Street. It was an area in which the teeming masses of unskilled labourers, dockworkers and the unemployed lived out a poverty-stricken existence. Two towering, cylindrical gasholders that stood within a high-walled compound dwarfed the houses, and we lived and played in their shadow. When fully inflated, the gas tanks loomed up through the smoke blotting out the light and making the workmen on top look like midgets as they were silhouetted against the sky. At other times, the tanks shrank so low that the superstructures surrounding them stood out above them. The locals took these monolithic landmarks for granted, scarcely noticing them within their encircling, skeletal framework of vertical iron columns, catwalks and metal steps.

The area was known as 'Foxheads' and it was probably named after a firm of iron makers called Fox, Head & Co. that had once had iron-rolling mills nearby. The doors of one row of houses had doorknockers in the shape of a fox's head, and similar motifs could be seen at the ends of the stone lintels of all the doors and windows. It had an unsavoury reputation, being a very rough area where the police, swinging their wooden truncheons, patrolled in pairs rather than singly as they did in the quieter and more respectable parts of the town. It was a lively and turbulent neighbourhood to say the least and disputes among the tough, hard-drinking men and women were usually settled by fists. In that rough and ready cauldron of teeming humanity it was not uncommon for drunken women to fight in the open street, the 'scraps' usually taking place outside the pubs from which they had just been ejected. As a crowd gathered they would punch, pull each other's hair and scratch until they were arrested and carted off in the police 'Black Maria'.

In the year between my birth and George's, Mam had given birth to a stillborn baby boy. They say that into every life a little rain must fall, and that summer it came down in buckets. 'The heavens must be weeping for him,' Mam said tearfully, as she carried his tiny body down the steep and narrow stairs in a battered, tear-stained shoebox. There is no loss more heart-rending to a mother than that of her child, and a few days later he was placed in the coffin of another person thus allowing him to be decently buried in consecrated ground. At that time, children who had not been baptised into the church were not allowed a Christian burial; it seems they were destined to spend eternity in limbo. Very close to tears, Mam said, 'His little soul has gone back to heaven whence it came. He will be loved and cared for by the angels. He is now a new star in the Milky Way, and if you look very carefully on clear nights you might be able to pick him out.' At times she was very worried that I might soon join him, as I was a weak and sickly child prone to picking up all of the illnesses common to the infants of our crowded and socially deprived neighbourhood. Every day I was given toast with Virol, the bone-marrow preparation, said to be the ideal fat food for children and invalids.

The year after George came into the world Dad was re-enlisted, this time into the Royal Artillery. In 1938 he was posted to the barracks at Hartlepool, a small town on the coast a few miles to the north of the river mouth, where he managed to find a tiny terraced house to rent. Mam's fifteen-year-old sister Renee came with us and was a great help. When war was imminent Dad sent us back to Middlesbrough, while he was posted to an ack-ack (anti-aircraft) site near Blyth in Northumberland on one of the great gun emplacements tucked away in the high sand dunes just to the south of the busy harbour where submarines were based.

In order to protect the harbour, Blyth Battery was reactivated in the early months of the war and Dad, being thirty-four years of age, was looked on as an 'old man' by the young conscripts. His earlier military service and experience of army life was – on the whole – much respected. A series of these anti-aircraft batteries formed part of the north-eastern coastal defences and they were located in large, camouflaged concrete bunkers and emplacements with their guns pointing seaward. The huge, long-barrelled guns ran on steel rails, and could be rotated through an arc of 180 degrees.

Our new home was in another small terraced house on Cannon Street, a little closer to the Newport Bridge. It stood in a low-lying area that tended to flood whenever we had heavy rain, and behind it was a narrow, cobblestoned back lane from which sacks of coal were tipped through a wooden hatch in the wall at the end of our yard. There were no gardens in our part of town; the dreary street was our playground, and in it crowds of small, noisy, undernourished children shouted and clamoured every day. Fishmongers would come round trundling two-wheeled handcarts shouting 'Caller Herren!' (meaning 'fresh herring') as gusts of wind blew gritty particles and filthy bits of paper around in the grey back alleys. The houses extended in row after grimy, monotonous row, all looking much the same with their chimneys belching out smoke for the greater part of the year. It was autumn but there were no rosy apples ripening anywhere near our treeless streets. Every week the window ledges and the round-edged front doorsteps that led directly on to the flagstones had to be scoured with a donkey stone. In our community, women were much respected if they scrubbed and polished until they were ready to drop.

Like all the other unbeautiful, unpretentious houses ours had no bathroom, even though the planners had called them 'dwellings for artisans'. At the end of the high-walled yard was a brick coalhouse and water closet that we called the lavvy. The swan-necked gas brackets were fitted solely in the two downstairs rooms and these provided only a dim light. To light our way to bed Mam used candles or, if she could afford the fuel, a paraffin lamp with a glass shade that was inclined to flare and smoke and need constant adjustment. In the tiny kitchen a coal-fired range provided warmth and was used every day for baking and cooking. The large black kettle always seemed to be simmering and steaming on the hob.

The house, rented from a local solicitor, was situated some 400 yards to the east of the Newport Bridge – one of the many bridges built by the local firm of Dorman Long & Co. Ltd. It spanned the tidal River Tees, once noted for its fine salmon but now badly contaminated by the effluents that had poured into it from the many industries along its banks over the years. The river formed the boundary between North Yorkshire and County Durham, and the bridge was unique in having a 270-foot-long (82.30m) stretch of roadway that could be lifted vertically to a height of 120 feet (36.5m) above the river by means of a system of huge steel and concrete weights and counterweights. This allowed high-masted ships to pass below it as huge pink-eyed rats with naked tails ran along its wooden pilings. The local people were proud of this technical marvel that was the first of its type in the country. It was the largest and heaviest bascule bridge in the world, and it was raised and lowered on average 800 times a month – twenty-seven times a day. Hundreds of workers crossed it to reach the growing number of industrial sites on the northern bank, thus reducing the long journey round to the next bridge, three miles upstream at Stockton-on-Tees.

Middlesbrough, with its population of some 140,000 inhabitants, was bordered to the south by the Cleveland Hills. Many people escaped from the dirt, smoke and noise of their day-to-day lives by going out to the hills at weekends. Some joined local rambling or cycling clubs to visit the lovely countryside, while others caught the train out of town and hiked for miles in the fresh air.

The people of Teesside often had to endure extremely dense fogs, and when the rising smoke met the cold, damp air stream, thick smogs formed. These yellow smogs sometimes persisted for days. They were real pea-soupers that turned day into night and at times it was impossible to see to the other side of the road. Emissions of chemicals, such as ammonia, mixed with the damp air of the river valley were thought to be a contributory factor. A large metal foghorn mounted on the superstructure of the new bridge was sounded to warn approaching ships of its presence. I vaguely recollect lying awake listening to the eerie, fog-muffled blaring. It was so loud that it seemed to be right outside my bedroom window.

The heavily polluted river between the two bridges was over 300 feet wide in places, and it formed a long, northward-sweeping bend that enclosed a roughly triangular piece of land known as 'The Ironmaster's District'. A network of railway lines and marshalling yards separated it from the grid-like pattern of our streets. Further down-river, beyond the Transporter Bridge, lay Smith's Dockyard with its crowded berths and its tall crane jibs that leaned at all kinds of crazy angles. The Ironmaster's District was packed with grimy iron and steel works; blast furnaces and coke ovens that reached up into the smoke-filled sky. Cooling towers belched clouds of white steam and noxious gases poured from smokestacks adding yet more filth to the already foul-smelling air. At night, as the furnaces were charged, a hellfire glow emanated and lit up the underside of the clouds, turning the whole sky a dirty orange. The ugliness of the scarred landscape was offensive to the eye but I assumed that this was the colour of the night sky everywhere.

The smoke-laden air left a permanent layer of smut over everything, settling on the washing that hung on the clothesline that was strung across our tiny back yard. There was the constant rattling and clanking of rail locomotives and heavy freight wagons being shunted; klaxons blared and screamed at shift-changing times and every day, prior to the sounding of the hooters, the streets were filled with crowds of grey, flat-capped men. These were the ones lucky enough to have a job to go to, and their segged and steel toe-capped working boots clattered on the stone setts echoing back from the grimy brick walls. Hissing steam poured from pipes and boilers; steam hammers clanged; drills whirred and the whole combined to produce a deafening and hellish cacophony. The hustle and bustle and the frantic activity never ceased and after a while people became inured to it. The endless din was part of the fabric of our lives.

On the northern bank of the river stood the huge British Oxygen Company, and close by lay the busy Furness & Company shipyard, with its massive dry docks and slipways. The activity had recently increased as it had received government orders for the construction of large numbers of naval vessels, and the increased employment was in marked contrast to the prolonged and catastrophic slump of the inter-war years. Now things were picking up, and on the south bank further downriver, Smith's Dockyard found itself in the same boat. Both yards were soon to be involved in the construction of warships.

The biggest economic event on Teesside in the inter-war years had been the amalgamation of a number of large works that now formed the Imperial Chemical Industries Limited (ICI). This sprawling complex lay to the south of Billingham just across the river from us on the Durham side and was the largest chemical plant in the country. The new chemical giant had played a major part in the provision of a wide and diverse range of products for the British Empire. With its many oil refineries, distillation towers and flare stacks, it was now working flat out and its oils, lubricants and high-octane aviation fuels were to be of vital importance to the Allied war effort.

These activities were to make it a prime target for the German bombers. Nitrogen was needed to manufacture explosives; fertilisers were vital to a much-needed increase in wartime food production, and perspex (formerly called Resin X), the first transparent plastic in the world, was produced here. The bomber and fighter pilots would now have the protection of perspex cockpit canopies and 'blisters' whereas in the past they had endured the bitter cold with open cockpits. Nothing was wasted. Hundreds of thousands of tons of high-octane aviation fuel was being manufactured from coal and creosote, and the coke oven gas was used within the works and in the domestic grid.

The effluents, which had been pouring into the local waterways for years, had turned the mudflats along the margins of the Billingham

Beck a sickly, bluish-grey colour. The polluted waters of the tidal beck then emptied into the River Tees turning it a dirty, greyish brown. The murky waters formed swirling eddies that we called 'whirlpools' before they swept the few short miles eastwards past Seal Sands to flow out into the vastness of the North Sea.

In the late summer and autumn of 1939 Mam saw squads of khaki-clad soldiers working on the nearby area of wasteland that the council called the Newport Recreation Ground. We called it 'The Common'. The soldiers belonged to the Royal Scots Fusiliers and the King's Own Scottish Borderers (known as 'Kosbies') and they were in the process of raising huge barrage balloons. The Kosbies seemed small men who wore Glengarry bonnets with a pompon on top and they were nick-named 'the bantams' by the local people. The balloons, which were about sixty feet long, looked to me like great, fat, floating pigs with huge ears. They were often called 'Blimps' after the well-known First World War windbag who went by the name of Colonel Blimp. They were attached to a winch by means of a long steel hawser and each was strategically placed with its nose facing into the wind. They were raised to a height of about 5,000 feet and the thick, mooring cables were strong enough to bring down low-flying aircraft. When it was windy we could hear them twanging and humming, and in high winds they had to be storm-bedded, which involved anchoring them down to concrete blocks. On one never-to-be-forgotten stormy night, one was struck by lightning. Just prior to the blaze, eerie bluish-white lightning had been seen arcing from one steel-wire cable to the next.

There were also odd contraptions called Thompson-Haslar units, which looked like large metal dustbins with funnels that emitted black, oily smoke. They were mounted on the backs of special, wheeled trail-ers pulled into position by army vehicles. The smoke units were being tested and would later be used, taking into account the prevailing wind direction, to screen the industrial sites. The Common covered a large part of the open area at the Newport Bridge end of Cannon Street and a long wooden fence, constructed from upright railway sleepers, hid the railway lines. Here, workmen had dug a network of nine-foot-deep, interconnecting slit trenches that were lined with wood, and the roof was supported by timber props. Along the sides were low wooden benches, or 'forms'. Rows of wooden, double-storey bunk beds had been installed and the local people entered the new, underground air-raid shelter by means of a concrete ramp, which led down to thick, metal, blast-proof doors. The tunnels were lit by rows of electric bulbs powered by a generator and the timber-framed roofs were covered with corrugated metal sheeting, which had a deep layer of soil on top. In an emergency an exit could be made by means of wooden ladders that were fixed to the sides of brick-lined shafts placed along the tunnels at intervals. These and the brick street shelters were to be used by hundreds of local people.

On the far side of The Common there were rundown allotments with the fences and sheds patched up with roof felt, bits of rotting wood and rusty corrugated metal sheeting. Close by stood a pigeon park, now in a state of disrepair, with the white paint of its wooden lofts flaking and peeling – all symptoms of the recent hard times.

Groups of poorly clad men regularly gathered on a corner of The Common, most wearing 'art silk' mufflers tied in a tight knot above collarless shirts. Many of them had the gaunt-faced look of the long-term unemployed, depleted by too many years of hardship. Depressed and broken in spirit they felt that they were of no use to their families or anyone else, and could be seen slouching around at the street corners or on that particular area of The Common day after day. Several had hacking coughs, spitting great gobs of phlegm on to the ground or sucking on an empty tobacco pipe and staring blankly at nothing. A few, fortunate enough to have a few halfpennies in their pockets, played pitch and toss in the constant hope of winning a few more coppers to spend on beer and tobacco. A couple of scruffy lads stood cavy (lookout) for them, giving warning should the other type of 'copper' appear.

Our house backed on to The Common and one day the rozzers (a local term for policemen) turned up in force. The hapless illegal gamblers scattered and one tried to make his escape by climbing over the wall into our backyard where Mam was hanging out the washing. She was heavily pregnant and the man's sudden appearance startled her, making her cry out, at which Dad dashed out through the kitchen door. He was really angry and grabbed hold of the man saying, 'Bugger off sharpish mate or I'll punch your bloody lights out.'

As a young man, Dad had brought home numerous presents from his postings in the Far East, one of them being the large tortoise that we kept as a pet. A beautiful ivory model of the Taj Mahal at Agra that he had brought back from India stood on the sideboard and could be lit from the inside. One of my earliest memories is of bleeding profusely after pushing George down Booth Street on his three-wheeler trike.

We had been to visit Gran, who now lived round the corner on King George Street, when I slipped, and as I landed on my left knee a sharp piece of gravel cut deeply into it. I still have a small pyramid-shaped scar to show for it. In another incident I was wearing semi-transparent, rubberised pants that were elasticated and fitted tightly round my chubby thighs and, desperately needing to go to the lavatory, I could hold on no longer. I passed water, which soon saturated the Terry towelling of my inner pants and, when it could absorb no more, the 'pee' could be seen slowly filling up the 'see-through' pants. I remember the lovely warm feeling of it before it seeped out and turned cold as it trickled down my legs.

My maternal grandmother, Florence Emma Bradford, a small, plumpish, fifty-year-old widow, lived a little closer to the bridge than us. Her fifteen-year-old daughter Irene (always known as Renee) was a slim, attractive, auburn-haired girl. A great bond of unspoken affection had developed between my parents and Mam's winsome young sister. Dad used to call her his 'Little Princess', and he spoiled her rotten.

Gran's eldest son, John, was twenty years old and was serving his apprenticeship as a plater at the Britannia Steelworks, a large, steel-plate rolling plant in the Ironmasters District. In February of the previous year he had joined the Territorial Army attending meetings in the Drill Hall every week and going on weekend training camps. The part-time soldiers were known colloquially as 'the Terriers' or, as some said, 'Saturday Night Soldiers'. Uncle John had joined chiefly for the excitement, the sense of adventure and the glamour of the uniform, which seemed to attract the girls. The extra money was also very welcome. In late autumn 1939 he received a letter from the local office of the Ministry of Labour and National Service, stating that he was now liable for conscription into the regular army and was to report for a medical examination. Small but strong, he passed A1.

Soon afterwards his call-up papers – with a four-shilling postal order to cover his travelling costs – were delivered. In the meantime, Gran fed him well, as like most women of the time, she considered it her duty to wait on the men hand and foot. Uncle John was just one of the thousands being mobilised and in early February he made his farewells. Travelling with several other young men to the army barracks at Richmond, North Yorkshire, he swore the oath of allegiance; 'took the King's shilling', was read the Riot Act and became number 4390218 with the rank of private. After being vaccinated he was issued with a uniform and kit, which included two enamelled tin plates; an enamel mug; a knife, fork and spoon, and was put into the 5th Infantry Battalion of the Green Howards.

The recruits were broken down by hard work and strict discipline before being built up again into an efficient fighting unit. They learned to work as a team, which was to stand them in good stead when they eventually went into battle, and as an unmarried private he was paid just fourteen shillings (70p) a week plus bed and board. Each week during the long basic training he managed to send part of his meagre pay to his mother. A few weeks later, following the outbreak of war, he was sent on embarkation leave. He sailed from Southampton as part of a naval convoy – with a fighter escort overhead – bound for the French port of Cherbourg. It was too dangerous to take the shorter, more direct route to Calais through the Straits of Dover, as the ship would have been within the range of German bombers. The 5th Battalion of the Green Howards then moved up to the Belgian border that had seen so much bloodshed during the First World War.

Gran's other sons, Archie and Harry, were aged thirteen and eleven years old respectively. Her other daughter, twenty-six-year-old Hilda, and her son Jimmy, were living with Gran's younger sister Ruby, having left Hilda's Irish Catholic husband, John Nolan. His faith frowned on mixed marriages at that time and throughout her turbulent and unhappy marriage there had been prolonged and bitter conflict with much ugly name-calling. Gran, who was a forthright God-fearing woman, declared, 'I've got no time for the Nolans with their hypocrisy, boozing and excessive religious humility, and John's mother is a hard-bitten, intolerant, religious bigot. I'll never forgive her for bawling after them in the street "I hope you die in your bed and rot in hell you Protestant bitch!" just after their marriage in the Register Office. She called Jimmy a bastard – because to her mind the marriage was not legal – saying, "If you are not married by a priest you are not married at all".'

There was a fair amount of resentment of the Irish at that time as there had been more than a hundred IRA bombings on the British mainland. Aunt Hilda had fallen for John Nolan's smooth talk and they had married in 1934 – the same year as Mam and Dad – and had rented a house just round the corner from Gran. When in drink, John Nolan was inclined to be violent and after he had been sent to prison for theft in 1936 they separated, leaving Hilda on her own to bring up their young son.

Great-great-grandfather John Knights worked on the colliers that sailed up and down the east coast, and reputedly became quite wealthy after moving up through the ranks to command various ships. It was said that in later life he lived in some style in large and impressive houses in the more affluent parts of the town, with one story alleging that he had a sock full of gold sovereigns hidden up his chimney.

John's eldest son, Henry Knights, was Gran's father, and he too was a merchant seaman. In 1886, at the age of just nineteen, he married a twenty-year-old local girl called Caroline Martha Wanless who we always knew as 'Granny Knights'. She was a live wire and a real character who was not averse to the odd tipple or a regular 'flutter on the gee-gees'. By the time Gran was born, the family had fallen on hard times.

In 1906, when she was just sixteen years of age, Gran eloped to get married, leaving home wearing work clothes on top of her best clothes so as not to arouse suspicion. She knew all too well that her mother was dead set against the marriage to her twenty-six-year-old boyfriend. He was weather-beaten and had skin like brown leather as a result of working on the River Tyne in all weathers. Granny Knights called him a foreigner, as she was barely able to comprehend his broad Geordie accent. He had been blinded in one eye by having sand kicked in his face as a young boy. The couple had married at Trinity Church, North Ormesby, on the eastern edge of the town. Grandad always called her Lol and they had a hard but happy life for more than thirty years before death intervened.

My maternal Grandad, Archie Bradford, hailed from South Shields, County Durham, and was a chronic asthmatic but he nevertheless managed to find fairly regular employment. He worked mostly as a dock labourer or as a lighterman on the two rivers and his job involved unloading ocean-going ships on to the lighters. The ships, being of too deep a draught, had to be anchored in the deep channel in midstream. A lighter was a kind of wide barge with a shallow draught on which the goods were taken to the wharves to be lifted ashore by cranes and derricks. Grandad worked long hours over many sweltering summers and chilled-to-the-marrow winters, until two years before the war, he died after an asthma attack. He would 'fear no more the heat of the sun nor the furious winter's rages'. He lived just long enough to see his two eldest daughters wed and the first three of his grandchildren come into the world, these being Jimmy, me and George. Three years prior to his untimely death he had promised Renee that he would take her to see the opening of the Newport Bridge, but she developed several septic abscesses on her neck and was bitterly disappointed. Boils were all too common amongst the undernourished children of the area at that time.

Gran had endured a very hard life. It had been a long grim struggle for survival throughout the late 1920s and '30s, the years of the terrible Great Depression, and, as a result, she had 'lost' five of her eleven children. It appears that great poverty invariably leads to a higher birth rate as having lots of children improved the odds of some reaching maturity. Three sons and a daughter died in their infancy, one of them being her firstborn son Archibald, named after his father, and a little later, a much loved, gentle and delicate daughter – named Florence after her mother – died at the age of only eleven years. She became ill after a rusty nail sticking up through the paper-thin sole of her boot punctured her foot. The tiny black spot under her big toe became infected leading to the septicaemia that killed her.

For many years Gran had lived on the edge of an abyss of uncertainty, just one of a warren of people who had to endure real hardship in squalid and wretched conditions. Fortunately for her, her eldest daughters were in work as domestic servants, enduring interminably long hours for miserably low wages. Like many sisters they didn't always see eye to eye and Gran, losing patience with them, would say, 'Can't you two go five minutes without arguing?' Mam worked as far away as Leeds for a time, but they managed to send a little money home to keep the family's head above water. After marrying they were obliged to support their own families, but, luckily, Uncle John had started work as a trainee crane driver in the Teesside Bridge Steelworks on leaving school in 1933, and Renee became a domestic servant on leaving school four years later.

During the long hard years of the Depression, Grandad used to walk down to the nearby Newport wharf early every morning to see if the foreman was taking on any men, and, if he was lucky enough to get a day's work, Renee would take him his bait (food) tin and a can of cold tea at the midday break. The work was hard and could be dangerous or even fatal. Gran's elder brother John had died of suffocation after falling into a container of red ore powder. Gran was tough, resilient and stubborn and, although entitled to poor relief, she was far too proud to accept any form of charity. Although close to destitution at times, she would never beg, suffering her many and repeated hardships in silence.

She would never let others see her emotional pain and gradually this rigid, grin-and-bear-it stoicism became the norm. She just got on with it because if she didn't, she would go under.

Gran had an inner strength that seemed to be a strange mixture of fatalism, resignation and faith, and she somehow managed to maintain her dignity and the small decencies of life, accepting whatever fate threw at her. Although close to despair at times, she was never completely vanquished, saying, 'There is always someone that little bit worse off than you.' Sadly, the long years of grinding poverty, unremitting toil and repeated knock-backs gradually hardened her soul and the long years of struggle turned her into a sad and bitter woman in her twilight years.

Her neighbours – although rough and ready – were a plucky, strong-willed, independent lot, who were never servile. Desperation has a way of binding the poor together and the people of that close-knit community helped each other out in order to make ends meet. There was a powerful sense of belonging and they knew they could call on 'Florrie' for help in times of crisis. The strong helped the weak and the elderly, but most of them were worn out by the age of thirty-five and were old by forty-five. They believed and hoped that better times were just around the corner and things could only get better, unaware that there would be many more years of self-sacrifice and personal loss before their living conditions would improve.

Religion was their prop and hope of eternal salvation, offering material as well as spiritual help. It offered the promise of a final, blessed release from their earthly sufferings and misfortunes. Marx had called it 'the opium of the people'. The local church, with two sombre, square twin towers at its westernmost end, was never a beautiful edifice. It stood dark and severe-looking, but solid and strong – an enduring refuge in times of adversity and an appropriate symbol of the gritty fighting spirit of the poor, long-suffering folk of our crowded neighbourhood.

2

Evacuation

By April 1939, the threat of war had grown and the government announced a scheme – called Operation Pied Piper – to evacuate some two and a half million children. Some adults, not directly required for the war effort, were also to be sent from the danger areas and would include many mothers, the elderly and the infirm. The word 'evacuate' means 'to empty', and it became an exercise in emptying the towns and cities likely to be targeted; the emphasis at the sending end being to get the evacuees out as quickly as possible. The fact that they were dealing with young and vulnerable human beings was often overlooked and the upheaval sometimes led to great distress and emotional pain. Powerful blood ties made it difficult to break up the clannish family units as life had little meaning to them except in terms of flesh-and-blood relationships. There was much fear of the unknown as mothers realised that they would be delivering their loved ones into the hands of 'borrowed parents'. They would be living with complete strangers whom they knew nothing about. Many were extremely reluctant to let their children go, especially since so many sons, husbands and brothers had left to join the forces.

Governmental pressure was brought to bear on the wavering mothers and they were made to feel selfish and uncaring. It was implied that only bad parents would allow their children to stay at home to face the dangers of enemy bombing. In many families the father was unemployed but they were proud men who hated having to go cap-in-hand to the National Assistance Board. It meant that they would have to eke out a meagre living from the pittance provided by the means-tested scheme known as the dole. They received dole money for each child and if the children were sent away they would lose it and find it very difficult to survive at all.

There was now much more government intervention in people's lives and during the year leaflets had been issued setting out the details of the mass evacuation plan. Mothers of pre-school children could accompany their children to the relative safety of the countryside if they so wished, but all were required by law to register first. What thousands of mothers had secretly dreaded had come to pass. Schools were to be evacuated en masse, including many of the teachers, and the red-brick Victorian School on Greta Street, Middlesbrough, was just one of the many involved.

Poison gas, which had been used by both sides in the First World War, was the greatest fear and the government made plans to provide the whole population with free respirators. It was a mammoth task. Millions were boxed up prior to distribution and in Middlesbrough they were to be given out from the blue wooden police boxes dotted around the town. The schools handed out gas masks to the children and practices at using them were regularly carried out. The under-fives were to get a bright red-and-blue model known as a 'Mickey Mouse' mask, which was designed to make toddlers more willing to wear it, but these were not issued until later in the year.

In readiness, rehearsals were carried out involving my uncles, Archie and Harry, and my young cousin Jimmy. They lined up in pairs and practised marching as part of a long crocodile formation, carrying their gas masks in buff-coloured cardboard boxes that were suspended on a long loop of string. Plans to raise the school leaving age had recently been suspended and Archie was just about to start his final term in school when Gran decided that he should go and take care of the boys.

On 31 August further notices were sent to every household stating that the evacuation was imminent. Each school was given a number; the names of the children, with their school number, had to be written clearly in block capitals on a cardboard label or on a piece of thick, brown paper. This was tied on to the lapel of their coats and they were repeatedly told their school number in case they got lost in the crowds. Initially it seemed to be great fun and many of them thought that they were going on holiday to the country or the seaside. Most of the parents believed that the war would soon be over.

Gran became more upset as the day of the evacuation drew near. The night before they were to leave, the boys had a good scrub in the tin bath in front of the fire. After they had gone to bed, Gran sat staring with unseeing eyes at the changing shapes in the coal fire, trying to put the next day out of her mind, but to no avail. She had already lost her husband to chronic asthma and John was in the army; now her other two boys and her grandson were going away and she had no idea of where or to whom they would go. She asked herself, 'Will they go to nice people who will understand their mischievous ways? Will they be able to tolerate their likes and dislikes? Mind you, they're not fussy eaters and Archie will keep them in order. He's a level-headed lad.'

Evelyn was also planning to go away with her two youngsters and at the thought tears welled up in Gran's eyes, but she managed to pull herself together. She had to stay strong for the children's sake. At least Hilda and Renee would be staying so she would not be entirely alone. A mass exodus of over 6,000 evacuees from Middlesbrough began on 8 September 1939. Archie, Harry and Jimmy would never forget the feel of the small cardboard boxes that bounced against their legs, and the day they left home with their scant belongings would dwell in their hearts and minds forever.

Before the war broke out, George and I were attending the Settlement House Nursery School where our mother had been working as a voluntary part-time helper for the last year or so. The nursery was in a Victorian town house with massive rooms and large double bay windows that stood behind an elegant wrought-iron gate and ornate railings. Set back behind its low brick wall it faced out onto busy, grey-cobbled Newport Road, that had been nicknamed Poverty Row at the time of the Depression. The place was once described as an oasis in an urban wilderness.

Our play room had large south-facing windows that let the sun in; the floorboards were kept smooth and highly polished so that we didn't get splinters. My best friend at the time was a little lad called Eric Ward, the youngest of ten children, who lived in a crowded two-up, two-down, back-to-back terraced house nearby. We played together most of the time and where one was, the other was sure to be found. He had five sisters and two brothers, and his eldest sister Edna was thirty years old by the time he came into the world. Just behind the big house was a long cobbled lane called the Bull Alley that led to a large slaughterhouse and, as the nursery was at the rear of the house, we could not fail to hear the lowing and the clattering of hooves as the cattle were driven down it to their deaths.

We were well cared-for by the nursery assistants – whom we addressed as 'Lady' for some reason – and they read lovely stories to us from *The Blue Fairy Book* and suchlike. Every day after dinner we were tucked up for an hour's sleep on little canvas beds that could be folded up and stacked away. My favourite assistant was cheerful and pretty sixteen-year-old Kathleen, who laughed a lot and was always singing classical songs. She had a lovely soprano voice that was delicate and high, and she used to sing *One Fine Day* from Puccini's opera Madam Butterfly for us. My other favourite was *O, My Beloved Father*.

In the summer months just before the war, Eric's fifteen-year-old brother Len, and his mate Bobby, used to come to the nursery play room every day. They would appear just as the Ladies were clearing up the toys and books that we had scattered everywhere. Their excuse was: 'We have come to take Eric home'; but once there they were in no hurry to leave. Their true motive was to try to get off with the two attractive nursery assistants. Unfortunately, their efforts were of no avail as the girls' interests lay with older and more 'mature' youths.

Separating Russon's Coal Merchant's yard from us was a high brick wall, behind which there was stabling for their eight huge draught horses and room for their flat coal carts. The coal deliverymen worked long hours and at the end of the day they would bring the horses and the coal-begrimed rulleys back to this yard to be hosed down. In the summer evenings the coalmen had to walk their horses across the Newport Bridge to the rough, coarse-grassed pastureland on its northern bank. They then had to make the long walk back, as they were not allowed onto the buses in their coal-blackened state and, by the time they'd had a bath and changed their clothes, it could be nine o'clock. To give themselves an earlier finish they were prepared to pay lads, like Len and his mate, four shillings (1.7p) a time to ride the heavy horses over the bridge. Once there they tethered them, left them to feed and ran all the way back to take another one. This arrangement benefited both parties as it gave the boys a bit of extra pocket money and the coalmen had time to go for a drink or to the pictures.

The Settlement was a charitable organisation that had, for forty-seven years, provided a great deal of help to the poor and needy folk of our area, which was officially classified as socially deprived. We, of course, were totally unaware of this; there always seemed to be some-one worse off than us and we didn't think of ourselves as poor, we just didn't have much money. Our parents were proud and tried their best, saying, 'If you have love and care you are rich indeed.'

Over the years, hundreds of women had received aid and support here when opportunities for them were extremely rare. Apart from material help, they provided lectures, courses, and books to help them better themselves, raising funds which were used to provide clothing, day-trips and free holidays. The Settlement had set up several youth organisations, ran a thriving cycling club, and Mam and Renee often took part in the concerts they put on. Mam regularly attended the mothers' meetings and the Bible-reading classes. Plans were under way to evacuate the children to the safety of the countryside. Mam, who believed in the family as a sustaining force, was concerned for us and the thought of an indefinite separation filled her with horror, therefore she applied for and got the job of assistant cook at the new place.

It was mid-September by the time we caught the rattling motor bus that had the letter 'O' on the front. Mam, my little fair-haired brother and I had barely sat down on the hard, upholstered seats before my pal Eric and his mam got on. Getting off at the magnificent town hall we walked to the railway station where we met up with a nursery assistant and a few of the other children. We were so excited, holding hands as we hopped and skipped along, and we were really looking forward to the coming train journey. Mam led us past the sandbagged booking hall and on through the central concourse to the stone-flagged platform. Our voices echoed back from the iron girders and glass panels of the grimy roof that soared above us.

On realising that the carriages were of the non-corridor type, Mam took George, me, Eric and the three other toddlers to the lavatories on the platform. We gaped, wide-eyed with wonder, taking in the sights and strange sounds, but I was rather apprehensive on passing the huge steam locomotive. It reminded me of a fiery dragon resting in its lair, hissing faintly as it slowly breathed in and out. As the fireman opened the door of the firebox, an orange glow illuminated his red, sweating face and the glare of the burning coals reflected back from an array of shiny copper pipes and brass gauges. As he wielded his long-handled shovel to throw coals from the tender into its gaping maw, it seemed to me that he was feeding it. The great shiny beast stood creaking and groaning with pungent fumes rising up as oil came into contact with hot iron. White jets of steam squirted out from cylinders down by its gleaming pistons and the metal rims of its massive wheels reflected the light. The minute droplets of steam that landed on my face were reminiscent of the spindrift on a windy day in summer when Mam had taken us to the water's edge at Redcar beach. At this point Mam helped us up the steps and into a carriage.

Steaming on past the wooden platforms of the tiny, outlying, sub-stations of Ormesby and Nunthorpe, we caught a glimpse of Ormesby Hall surrounded by its fine parkland. Mam remarked to a lady who had got into our carriage that it was here, on a fine day just over two years back, that Neville Chamberlain had addressed the assembled crowds seven weeks after becoming Prime Minister. The Hall had been the home of the Pennyman family for 400 years and Colonel Pennyman's grandfather had helped to raise the money to build Holy Trinity Church in the market square in nearby North Ormesby. 'That's the church which your Gran got married in,' Mam said, as she pointed it out in passing.

As we stopped to pick up a few passengers at Great Ayton, Mam said, 'The old village is about a mile away and it was here that Captain Cook's family used to live. It's only five years since his parents' cottage was sold, taken apart stone by stone and shipped out to Melbourne in Australia. You'll no doubt learn all about him when you start school.' From here the train gradually climbed onto the lower slopes of the Cleveland Hills and we caught a glimpse of a towering, stone obelisk silhouetted starkly against the clear sky. It stood on the crest of a high hill on nearby Easby Moor, and Mam said, 'It was erected in honour of Captain Cook, the famous explorer.'

The train halted for a few minutes at Battersby Junction where we could see a row of tiny railway cottages, each one with a pigsty behind it. As we clattered onwards and upwards towards the high moors, we gazed out on a patchwork of pale-gold, stubble-covered fields, thorn-hedged green meadows and isolated farmsteads.

As Mam dandled George on her knee, Eric blurted out, 'I'm not coming to the new nursery school with you, like.' It seems that arrangements had been made to billet him in a nearby village and, taken aback by the news, I sat thinking about it. I gazed wistfully out of the window as we gradually climbed towards the higher moorlands. Lush shoulder-high fronds of green bracken, some of it just turning brown, caught my attention as it formed a mosaic on the sheep-cropped, grassy slopes. We then beheld the fawns and browns of sere, bent grasses; the russet of reeds and the yellow of gorse that clad the airy heights of the beautiful North Yorkshire Moors.

It was a glorious day and sweet, heady scents of sun-warmed heather and gorse wafted in through the partly open window. We, still with our young child's capacity for wonder, were awe-struck and entranced by the vast openness of it all. Journeys are always exciting to young children and I was loving this one. We climbed steadily up to broad uplands where great clumps of sunlit purple heather stretched away as far as the eye could see. I gazed out on a vista of purple hills and the vivid, green hues of stream and river valleys. I was enthralled and exhilarated by the wide, limitless expanse of these treeless uplands, as this was my first experience of such hazy and gloriously melting distances. It was so different to the urban world we were used to and I had never realised that such wild and lovely countryside existed. Sparkling, crystal-clear streams rushed and tumbled down beneath a wide, unclouded Indian summer sky; it was the start of a lifelong love affair with nature.

George, nestling up close to Mam's soft and rounded Mother Earth figure, was lulled to sleep in the warmth and comfort of her lap as she sang a gentle lullaby, the words of which went something like, 'Golden slumbers kiss your eyes. Smiles awake you when you rise. Sleep my darling one, gently sleep and I will sing a Lullaby.' One or two of the younger children, who had been woken much earlier than usual that morning, also nodded off, lulled by her quiet singing. The soporific rocking of the carriage, and the rhythmic, clackety-clack sounds of the train as it rolled over the jointed rails, added to the languorous atmosphere, but I sat there wide-eyed with childish wonder. I was not at all apprehensive about leaving home, as I knew that our mother was going to be with us.

By the hamlet of Kildale, the track ran close to the meandering course of the upper Leven as we rattled along through Commondale Moor. Occasionally the train stopped at tiny rural halts to let the odd passenger off and we saw greyish-white, greasy-fleeced Swaledale wethers scattered far and wide across the moors. At first I thought they were boulders, until they moved. Most of the hardy curly-horned sheep continued their endless chewing, unperturbed by our train as it thundered by on that fine, sunny autumn day. Their continual grazing had given the grassy areas the look of neatly mown lawns and they seemed to be making a better job of it than any lawnmower could.

The train steamed on by sleepy moorland farmsteads and narrow winding lanes before we passed close to the relatively large village of Castleton and on to Danby station. On the hilltop we could see a number of tall, steel-framed towers, unaware that they were top-secret radio transmitting stations. From the train I could see the steep earthen banks of the meandering upper reaches of the River Esk, as it wended its way down to Whitby. From here the track ran on embankments and passed over small stone road bridges on its way to the tiny, quaintly named hamlet of Howlsike. High above to the south, we could see the beautiful purple heights of Danby Moor.

Descending slightly, we passed the patchwork fields of Fryup Dale before halting briefly at the little station at Lealholm Bridge. A network of dry-stone walls dipped and arched following the contours of the land. In the damp, boggy areas the grass was tussocky with clumps of brown rushes and the stones were moss-covered. Black-faced, white-muzzled Swaledale ewes scattered, running stiffly on grey-mottled legs as our train clattered by before it crossed a five-arched stone viaduct. Close by stood humpbacked Beggars Bridge with its old weatherworn stones and Mam told us that we were close to the picturesque moorland village of Glaisdale. Smugglers and wandering traders had used these old moorland tracks for hundreds of years, carrying their wares in pannier bags slung over the backs of their patiently plodding packhorses. The tracks are paved with sandstone slabs in parts, and are called trods or pannier ways, and these ancient tracks cross many miles of high wild moorland that lead to and from the old bridge. The low parapets were designed to lean outwards so as to allow for their wide bulky packs.

At Grosmont station, which was to feature in the television series *Heartbeat* many years later, Mam lifted us out onto the platform with our luggage. A black-clad porter, after shouting, 'All change for Pickering', brought George's pushchair to us from the guard's van. As we waited, an elderly lady said, 'I'm goin' to Pickering an' all. D'yer mind if I travel with yer?'

'Not at all,' Mam replied. Boarding the train, we slowly huffed and puffed over the level crossing, passing the old *Station Tavern* and, as we passed St Matthew's Church, the lady said, 'That were built by the local ironmasters and mine owners, and this railway were once a lifeline to all the little villages along it.' The line now ran close to the course of the Murk Esk and beside it we saw abandoned sidings, ventilation shafts and cottages.

We climbed up through a lovely wooded area towards Beck Hole, and below us, through the canopies of the alders that clung to its steep banks, I caught sight of a pretty, stone-walled, humpback bridge and a shady beck with tumbling waterfalls that glinted in the sunlight. The lady told us that in the early days of the line, there had been a steep incline near here. There was a fatal accident on it in 1864 when the rope snapped and the coaches raced back down the incline killing two people and injuring many others. Plans were drawn up to prevent it happening again, and the four-mile stretch of line to Goathland that we were now on was laid in 1865. The old incline was on the other side of Eller Beck.

I was discovering so many new and exciting things; it seemed to me like a magical journey through an enchanted land. Passing on again by the pretty village of Goathland, the steam train headed south into Goathland Dale and the wild and narrow gorge of the Eller Beck. Many years later, Goathland was to become known as Aidensfield in the popular TV series *Heartbeat* and it was called Hogsmeade in the Harry Potter film, *The Philosopher's Stone*. On the open moors we saw several hurdles before the line began the long drag up from the Raindale area to Fen Bog, where I was spellbound by the stunning views and refreshed by the purity of the moorland air.

Beside the single-track line the sun glinted off the clear purling waters of the lovely Pickering Beck. The word beck comes from the Norse 'bekk', meaning a stream, and in these parts a small waterfall is called a 'foss'. A little further on, to the east, lay the huge natural amphitheatre called the Hole of Horcum. The line skirted this strange but natural phenomenon that was a quarter of a mile across and 400 feet deep. Mam told us about the legend of the Hole. Some call it 'The Devil's Punchbowl' and local legend has it that Wade, an angry Anglo-Saxon giant, was having a row with his wife Bell. He scooped out a handful of earth to throw at her and left this deep depression. Having missed her, the resulting heap of soil formed the high hill called Blakey Topping a mile or so further east. Some say it was the devil himself who dug out the great hollow. The deep grooves near the bottom looked to me like gigantic fingermarks. Round here nature was wild and untamed, and perched high up on the eastern flank of the marshy hollow Mam pointed out the old *Saltergate Inn*, saying, 'The Devil was once trapped in its kitchen and a peat fire was lit to keep him in and it has been kept alight ever since.'

My imagination ran riot and I prayed that the fire would never go out. In reality, the 'Hole' had been formed by the power of glacial melt-waters and collapsed springs following the last ice age. Above it masses of blooming heather turned the rolling moorland purple with tall sere grasses and reed clumps standing out in fawn and umber. I glimpsed isolated stone cottages and farmhouses and the beauty and serenity of it all took my breath away.

After skirting the high bluff of Pickering Moor the train began a long gradual descent. In places the steep sides of beautiful Newtondale rose up to about 450 feet; in the old days the trains had rolled down here under their own gravitational pull. The slopes of the deep and lonely gorge were clothed in lovely trees and shrubs, and Mam said, 'I've never seen such glorious autumn tints.' The beauty of this remote eleven-mile-long stretch made a powerful impression on my young mind. I was seeing Mother Nature in her natural state, and her clean vibrant colours and leafy grandeur contrasted so sharply with the grime of our mucky old town.

Steaming onwards we passed close to a flat area on the eastern side of the line where a derelict, partly overgrown track bed led off to mounds of fallen stone. The area was gradually being colonised by grass and weeds. An old dried-up reservoir overlooked the former mine workings and ruined stone buildings. There was an air of neglect and melancholy about the place and bits of rotten wood swung back and forth on creaking, rusty hinges. The ugly scars were sad reminders showing where the bowels of the earth had been ripped open and turned out in the frantic search for iron ore; the ore on which my hometown's very existence had once depended. Close by, an old fifty-foot stone chimney that had once been an air shaft for the underground workings still dominated the skyline. It was to be demolished for safety reasons some twenty-one years later and the stones and rubble were used to fill in the 300-foot-deep pit shaft.

High above on the cliffs stood a dark, derelict, square tower, which seemed to teeter on the very brink of the precipice. The elderly lady said, 'Yon ruin is Skelton Tower. It's all that's left of an old shooting lodge that once 'ad stables on its ground floor.' It had been built for an allegedly dissolute reverend gentleman of that name.

The train began to slow by a tall white signal post at the point where the single line became a double track, and we passed over a narrow level crossing by a wooden coal storage hut. We rumbled over a wide wooden-gated level crossing that stood close to a tall, brick-built signal box with blast-taped windows. Just past the ticket office, we pulled in alongside the neat and tidy stone platform of a little station called Levisham Halt. On the platform were a couple of paraffin lamps mounted on cast-iron posts that had been freshly painted in cream and maroon.

A few people got off and, as the red-and-white arm of the signal went up, we continued on our journey. Crossing over the points, the double line became single track again for the next six miles and the train rattled southwards on a flat, straight stretch bordered by the tree-covered slopes of Blansby Park. Here the valley widened out and the track had several bends. We could lean out of the window and see the steam and smoke-shrouded engine and, in the other direction, the guard's van. High above stood the curtain walls of Pickering Castle.

Pickering Beck was always in sight and we finally rumbled over it and into Pickering station where a wooden newspaper and magazine kiosk stood at the end of a long platform. The walls and doorways were piled high with sandbags that almost reached the glass roof. The great black engine gave out a long echoing hoot as, with an agonised squeal of brakes – amid billowing clouds of steam – it slowly clinked and clanked to a halt. To a staccato clattering of carriage doors, we climbed down onto the platform to be met at the W.H. Smith bookstall by Miss Florence Thorne, the auburn-haired, middle-aged matron of the new nursery school, who had travelled down from Middlesbrough a week or so before to get things organised.

We followed her slim figure out of the station, through a wrought-iron gate to a single-decked motor coach where the driver loaded our cases and we set off. My friend Eric was on the seat behind me as we travelled through a couple of villages and turned north up to Cropton. After passing the *New Inn*, the road forked to either side of a large chestnut tree with a low wooden seat encircling the wide girth of its gnarled trunk. Miss Thorne said to Mam, 'The local gentry and land-owners used to assemble here for the Sinnington foxhunt, a regular event before the war.'

Bearing left onto the Rosedale road, we travelled down Cropton Bank, with a grassy mound on our right that was once the site of a Norman motte-and-bailey castle. Heading north, we passed through a pleasant river valley lined with sunlit meadows and hedges; we drove up the narrow country road for another four miles, passing the inn at

Hartoft End on our right. Beautiful spruce and pine-clad slopes rose up on our right-hand side before we pulled in at the large inn on the square in the village of Rosedale Abbey. Small groups of people were waiting as Miss Thorne, the other mothers and a few of the children got off. I was quite upset to see that my pal Eric was one of them. However, young children adapt quite quickly and I soon got over it.

We went back the way we had come before turning left at a wooden gate; this led onto a narrow stony road and passed between the tall sentry-like conifers whose tangy aroma scented the air. At the side of the tree-shaded track – that led up to a large stone farmstead called Spiers House – small brightly coloured birds darted about. We climbed ever upwards through the hushed beauty and solitude of the forest until the coach turned right by the big farmhouse that stood in an open area of wide grassy meadows.

Climbing up from a gurgling runnel the track passed between hundreds of densely packed green giants. Tiny black and brown birds flitted in and out and Miss Thorne said, 'Those shy little birds that you see there are coal tits.'

Halfway down, a short track led eastwards to the rear of Sutherland Lodge, which was owned by the Stancliffes. A short gravelled drive, big enough for a car to turn round on, ran along the back of the house that had no formal gardens as such. There was just the odd grassy area to the south and east, otherwise it was hemmed in on all sides by the vastness of the forest.

On our arrival, the driver carried our luggage through an old nail-studded oaken door and left it in the passageway. From here a narrow servant's staircase led straight upwards and a door on the left opened into a large kitchen. We were warmly welcomed and shown round by the deputy matron Miss Rosemary Waters, a tall young woman with short, fair wavy hair that was parted in the middle. Mam was shown around the huge old-fashioned kitchen at the eastern end of the house where there was a large well-scrubbed wooden table in the middle of its stone floor. A Welsh dresser stood against the back wall and a wide stone fireplace and chimneybreast occupied most of the gable end. In front of it was a range of fire irons and an old wooden rocking chair stood to one side.

''Ere, I'll 'elp thee with thy baggage,' said an elderly, bow-legged man and Mam left to go off with him. He was wearing a soft, checked flat cap; a waistcoat; riding breeches and leather gaiters, and we learned that he was called Spaven. He carried Mam's luggage along an earthen path to her lodgings and she told us later that the trees had a tangy smell similar to carbolic soap. Between them she caught glimpses of lovely wooded hills stretching away into the distance. She was to lodge in an old stone farmworker's cottage, called Keldy Cottage, which stood in a forest clearing about a mile away. Her cosy bedroom lay directly beneath the red pantiles of its steeply sloping roof and she said the view from her dormer window was magnificent. Spaven, who took care of Mrs Stancliffe's horses, lived with his daughter and her husband in a large stone house at the far side of the meadow to the east of Sutherland Lodge. It had been the estate gamekeeper's house at the turn of the century. In time, we learned that Spaven was a little too fond of visiting the local hostelries, and he sometimes arrived back a bit tipsy after sampling the potent ale available at the *New Inn* at Cropton. We would see him reeling around like the top of a spruce tree in a gale. He was a smallish man of medium build and it was said that he thought more of his beloved horses than he did of people. He was convinced that they were plagued by witches saying, 'T'osses 'ave bin found first thing in t'morning agitated and lathered in sweat after bein' 'ag-ridden durin' t'neet.' As a preventative measure he hung small stones that had a natural hole through them above each of the stalls. These were known locally as hagstones.

Mam was kept very busy in the kitchen, but on most days she would stay with us for a while when her work was done. We were taken to her cottage on her off-duty days, and this helped us to adapt more readily to the sudden changes in our life, but in the early days we cried a lot when she was obliged to leave us.

Sutherland Lodge with its impressive double-gabled, ivy-clad frontage stood on rising ground and had magnificent views to the south. It overlooked dense green forests, rolling countryside and the green fields round Cropton way. The eaves of the house had intricately carved bargeboards with a series of alternating diamond and bow shapes cut into them along their whole length. Delicately carved wooden finials crowned the apexes of the gable ends with, below them, a matching inverted finial. High up on the gable at the western end there was the gauntleted forearm of a knight grasping a short dagger on a stone shield, with the word PERSE engraved below it. It was probably the crest and motto of a noble family, with the word meaning 'perseverance'. We would need a good deal of that in the times to come.

Three stone steps led up to a pair of studded oak doors which were flanked by stone buttresses. Above them an elegantly carved Gothic arch framed a stained-glass window with a leafy stemmed rose (the flower of secrets) in the centre of it. A pair of finely carved, winged gargoyles – which always frightened me – jutted out on either side of it. At one side was an old-fashioned, brass bell pull and directly above the doorway there was a stone-mullioned, three-sided oriel window.

A wide gravelled drive ran along the front of the house and we were told that the upper west wing was for the exclusive use of the resident Stancliffe family. From the drive, a wide flight of steps flanked by low stone walls led down to a rustic fence that surrounded an open paddock; a couple of horses were contentedly grazing on the meadow grass that was still lush and green.

Part of the house had been requisitioned on behalf of Middlesbrough Borough Council to be used as a nursery school for evacuee children below school age. It was about a mile and a half north-east of Cropton as the crow flies, but it was three miles or so by road and forestry track. It stood in a small clearing at the southern edge of the vast Cropton Forest where English kings had once hunted deer and wild boar.

Much of the land had been in the care of the Forestry Commission since 1930 and they had provided sorely needed work for the locals and those who came here from farther afield. A huge area of land had been planted with conifers, although many of the indigenous trees remained and rhododendron shrubs grew in profusion along the edges of the forest tracks. Our new home (built in 1870) had originally been a shooting lodge belonging to a Lieutenant-Colonel Daniel Thompson, a retired veteran of the Crimean War.

The fine three-storey stone building, with its eleven bedrooms, had later been the property of the Ringer family who were much involved with fox hunting and grouse shooting. They had made good use of the long range of stables and kennels that stood to the east of the house but most were now unused. A couple of the stables housed the horses of the present owners, Captain and Mrs J. Stancliffe, who had bought the house between the wars. They were deeply involved in local church and village affairs, although Captain Stancliffe, like so many others, was away serving with the army.

Mrs Stancliffe, a refined and attractive middle-aged lady with dark curly hair, was always kind, gentle and ladylike in her dealings with the nursery. We thought her very posh as her daughters Susan, aged seventeen, and Rosemary, aged fifteen, were away at a private boarding school. Her mother was a leading light in the local Red Cross and Women's Institute and they owned several farms and a good deal of the land in the area.

Mrs Stancliffe employed a young German Jew as her housekeeper and her living quarters were in the topmost room of the ivy-covered tower. To me it seemed like a scene from a fairytale. Apparently she had recently been reported for letting a light show after dark as the blackout regulations were being strictly enforced and a light had been spotted at her window. Malicious rumours concerning the Jews were circulating in some quarters and there were real fears of infiltration by secret agents. Stories concerning the unseen presence of German sympathisers were 'doing the rounds' and the press called these fifth columnists 'the enemy within'. The suspicion became even greater if they were German nationals. This atmosphere of mistrust may have had a bearing on the governess being reported and she was fined and sternly reprimanded at Pickering Magistrates' Court.

Within a few months all German nationals were to be classed as aliens and interned. Most were kept behind barbed wire, patrolled by armed soldiers, in requisitioned hotels and guesthouses on the Isle of Man while their credentials were examined, but most turned out to be genuine refugees escaping Nazi persecution.

Mam had had a good deal of experience as a domestic servant, having worked for middle-class families in a number of large residences over the past ten years. This stood her in good stead as she assisted Mrs Winnie Ruonne, an excellent cook who always managed to feed us well even in those increasingly austere times. She was a short, plumpish lady with small features and a pale, freckled complexion, and we always called her 'Dinner Lady'. She was actually a middle-aged woman but her round baby-face made her seem much younger. She always wore a white wrap-over pinafore and an elasticated mobcap that hid most of her ginger-coloured hair, which she plaited into a thick pigtail that hung down her back.

Winnie's husband was a railwayman, and she saved up her off-duty days so that she could go and stay with him from time to time. Mam and Dinner Lady worked happily together in the cosy warmth of the kitchen where there was a large open fireplace and a Yorkist range of cream-coloured, enamel-coated ovens. They rose early and were

getting breakfast ready long before we got up. As the porridge bub-
bled away in a huge pan the great black kettle steamed on the hob, and
the distinctive mouth-watering aroma of home-made bread and cakes
often permeated the whole house.

Across the corridor from the kitchen was a large well-stocked storage cupboard with its shelves full of tins of ham, soup, baked beans and
the like. There were even 7lb tins of bully beef in it. At the other end of
the kitchen there was a walk-in scullery and a large copper for washing
the masses of dirty laundry that we produced every day. A local woman
used to come in on a Monday to tackle it and on the following day she
did the ironing. Whole days were set aside for particular domestic tasks
in those times.

A doorway led out into the side yard and diagonally across it was a
coal store and the garage where Mrs Stancliffe kept her big shiny-black
Humber car. Next to it was a tack room with a converted bothy on the
floor above, and beyond that lay the stables and kennels. It was not until
many years later that I learned that the sensuously curving pantiles on
the roofs had been brought to this country from Holland as ballast in
the old sailing ships.

On my first night I was put into one of eight small beds set up in
the large ground-floor dormitory that had a polished wooden floor
and no carpets. There was a small rug by each bed and a wooden frame,
covered in a layer of thick black material, was placed over the windows
at dusk. It took me a long time to get to sleep and, in the dead of night,
I woke with a start not knowing where I was; I felt lost and frightened
in the unfamiliar blackness and had the urge to go to the lav (as we
always called the toilet). Trying desperately to hold on, I searched under
the bed for the po (chamber pot) only to find there wasn't one. I had
not been there long enough to know the whereabouts of the bathroom
and, in any case, there had always been a smelly po (often called a jerry)
under our bed at home; a necessary evil as the lav was outside. When
we went to the toilet during the day we always said, 'I'm just going
down the yard.' Unable to hold it any longer I wet the bed and, fearful
of the consequences, I cowered under the covers on the damp warmth
of the saturated sheets. I lay there full of shame and guilt and I thought
the reek of ammonia must surely be noticed and I would be found
out, but nothing happened. I lay there choking on the fumes that rose
from the stinking palliasse wishing it would go away but, like me, it had
nowhere else to go. Trembling with cold, I tried to smother my sobs

in the now wet pillow. I lay there – a lonely, home-sick, ashamed four-year-old who badly needed his mother – shivering in the darkness for what seemed like hours until, exhausted, I dozed off, wrapped uneasily in a ragged veil of sleep.

The following morning, when my 'crime' was discovered, nothing was said and I was bathed and dressed by Miss Waters who was a caring, sympathetic and likeable young woman. The thin mattresses on our small metal-framed beds were filled with straw and chaff and were, fortunately, easily emptied, washed, dried and refilled, and when Mam came to work that morning and learned of my accident she gave me a big cuddle, a hug and a kiss.

'I couldn't help it Mam, it just came.' I mumbled tearfully.

'Never mind darling, just forget about it. Things will soon get better,' she said in her soothing manner. It was not an unusual occurrence, but I was to live with the guilt and shame of it for some time to come.

A few days later the gaunt-featured and prim Miss Thorne took George and I to have our hair cut in Pickering. Her auburn hair, parted on the right, was tied back giving her a severe appearance but she was nice to us, although firm when necessary. Spaven brought out and yoked up the trap. In retrospect, his surname seemed a little inappropriate for a man in charge of horses, as the word 'spavin' is defined as 'disease or distension on the inside of the hock of a horse'. Miss Thorne sat with us in the trap, which was always readily available for our use, and which she referred to as a Governess cart.

It was our first time in one and we loved sitting on the hard, wooden side seats of the highly polished carriage. The wooden-spoked wheels were twice my height and the burnished brass rail at the front gleamed in the autumn sunshine as Spaven busied himself with the harness. As we set off, the rhythmic rippling of the horse's sleek flanks fascinated me; the muscular haunches twitched constantly and it swished its long tail about to stop the swarms of tormenting, stinging gadflies from settling. The sharp resinous tang of pine-scented air mingled with the faint leathery smell of horse.

We travelled on a different route this time and, as we headed south on the long straight forest tracks, we quietly absorbed the stillness and gazed at the luxuriant greenery. We watched red squirrels collecting nuts and cones to store up for the winter. The forest was mostly made up of sentinel-like spruce trees with greyish-brown flaky bark, but the pine trees had more deeply fissured, crusty-looking trunks. The brooding stillness was broken only by the gentle rustling of leaves and the rhythmic and leisurely clip-clop of the hooves of the sleek brown mare. A slight autumnal haze hung over the leafy vale and we could hear the soft murmuring of a beck.

The bay mare crossed a shallow ford, or water-splash as we called them, beside which was a stone footbridge with white handrails. It nestled in the depths of a small valley and a little way past it a path led up to Kelton Banks Farm. 'Mr Ward owns that farm,' Spaven told Miss Thorne. 'They keep several Shire 'osses stabled there. They do various jobs on t'farm as well as pullin' t'snowplough, which is kept ready in case it's needed locally durin' t'winter.' The narrow, twisting road climbed a steep bank between tall, overgrown hedgerows before we turned right onto the Cawthorn–Cropton road. We travelled beside wild briar bushes that were heavily laden with blushing hips. 'In t'winter months this road often gets blocked by deep snowdrifts,' said Spaven. As we got closer to Cropton the tightly packed conifers gave way to mixed woodland interspersed with ploughed fields and grassy meadows. We turned into the top end of Cropton village and on our right a narrow earthen track led up a grassy slope to the church gate. Behind it lay an old graveyard with its grassy hummocks and leaning headstones, clustered around the pretty parish church in which Mrs Stancliffe was a Sunday school teacher – as Mam had been at home.

We thoroughly enjoyed that lovely carriage drive of about eight miles through the sights and scents of the countryside. The leaves whispered in the gentle breeze with the odd one spiralling silently down; Miss Thorne called them 'harbingers of autumn'. The trees seemed, to me, sad at their loss. Apples were ripening in the orchards and blackberries hung in red clusters in the hedgerows. Once in the small market town of Pickering we walked up the hill to the old stone building called The Vaults where Fred Pickering's barbershop was situated. We had our hair cut in the bobbed style of those days. The barber put an enamelled tin bowl on my head and cut up to it, and I vaguely recall the masculine scents of bay rum hair oil and shaving soap. I remember the click and snip-snip of the scissors as my fair locks tumbled to the floor, and as we came out the old, octagonal-shaped clock on the square, church tower struck four. We giggled when we were told that the top part of Potter Hill, facing east, was once called High Backside. We were taken to the Central Café above a tobacconist's shop and were treated to a lovely iced fairy cake with half a glazed cherry on it, and a glass of orange fizz.

The long, fine sunny spell came to an end and October was very wet with heavy and persistent rain that rushed down the forest runnels to swell the waters of Sutherland Beck. The streams became engorged to overflowing as the seemingly endless rains drained down from the saturated uplands. As the appalling weather continued unabated, the once shallow beck became a deep, raging torrent that raced down the narrow valley to join the roiling waters of the River Seven, now in full spate on Glaisdale Moor. Lower down it became a man-deep torrent that angrily thundered, foamed and surged southwards threatening to sweep away the picturesque old footbridge at Nutholme. Further downstream the full, muddy river caused extensive flooding when it burst its banks in the low-lying areas.

On those cold, dark and dreary days the paraffin lamps were on all day, and the doors and windows were kept tightly shut as incessant rain lashed against and streamed down the windowpanes. The wind howled, rattling the tall sash window frames as it boomed and echoed in the wide, stone chimneys. The torrential rain saturated the land and clattered onto the portico roof making the glass sing before rushing down to flow along the old cast-iron guttering. It drip-dripped interminably from the trees and bounced high in the puddles, and the packed soil of the pathways became sodden and slowly turned to ooze.

3

Little Man You've had a Busy Day

Around that time two new twenty-year-olds, Catherine Todd and her friend Mary, joined the nursery staff. Ten years earlier, when Catherine was only ten, her mother had died in the family home at Berwick and she was sent with her younger sister to a children's home in Scarborough. After leaving school she worked as a housemaid in Leeds, then in the early 1930s she got a job as a housemaid at Queen Margaret's Girls' School for well-bred young ladies on Filey Road, Scarborough. It was a private school; a kind of finishing school for the well-off, where she became a close friend of another maid who came from Middlesbrough. Mary, a tall, slim, dark-haired girl, went home on holiday taking Catherine with her. The family was living on Cannon Street when war was declared and the pair went to a 'keep fit' session at The Settlement Club where they heard that staff were urgently required. They applied and in early October were delighted to learn that they had obtained posts at Sutherland Lodge. Catherine was 5 feet 4 inches – quite tall for a young woman in those days – slim, fit and attractive with soft mousy hair (with a 'kink' in it) that rested on her shoulders.

The two young women really loved children and, from the outset, Catherine used to sing us to sleep at night after tucking us in and giving us a hug and a kiss. These little gestures of affection were much appreciated by the children who, like me, were so far from home. She used to sing a song that began, 'Little man you're crying, I know why you're blue', and went on to say, 'Time to go to sleep now, little man you've had a busy day.' I learned later that the lyrics were from a song recorded by Kitty Masters – a popular and well-known singer of the time – who was a vocalist with Henry Hall's BBC Dance Orchestra. During the '30s the band, with its signature tune of *Here's to the Next Time*, was often heard on the wireless and we called Catherine 'Kitty' from that time on.

We took to her and came to love her, and she returned our love a hundredfold. She was a sensible, capable and level-headed young woman who believed that children are precious and should be protected and loved if they are to become stable adults. When we had to stay indoors Kitty kept us entertained and happily occupied by playing music, singing and dancing for us, and her youthful exuberance ensured that we did not mope or brood about home too much. She kept us busy drawing and playing with toys and she devised guessing games that lifted our spirits and encouraged us to think for ourselves. When we were with her we scarcely noticed the rain that fell pitilessly day after dull, dismal day.

The cosy day-room was in the bothy on the floor above the tack room and in it we sat on tiny wooden chairs that were arranged in a circle around her. In times long past, the bothy was the place in which the unmarried farmhands used to sleep and eat, and to get to it we had to go up a narrow wooden staircase. A log fire burned in the grate of the open stone fireplace behind a wire-mesh fireguard, and on the green-painted wood panelling of the dividing wall there were brightly coloured pictures of children at play. A row of five elegant, mullioned windows faced north, and beyond the garage, the stables and the soggy meadow, the deep dark forest crowded round us in all directions.

Mary and Kitty read to us and we learned to chant 'Incy Wincy Spider' and many other popular nursery rhymes. We sang children's songs like *Twinkle Twinkle Little Star, I Had a Little Nut Tree* and *Hickory, Dickory Dock*, and I particularly enjoyed singing 'You push the damper in and you pull the damper out and the smoke goes up the chimlee [as we called a chimney] just the same' at the top of our voices. We made 'atishoo' sounds and flopped down giggling when the music stopped. We played 'Ring-a-Ring-a-Roses', never realising that we were re-enacting the sneezing that was a symptom of the bubonic plague that 300 years back had caused thousands of tragic and painful deaths.

At other times Kitty read us stories from *Aesop's Fables, Grimm's Fairy Tales* and *The Arabian Nights*, that told of wicked giants, flitting fairies, fearsome ogres, and fire-breathing dragons. There were men in turbans wearing slippers that curled up at the toes and huge genies that came out of oil lamps, and little children got lost in deep forests and were in danger of being eaten up by gnarled old witches. Our reactions to them told Kitty much about us and the tales helped us to learn right from wrong.

In the cosy warmth of the day-room I felt loved and secure, but some of the tales frightened and thrilled me at the same time. I would sit there wide-eyed, totally engrossed and enraptured by Kitty's lilting and mesmerising voice as her stories weaved their magic spell. From that time on – in my mind – I was able to transport myself into enchanted realms as she had given me the key that opened the door to hidden treasures.

The room across the landing contained several small camp beds, each with a feather-filled pillow and a straw-filled palliasse. There were white cotton sheets and warm woollen blankets on every bed and the row of tall, narrow windows were shuttered against the fury of the raging tempest. The regular routine of The Settlement Nursery School was continued here and we were kissed and tucked up in bed for a nap every day after our midday meal, which we ate at the tiny tables in the day-room. We always called it dinner and never lunch because we had been brought up to believe that only posh people called the midday meal lunch or luncheon. Every time we turned over in our little beds the hooked wire springs made a metallic, twanging sound and this, of course, encouraged us to try to outdo each other to see who could make the most noise until we got a telling off.

Sometimes, after Kitty had read scary stories to us, I could not get them out of my mind, and I was reluctant to be laid down. The low, dancing flame of the paraffin lamps threw out a soft light and had a distinctive smell, but the guttering candle threw grotesque, shifting shadows and, where they were deepest, I thought I saw horrible monsters and weird phantoms lurking, flitting and floating. Stifling my terrified whimpers I would curl up under the bedclothes and try to shut them out. Were they the product of an overactive mind or due to some trick created by the light and shade?

Upstairs in the main house, there was a spacious bathroom with a large white-enamelled bath enclosed within highly polished, wooden side panels, and in its capacious depths Kitty and Mary bathed us every night. Kitty always dipped her elbow in it to check that the water temperature was not too hot and one child was bathed while another was being dried. We were then put to bed, either in the large downstairs dormitory in the west wing of the house, or in a smaller room above the kitchen, in which Kitty slept. Here she was able to keep an eye on four children – usually those that required more care or supervision than the rest. I enjoyed the climb up the narrow, back staircase to that little bedroom, and I liked sleeping there, as I always felt more comfortable and secure with her around. The room had once been used as living quarters for the maids that worked in the grandeur of the old country house.

At bath times, Kitty and Mary had been told by Miss Thorne to examine our heads for lice and to check our bodies for signs of scabies. This happened more often after a puny little child arrived from a slum area of Middlesbrough where he had contracted scabies after sharing a bed with an infected person. He was showing the classic symptoms of the nasty and unsightly, contagious skin disease that was quite common in those days. It was caused by a female parasite, the itch mite. Skin eruptions occur in the webs of the fingers, on the wrists and buttocks and in the groin. The little boy was kept apart from us to prevent the disease spreading and was given hot baths in a small bathroom off the downstairs passageway. Kitty had to scrub his back and buttocks to lay open the lesions and we could hear him crying pitifully throughout this painful process. But she had to be cruel to be kind and, had it not been done, further complications could have arisen. A yellow emulsion was then very gently applied and the messy stuff covered a good part of the skinny boy's little body from the neck downwards. Her heart went out to him, but the disease was caught early enough to prevent impetigo and he soon recovered.

By Halloween the rains eased a little and were succeeded by thick clinging white mists that often lingered all day. The trees of my 'enchanted forest' looked spooky in the dim, dreary light and the bushes became indistinct and assumed nebulous and ghostly shapes. The raw, chilly fogs that shrouded the damp and drearily dripping forest were known locally as 'roaks'. Kitty and Rosemary entertained us with games using apples suspended on a string, which we tried to bite, or we played at apple bobbing where we tried to get one from a barrel of water using only our mouths. Kitty dressed us up as witches, ghouls, ghosts and vampires and made lanterns from hollowed-out turnips. It was scary in the darkness of the bothy with the lights out and we were glad when they lit the candles.

I felt sad on seeing the number of trees that had been brought down by the gales as I looked on the fallen giants as my friends. On the afternoon of 5 November the gardener built us a bonfire from tree cuttings and deadwood, and Mam told me that, 'In the distant past bones were burned to ward off evil spirits, hence the name "bonfires".'

We were only allowed to have a fire during the hours of daylight and the fallen softwood branches and twigs, known locally as 'kids', spat and burned well due to the resin in them. Once the fire was well established we roasted jacket potatoes and the delicious, golden butter dripped down onto our chins and bibs. The fire had to be put out before dusk. We then sat in the semi-darkness of the bothy and watched wide-eyed as Kitty lit sparklers and a small box of indoor fireworks that were the Stancliffe family's leftovers from the previous year. Soon all fireworks were banned completely.

Kitty was well able to cope with most of our childish problems and small emergencies and she had an uncanny knack of knowing when things were troubling us. She started getting us up to go to the toilet during the night, thus greatly reducing the bed-wetting. The weak and pitiful little boy (the runt of his family) who had had scabies used to tremble and shake on being taken from his bed during the chilly nights and Kitty felt so sorry for him. She would often wrap a warm blanket round his thin little body and hug him close until he settled, and she lavished on him that little bit of extra love and attention that she knew we all so desperately needed.

With the air heavy with the odours of cabbage and onions, we would often catch sight of Mam in the kitchen amid great clouds of steam. There was a constant clatter of pots and pans, and rich, fragrant smells of tasty, savoury stews often assailed our nostrils making our mouths water. As she baked fresh bread and cakes, her hands were often white with flour and we came to associate her presence with the aroma of lovely food. More often than not, when I saw her she was smiling and she had a way of tilting her head as she spoke. She was to stay with us for just a few short, precious weeks and, as the time for her to leave drew near, there was a deep sadness in her speech, which is often the case before a parting. Her face was often red and blotchy from crying but we never saw the tears that undoubtedly dripped into the stew.

Mam knew that we were being well fed and looked after and had settled in well, and that pleased her, but sadly for George and me, she was obliged to go. On the day of her departure there was much hugging and crying on both sides and she tried to hide her tears, but I could see the slight movement of her throat as she swallowed them. She was unable to afford the rent on Keldy Cottage for any length of time even though she had managed to sublet our house in Middlesbrough while she was away. But she now felt that she should be there when Dad got a forty-eight hour pass, as the train journeys were too slow for him to come here. Her doubts and fears remained unspoken and we were told much later that leaving us had broken her heart, but she knew in her heart of hearts that she had done the right thing in getting us away to safety.

That was the bad news. The good news was that my pal Eric had rejoined us, as for some reason he had failed to settle, and I was delighted that he was back. Eric's mother Winifred, who Mam knew quite well, said to her, 'Rosedale Abbey is in a lovely setting but it's bleak and remote. Eric was billeted at a big house and I had a letter from there. It said that Eric was a nice little fellow and the woman asked for his birth certificate. During the recent wet spell she asked me to send him a pair of Wellington boots. He was thrilled to bits at the thought of wearing them, as he said he would now be able to help her to get the ducks in. That Sunday they had duck for dinner and he asked her if it came from Albert Park in Middlesbrough. That was the only place that he had ever seen ducks before.'

Not long afterwards, as we were playing outside on our tricycles, the garage doors were stood open and Mr Bentley – Mrs Stancliffe's chauffeur – was polishing the car. At that point something caught our attention and we dashed off to see what was happening, but Eric had forgotten his trike and left it by the garage doors. He was devastated to find that the car had backed out and flattened it.

We were told by Miss Thorne that, if the Germans came, they might use 'nasty smells to make us feel ill' and we had to practise putting on our newly issued Mickey Mouse gas masks. They had a bright red rubber bit at the front and the circular eyepieces had blue rims but some of the children were frightened of them and hated the choking, claustrophobic feeling and the rubbery smell. Eric and I thought it was just a funny game and we collapsed in fits of giggling when the red floppy bit fluttered as we breathed in and out.

There were large storerooms and wine cellars beneath the house, which were reached by a flight of stone steps behind a doorway in the kitchen. The cellars, with their whitewashed walls, were always cool during both the summer and the winter, and many foods, such as cheeses, apples, salted sides of ham and jars of preserves, were stored down there. There were no fridges in those days and eggs were preserved in buckets of isinglass, a kind of gelatine that was obtained from fish. Kitty assured us that if we were bombed or attacked from the air we would be quite safe down there. However, I always had an illogical fear of what might lurk in the darkness behind that spooky cellar door.

In mid-December it turned bitterly cold with severe frosts. The muddy ruts of the forest paths became as solid as rock and light snow flurries drifted down from time to time. On duty the nursery assistants wore a thin, floral-patterned cotton housecoat that buttoned up at the front to protect their everyday clothes, but it didn't keep them warm and these 'uniforms' had to be bought with the money that they managed to save from their meagre wages.

In the run-up to Christmas thoughts of home crowded in and Kitty kept us occupied to take our minds off them. We coloured in strips of paper, which we then made into links using a paste made from flour and water until we had a long chain. Kitty hung these up in the bothy day-room along with the colourful strings of twisted tissue paper. We beamed with pride when the staff hung up the paper lanterns that we had helped to colour and glue.

The stairwell was wide and deep enough to hold a seventeen-foot-tall Norway spruce from the forest and it was decorated using cotton wool as snow and a fairy was placed on the top. On it we hung a few of the long, light-brown, spruce tree cones that we had collected during our forest walks. We were lucky, but many families had to do without Christmas trees that year, as all timber was now badly needed for the war effort. We painted Christmas scenes and Kitty pinned them up on the walls and we repeatedly asked her, 'How many days is it to Christmas?' We were so excited and impatient for Father Christmas to come.

When Christmas Eve, which was on a Sunday, arrived at Sutherland Lodge, Mam paid us a short visit, but Dad was not able to get leave from the army and, unseen by us, she left presents with the nursery staff. At bedtime we excitedly climbed the wide, plush-carpeted staircase to our dormitory and hung our woollen socks from the mantlepiece above the fireplace. A small glass of ginger wine and a sugared mince pie were left on the tiled hearth for Father Christmas but, due to an excess of excitement, it took much longer than usual to get to sleep and we tried *too* hard. Kitty had said, 'The sooner you go to sleep the quicker the morning will come,' but to no avail. We had tried to be good in the days leading up to Christmas, as Miss Thorne had told us, 'Santa Claus brings bags of cinders to children who have been naughty.'

Eventually – on that night of all nights – he must have crept up on us unnoticed, for when we awoke on that most wonderful day of the year we saw that the glass and plate were empty. Santa Claus had been! What other proof did you need? Kitty rubbed our faces and wiped the remnants of gritty sand from our eyes with a warm, damp flannel and, full of childish glee, we emptied our bulging socks on the coverlets. George and I had a few sweets and nuts, an orange (still available at that time), a bar of milk chocolate and a big, shiny, rosy-red apple. Huddled over our presents, I found that I had a popgun and some brightly painted lead soldiers and George got a colouring book and crayons. Christmas morning's magic never failed to thrill us.

The rationing of food hadn't started yet; therefore Dinner Lady was able to cook us a huge and delicious roast goose for our Christmas dinner and we had slices of it with roast potatoes, Yorkshire pudding, vegetables, and thick, rich, steaming gravy in the bothy. We sat on tiny, rail-backed chairs at low tables covered with green-checked gingham cloths where we pulled crackers and drank lemonade. The main course was followed by hot, rich plum pudding with lashings of steaming hot custard. But George and I missed our Mam and Dad terribly on this, our first Christmas away from home, even though the staff did their utmost to try to take our minds off it. It never entered our self-centred minds that the nursery assistants, who were also far from home, might also be missing their parents.

We were too excited to sleep when we were tucked in for our afternoon nap and we were so delighted when Father Christmas came to our tea party. We never suspected that he was actually Lol Bentley, the chauffeur and odd-job man who was the husband of old Spaven's daughter and lived in the big house across the field. The Christmas tree was now fully decorated. The staff had hung up the little parcels we had made earlier, along with shiny baubles and strings of silver tinsel, and under it were the presents from our parents.

We were given presents from Santa's sack and every child was handed a toy or a book. We wore paper hats and played games by the roaring log fire. We gorged ourselves on cheese and biscuits, hot mince pies, cakes, sweets and crisps, and had a slice of the white-iced Christmas cake, until we were near to bursting. We laughed and giggled uncontrollably when Eric burped loudly after drinking too much gassy lemonade. Old Spaven's grandson and the two teenaged Ward girls who lived at Kelton Banks farmhouse came and joined in with our games and carol singing.

Our photograph was taken, and I was all eyes when the man ejected the burnt-out flash bulb. We sat on low wooden chairs and I was behind my friend Eric, who held his new cowboy pistol. Eric was two months younger than me, but he was tall and well built for his age and I thought that he must be older than me as I was at that stage of development when children judge age by height. I reasoned that adults are taller than we are, therefore, that makes them older. Our George was safely ensconced in the arms of Miss Waters and Kitty stood next to her holding the hands of Mary who was kneeling on the carpet in front of her. We had a lovely Christmas in the company of people we loved and who loved us in return.

The whole of January 1940 was bitterly cold, with snow falling thick and fast and the ground frozen rock hard. We had dense, freezing mists as an exceptionally cold wave gripped the whole of Europe and the snow lay deep on all the rooftops. The windows were often covered with intricate, lace-like frost patterns and there was even a thin layer of ice on the inside of the glass at times. The bare branches and twigs of the deciduous trees were pure white and were three times thicker than normal due to the frozen snow that coated them. The woodland birds were twice their normal size due to their feathers being puffed out to retain body heat; with their heads tucked under their wings they looked like little fluffy balls. Many did not survive the cutting Arctic winds of that long harsh winter when temperatures as low as -2°F were recorded in the area. We overheard Tommy Gibson telling Miss Waters that, 'One of our bombers was so affected by the thickness and the weight of ice on its wings that it crashed three miles away on the moors over by Spaunton.'

The icy wind wailed as it whipped through the trees and the tops of the conifers rocked and lashed about wildly. We were kept indoors, cosy and warm, as a huge spruce log crackled and spat in the grate throwing out blue and yellow flames that licked around it and roared up the wide chimney. The Reverend Illingworth, the vicar of Cropton and Middleton, had some difficulty in reaching us through the deep snowdrifts. After we had sung a hymn, he asked us to close our eyes and put our hands together to pray for the thousands of British soldiers and airmen, who, he said, 'are having to endure atrocious weather conditions of frost and deep snow as they prepare to defend France and the Low Countries from an expected German attack. The training is going badly as their gun mechanisms, their lorries and they themselves are frozen stiff as quite often a foot of snow falls overnight.' Uncle John was among them, and the vicar said a prayer which went, 'Pray for all who serve in the Allied forces by sea and land and air; pray for the peoples invaded and oppressed; for the wounded and for the prisoners. Remember before God the fallen, and those who mourn their loss.' We were too young and full of the joy of life to really understand what it was all about.

The walnut-encased wireless that sat on a shelf in the kitchen was often on and its fretted speaker was carved in the shape of a sun and sunbeams. On it Kitty heard that the River Thames had frozen over for the first time in sixty years and, during slight thaws, when winter deigned to ease its icy grip, huge icicles hung like long daggers from the eaves. We were only allowed outside for short spells, wearing our warm Melton coats, knitted mufflers, woollen balaclava hats and Wellington boots. In Middlesbrough we would never have had a hope of possessing such warm, top quality overcoats, which had been bought with funds raised by generous-hearted benefactors.

We snapped off icicles and sucked them and sometimes used them as swords and had mock fights until someone, inevitably, got hurt. Bursting into tears they had to be comforted by the staff. We made slides on the frozen puddles and played out until the frost nipped at our fingers and made our noses red. After crunching through the deep snow, we kicked the verandah steps to remove the thick chunks from the soles of our wellies. Taken inside, we were given hot soup and steaming mugs of cocoa or Bovril as we sat in front of the fire. The tops of my wellies had chafed my legs, so Kitty gently smeared the red, raw places with a soothing salve. Later that month the worst storms of the century swept the country, with several trees being blown down, and the becks were frozen so solid that we could walk and jump up and down on them with no danger of falling through.

Winter dragged on and it often grew dark, making it seem later than it really was as snow fell softly and silently. Large flakes floated and spun in the air as the snow hid our deep footprints, and the dense forest was hushed as the house lights came on in the gathering gloom. When Jack Frost bit at our noses and the icy air hurt our lungs, Kitty ushered us inside. The blackout curtains were drawn and the rooms were flooded in golden light and we warmed ourselves at a fireplace built not for coal but for a raging log fire. At bedtime Kitty rubbed our chests with Vicks or camphorated oil, and the pungent, soothing vapours crept up from under our wincyette pyjamas to clear our clogged-up nostrils. She always gave each of us a kiss after tucking us into our beds, which had been warmed by means of glazed, earthenware ginger-beer flasks filled with hot water. There was much human warmth and loving kindness in that isolated place so far from home and it helped to make the disruption a little more bearable.

Those northern winters were harsh indeed and in February the countryside lay asleep under a creased and rumpled white sheet. A wan winter sun reflected back from the freshly fallen snow that thickly blanketed the grounds as Kitty dressed us warmly to go outside following a long spell indoors. We wore thick socks under our wellies, and our woollen balaclavas were pulled over our heads to keep our ears warm. Long knitted scarves were crossed over our chests and pinned at the back, and we had thick coats and warm mittens on as we excitedly ventured out, squinting into the blinding glare. Kitty brought out the Stancliffe's beautiful, highly polished, wooden sledge, named 'The Yankee Clipper' after a fast nineteenth-century Royal Navy cutter that had won the Blue Riband in sailing schooner races across the Atlantic. She sat on it with two excited, giggling children at a time sitting between her legs and, starting slowly, it picked up speed as it slid down the long, snow-covered forest drive. Kitty tugged on the rope and dug in her heel to make it shoot round the sharp right-hand bend at the bottom and this was repeated over and over again, until every one had had at least one turn. It was a long hard trudge for her as she repeatedly dragged the heavy sledge back to the top of the track that was like a long white gash as it cut through the avenue of dark-green trees. Giant spruce trees with their distinctive greyish-brown trunks lined the sides of the woodland path in their serried ranks, towering above us like majestic, sylvan gods. Masses of glossy, waxy-leafed rhododendron shrubs crowded the sides of the track beneath them. It was great fun, and in between our turns we threw snowballs at each other, waiting for Kitty to trudge back to the top where we clamoured impatiently for another go.

4

Kitty

Kitty was an attractive young woman who always kept herself neat and well groomed, and she liked to varnish her toes and fingernails in bright colours when she could get it. She was always cheerful, but around that time she seemed to be happier than usual and she positively glowed. It seems that she had been going out for some weeks with a chap called Alan Brown who was a Forestry Commission worker, and the first time she came across him she had been taking us for a walk in the forest. After hearing someone whistling a happy tune, she had caught sight of Alan up a tree. She learned that he was living with his parents in one of four rented red-brick cottages that had been built by the Forestry Commision in 1930. It was officially called Sutherland Beck Bungalow, but the locals always called it Peep o' Day Bungalow as 'Peep o' Day' meant dawn. It stood at the edge of the forest about a mile west of Sutherland Lodge and to get there you had to walk down a gradually descending grassy track. The walk, a right of way used by the postman and local tradesmen, involved the opening and closing of five wooden field gates.

In the fields next to it was Peep o' Day Farm, the home of old Willie Hammond; a little, wiry man with a bushy moustache who usually wore a flat cap, a dark three-piece suit of thick, hardwearing fustian and on his feet he had hobnailed boots. His leather gaiters only served to emphasise the bandiness of his legs. Born at Levisham seventy years earlier, he had run this small farmstead for more than forty years. Nearby there were other farmsteads called 'Rising Sun', 'Flowers o' May' and 'Cuckoo's Nest'. These lovely poetic names had given rise

to a local song called 'Spring in Ryedale', the chorus of which went
something like:

> The rising sun brings the flowers of May
> See the cuckoo's nest at peep o' day.

We learned that Kitty, one of life's givers, had been going to the three-
penny (1¼p) hop (dance) at Cropton village hall on her evenings off
and she had grown fond of Alan. She and Miss Waters would get us
bathed and tucked into bed before they set off along the track to Peep
o' Day Bungalow to meet him. They then took the short steep path
down from the bungalow to the beck, where Alan and his dad often
fished, crossing a narrow wooden bridge before walking up the hill
into Cropton; which took about thirty minutes. They enjoyed and
keenly looked forward to the dances on those dark winter nights as
snow lay thick on the ground. Glad to be out of the cold and the darkness, she would change her shoes and leave her favourite green coat
in the warmth and brightness of the cloakroom. It was at the Saturday
night hop that Kitty, after mingling with the locals, had first spoken
to Alan. She had been wearing a home-made, checked, cotton frock
with puffed out, leg-of-mutton sleeves, and on her feet she had blue
Cuban-heeled court shoes. The young people were dressed in their
best clothes, with most of the girls wearing floral-patterned frocks and
peep-toed shoes. The youngsters enjoyed the high-spirited fun in the
cosy atmosphere of the small hall, but many were obliged to dance
together as there was an acute shortage of males, with most of the men
away in the forces. Footloose and fancy-free, they performed the popular sequence dances of the time, including the lively Gay Gordon's; the
Valeta; the St Bernard Waltz; the robust and regimented Military Two
Step and the energetic Dashing White Sergeant. In between there were
various old-time Viennese waltzes, foxtrots and quick steps.

Alan was a good dancer and had a passion for it and, during the strict
tempo quicksteps, he would throw in a few twiddly bits, chasses and
fleckles. Kitty was not so good but she enjoyed the soft, sentimental,
romantic dance tunes, such as the haunting *Laura* and the recent hit *A
Nightingale Sang in Berkeley Square*. The music issued from an upright
piano in the corner of the wooden-floored room, played by a middle-
aged lady reading from sheet music. The village hall was on the main
street and was known locally as the Reading Room, and the pianist's

husband, who had a motorbike, brought his wife over on the pillion seat every week.

Kitty and Alan held each other very close, moving as one in a slow foxtrot to the tune of *Falling in Love with Love*. The atmosphere was romantic under the dimmed lights and in the warm, intimate and cosy setting they let the music take them. He even gave her a peck on the cheek, which was looked on as quite daring in those days. The last waltz was always danced to the tune of *Who's Taking You Home Tonight*, and whoever was chosen as a partner for this was generally recognised as your best girl. Alan chose Kitty. Just before midnight everyone stood to attention while the National Anthem was played, as Sunday was still observed as a day of rest. Everyone knew almost everyone else and the hops were always pleasant and friendly occasions. They were a much-needed antidote to the social isolation of the big house in the forest, and they helped folk to forget their wartime anxieties for a little while.

Kitty was pleased to learn that Alan's work was considered important to the war effort and his job was – like that of the farmhands – a reserved occupation that exempted him from military service. Whenever they had time off work they would meet up. Alan, who was ten years older than Catherine, was a strong, but smallish (5 feet 5 inches) man with straight brown hair that had gingery flecks in it. He was a rugged, tough and resourceful man, like most of the miners and steelworkers of the North-East who were reputed to be as hard as that which they produced. His friends called him Geordie, and Kitty soon learned that he had a quick and fiery temper when aroused. His teeth and fingers were stained brown with nicotine from the Robin and Player's Weights cigarettes that were his favoured smokes. He had come down here from the mining village of Chopwell, a typical County Durham pit village, in 1930 during the Slump, when droves of young men were desperate for work and prospects in forestry looked promising.

Alan's father, an ex-miner called Joe, was a small, jolly, placid man who was, like many another at that time, unemployed. His mother, Minnie, was an outspoken Geordie with a broad accent who was inclined to speak her mind, even if it sometimes hurt the people around her. Alan was her favourite; his older brother Fred was still working in a coal mine in Durham. Alan and his father had been glad to take any employment, especially when it included a cottage and a bit of land. The bungalow, and the smallholding that went with it, consisted of three fields at the front and one at the rear and it had a large garden where they could grow vegetables and keep a few pigs and hens.

Kitty told Mary that 'a woodman never works in the forest alone'. They worked in gangs for safety reasons as a man could easily wound himself in some isolated spot and lie there for hours before being found. Two men would use a long saw with a wooden handle at each end to fell the great softwood trees when they reached maturity, and the job was essential to the war effort as timber was in great demand for making pit props, telegraph poles, railway sleepers and such. The small side branches were used for fencing and for rustic work. The men also had to know how to handle the big, powerfully muscled Shire horses that were used to drag the felled trunks out of the forest. Harnesses and chains were attached to a long timber shaft fixed between two huge wooden wheels and the straight, newly felled giants were slung beneath this contraption which was then pulled along by the horses. It was a tough and often dangerous job.

Often completely shut off from the outside world, the roads and forest tracks had just been reopened by soldiers stationed in Pickering. With the wind whipping the snow into their faces, they had dug through the deep drifts in the more exposed areas. The powdery snow-drifts, blown through gaps in the hedges by the easterly winds, were known locally as 'stowerings'. Squads of soldiers were also sent out to help the local farmers to dig out buried sheep that had been sniffed out by the hard-working Border collies. At times the snow on the surface of the drifts froze so hard that the soldiers were able to walk over them. They said it felt really strange to be walking on top of buried hedges and stone walls. It was said to be the coldest winter of the century.

When a slight thaw set in Mam visited us again, and the taxi had great difficulty in getting through the slushy lanes and the snowbound forest tracks. She had come down on the train with her friend Winnie Ward, Eric's mother, who she had known since The Settlement days. Winnie showed Mam a nice letter she had recently received from Miss Thorne, in which she had written, 'I'm pleased that you sent Eric such warm and sensible clothing for this time of the year. He was delighted with the skittles, the comics and the sweets. He asks such intelligent questions about everything he sees.' Eric had shared some of his sweets with me and we had great fun playing with the skittles in the bothy.

By this time I was getting a feel for the countryside and was slowly but surely changing from a child of the town into a child of the forest.

Like many children of my age, I seemed able to identify with the intangible forces of nature, *feeling* as much as I saw. It would appear that the developing child is often open to influences that adults are not and I would sometimes sense that 'other' spirit world that lies just beyond this one. Young children, at times, have an uncanny intuition about such things and I believed that all natural things had good or evil spirits within them. I felt that the tall green giants were my friends spreading out their long arms to protect me. It may be that the young child retains fleeting recollections of their soul's early origins and this may enable them to peep through a tiny chink in the door to see things older folk are blind to. I seemed to dwell at times in a private, secret and mystical world of my own; a world that, sadly, becomes buried and lost forever as we grow up. There are many psychic things that can never be explained and it may be this that causes young children to behave so unpredictably at times. It seems that I had several invisible friends that I openly talked to and played with.

On Shrove Tuesday it was still dark as we got out of bed to be washed and dressed, and the thickly forested countryside was still snow covered and the cold thin air was crisp, clear and bracing. It was just getting light as we sat down to our breakfast of cornflakes with hot milk and toast and marmalade in the day-room. The Robertson's marmalade jar had a golliwog on the label, which led to arguments as to who should have it, so Kitty devised an alphabetical rota of our surnames. This, of course, meant that I was last on the list to get one, which was to be the case throughout my schooldays.

At tea time we watched wide-eyed as Dinner Lady expertly tossed pancakes high in the air and flipped them over before we ate them steaming hot and covered in sweet, sticky golden syrup, spooned from a large yellow tin with the word 'Tate's' enclosed within a red diamond shape. Miss Thorne told us that, 'In Pickering it is the custom to ring the pancake bell at 11 a.m. on this day and on hearing it all the shops close and the children have a day off school.'

For parents wishing to visit their children the L.N.E.R (London and North-Eastern Railway) had started to provide cheap day returns at weekends and Mam – sometimes with Dad when he could get leave – took advantage of these special offers. They visited us as often as they could afford to, which was not as often as they would have liked. It was such a long and difficult journey to get to and from Sutherland Lodge and they had to set off very early in the morning to catch the train from Middlesbrough to Pickering. The trains were slow and stopped at every station and they then had to catch the Helmsley bus and travel the two and a half miles west to Wrelton village. It was four miles on shank's pony through Cropton to Sutherland Lodge but occasionally, if they were in luck, they managed to hitch a lift on a passing farm wagon. On bitter raw days, as rain swept across the fields and forest, they arrived bitterly cold with the wet penetrating to their very bones and they were glad to dry out by the flames of a nice log fire. They then had to face the long walk back or share a taxi with other visitors, which they could seldom afford to do, and taxis were getting harder to find due to the petrol rationing. In the hard winter months this was often the case and Mrs Stancliffe would sometimes ask Spaven to take them to Pickering station in the pony and trap. The Lodge was in an ideal setting for us but it was far from ideal for our parents who often arrived back at Middlesbrough railway station well after midnight.

In the early part of the year catkins hung on certain trees and shrubs. The willow catkins were soft and fluffy, like a rabbit's paw; the alder catkins were dark and hard while the hazel catkins were long and pendulous with a dusting of yellow pollen when they first appeared in late January. They reminded us of lambs' tails, as they shook in the gentle, chill breeze and, as the winter days passed and the severe weather eased its icy grip, the birds began to sing. New life began to stir as the cold earth started to warm up and we noticed the first hints of spring. Green shoots of snowdrops pushed through their icy blanket to hang their white, droplet-shaped heads and Spaven said, 'They're known as Fair-Maids of February round these parts.' Soon after yellow, mauve, white and lilac crocuses thrust their way through the slowly yielding earth.

On Palm Sunday, at the start of Holy Week, we were presented with small raffia crosses and Spaven said, 'If yer keep 'em till this time next yeer, yer'l 'ave good luck.' On Good Friday we ate home-made hot cross buns and on Easter Sunday Miss Waters hid hard-boiled 'pace' eggs that had been dyed in bright colours around the grounds and we had to search for them. We then re-enacted the age-old custom of rolling them down the grassy slope at the edge of the paddock to see who could get the farthest. We loved seeing the fluffy, yellow chicks that were hatching out in the warmth of the incubators.

On Carling Sunday we ate the delicious, brown-skinned peas known as carlings. Dinner Lady had soaked them in water overnight and then fried them in butter and we called them sheep droppings, because that's what they looked like to us. Miss Thorne, who hailed from South Shields, told Kitty, 'It is an old northern custom which stems from a time of severe famine. It seems that many, many years back the River Tyne was frozen over and no ships could get in with food. The first one to get through was laden with these peas. They had a great public feast to feed the starving people and the story lives on in folk memory.'

In their due time, the green daffodil shoots budded, burgeoned and bloomed and there were large clusters of them around the stout, stone walls of the old house. They nodded their bright yellow trumpets and rocked in the wind as Spaven said to Kitty, 'Don't bring yon snow-drops or daffy-down-dillies in t'house. Flowers that 'ang their 'eads are unlucky indoors and they stop t'ens eggs from 'atchin out.' Pale yellow primroses and deep yellow celandine broke through and peeped from under the hedgerows around the paddock where the horses would soon be put out to graze.

The swelling buds created a green haze as the emerging foliage misted the hedgerows and shrubs beside the forest tracks. Mrs Stancliffe told Kitty that during the lambing season, catkins are put round the fireplaces of some of the local farms as they swear that it aids the birth of the animals. Some of the country folk secretly clung to the old nature worship and this was a clear example of their belief in sym-pathetic magic. Many of them still believed in the spirits of the trees, the water, the sky and the plants; animism – the attribution of a soul to living objects – is said to be one of the oldest religious beliefs. To the Brigantes, the ancient Celtic tribes of the region, stones, water and trees held real spiritual significance and pools, springs and rivers were regarded as entrances to and from the underworld. Many of the villages and farms were said to have their resident 'wee folk' and some said that creatures such as hobs helped with tasks, as long as they were not spoken to or interfered with in any way. There were stories circulating of folk being spirited away by the little people. Old Spaven added, 'Aye, not far from 'ere at Fairy Call Bridge near Lastingham, fairies used ter blow out t'lanterns on t'carriages; and other strange beings, such as bargests, if seen, foretell of a death in t'family.'

We enjoyed taking short cuts through the dense forest where, year upon year, the pine needles had drifted down to form soft brown carpets for us to bounce up and down on. We would often see Mr McDonald, the Keldy Castle estate gamekeeper, in his tweed suit as he patrolled the woods in leather gaiters with a double-barrelled shotgun broken over his forearm. To him and the local farmers, a gun was like a third arm. After the long winter we enjoyed playing in the fields on the fringes of the forest and were taken to the forestry workers' bungalows. Here we saw the gambolling lambs and thought it odd that the grey, slow-moving Masham ewes could give birth to such frolicsome offspring. We loved to see their long tails shaking from side to side as they pushed under their mothers' bodies to suckle. In the early spring sunshine, when everything was new, the dazzling whiteness of their wool stood out sharply against the lush green grass.

So, in these idyllic surroundings, I experienced the bliss of being and I loved the miracle of spring, the season most propitious to all living things. Wild violets, primroses and the blue periwinkle were now in flower and on April Fool's Day 1940 we played silly tricks on each other. George and I received birthday cards from our relatives and family friends in Middlesbrough, delivered from Cropton post office on foot by Ez Thorpe who wore a black, serge uniform and a flat-topped cap. He even worked on Christmas Day, walking long distances between the scattered farms regardless of the weather, unless the roads were completely impassable.

I was five years old on the fifth of April and George turned three the following day, which fell on a weekend that year. They were soft, warm days of changing sunshine and cloud and we were delighted when Mam and Dad came to visit us and stayed for a special birthday tea in the bothy where we had jelly and custard and fairy cakes. Mam usually managed to make the long, difficult journey about once a month, and whenever Dad managed to get leave and come with her, we were over the moon. We ran about on the springy turf of the lawns, and when he dropped to the grass we clambered all over him. We were given pick-a-backs and never gave him a minute's respite. It is amazing what young children can make otherwise sensible parents do; we were in raptures of delight and scarcely left his side. When Dad was with us we felt safe and secure and that all was well with the world but, all too soon, it was time for them to leave again. Each parting became harder to bear and Mam tried her best to hide her pain, not letting the tears round her heart come to her eyes in case it upset us. No doubt she let them flow once we were out of sight.

The next day we were taken to see Mrs Stancliffe's recently born foal, with its big, mournful, brown eyes and long eyelashes, while the shiny-coated mare grazed on the lush, new grass within the rustic fencing of the paddock. The foal stood wobbling on long stiff legs as it tried to nuzzle up to the black teats on the mare's underbelly, and its skin was as smooth and sleek as the skin of a mole. The mare was usually harnessed to the trap when old Spaven took it on errands but she was enjoying an extended break from her duties after her eleven-month pregnancy.

The harnesses that hung on the walls of the stable had an acrid smell of leather and linseed oil, and Spaven talked of horsey things while stroking and gentling the whickering mare as she stamped her forefoot and snorted. He tried to explain things to us but, on receiving the inevitable 'Why?' in response, he became so exasperated that he gave up. The horses were huge beasts to us but he lifted us up to help with the grooming using the body or the dandy brush. He loved his ''osses' and looked on them as close friends and I loved the feel of the mare's warm, sweet breath as I held out a few pellets in my cupped palm. I liked nuzzling up against her and stroking the long soft hair of her mane and the top of her long muzzle.

We would carry in small bundles of wheat or barley straw when the soiled bedding needed changing, and we were sometimes given the job of stirring the bucket of bran mash and mixing in the thick gooey molasses that old Spaven had prepared. In the winter he warmed it up for them. Twice a week he took a handful of linseed, put it in a pan and boiled it up, and when a crust formed on top of the oil he let it cool before adding bran and oats. He said this helped to give their coats a lovely glossy sheen and he warned us never to stand directly behind their back legs as they might suddenly take fright and kick out. On the insides of their legs we couldn't help but notice a network of thick veins that were so pronounced that we thought they might burst at any moment.

Tommy Gibson brought the tall, round milk churns to the kitchen of Sutherland Lodge every morning in his little van. On those warm, late spring days the twittering and trilling of a variety of small birds could be heard as our walks took us through green woodland glades. The tick-tick of the tiny jenny wren and the black-hooded bullfinch issued from the depths of leafy thickets and the low cooing of collared doves could be heard. The midges danced and bit in the damp umbrella of shade beneath the deciduous trees. As the sun shone through the branches, dappling the ground, it lit up the leaves making them translucent so that from below we could see every vein. I thought, 'if they have veins then they must have hearts', and as Mam used to say, 'You can see the hand of God in every living thing.'

Sometimes we saw buff-coloured hen pheasants, with their tiny chicks making weak, whistling cries of alarm as they scuttled for cover. Occasionally the clattering flight of a wood pigeon would startle us as it flew up, shattering the peace of the forest. The noise brought to mind that of a roller blind being released and we would catch a glimpse of white as the bird flew off. We nibbled on the tender, pale green leaves of hawthorn and called it bread and cheese, as it was said to taste like that.

Even in that idyllic setting things were not always of a pleasing nature. We often had to pass a gaggle of orange-footed geese (the gander was called a 'steg' in these parts). I had been terrified of them ever since one had hissed and chased after me, honking loudly with his neck fully outstretched and his cackling concubines also joining in. As I ran like billy-oh, blinded by floods of tears, he had torn my trousers with his vicious, stabbing beak and bruised my arm with his power-ful wings. That incident established a life-long wariness and distrust of them. Kitty said, 'They make good guard dogs because they honk whenever anyone approaches.' All the same, I liked to see the fluffy, white-downed goslings as they crossed the paths near the Forestry bungalows. At other times we glimpsed them on the wide grassy fire-breaks between the trees.

Another frightening experience occurred when we were confronted by a tall cross-eyed tramp, who occasionally turned up pushing an old pram that held all his worldly possessions. He had a dirty, straggly beard and long matted hair and wore torn and filthy clothes. We cowered behind Kitty's skirts as she assured us that, 'He is a well-educated man who has fallen on hard times and he is quite harmless.' But we were not so sure and kept well out of the way when we saw him begging at the bungalows. When he knocked on our kitchen door, Dinner Lady always gave him something to eat in return for small jobs, such as chop-ping up logs into sticks for the fire.

On the spruce trees the pale green tips of the year's new growth contrasted sharply with the dark green of the older leaves. A large area of the forest had recently been cleared and squads of soldiers were erecting Nissen huts. Army officers were moving into the recently commandeered Keldy Castle, which was a few minutes' walk away from Sutherland Lodge. The site was being made ready to receive the many infantrymen who would soon train here. Metal stovepipes stuck up through the semi-circular, corrugated tin roofs of the huts, which would soon house eight soldiers each. Large areas of the moors had recently been made inaccessible to the public as they were to be used for military manoeuvres and as firing ranges.

Keldy Castle was not really a castle at all, but it had been made to look like one. It was really a large, castellated, country house with land-scaped grounds, gardens and terraces. A long drive led up to an arched doorway with a two-storey wing at each side, and well-groomed lawns swept down from colourful shrubbery. The wooded estate covered some 7,000 acres that included around fifty farms and smallhold-ings. Purchased by Sir James Reckitt, the founder of the nationally known firm of Reckitt and Colman, at the turn of the century, it had a well-stocked fishpond with its own boathouse. Their products had been household names for many years and included the widely used Reckitt's blue bags for washing clothes and the world famous Colman's mustard. However, its huge factories at Hull and Norwich were soon to be bombed by the Luftwaffe.

The main structure had been rebuilt to Sir James's specifications. Its battlemented walls surrounded an inner courtyard, and merlons and embrasures crowned every parapet and corner tower. We were taken through the trees to the fishpond where we expected to see frogs bask-ing on the shiny lily pads. As we got there we heard them croaking, snoring and bubbling contentedly but we made too much noise and they rapidly plopped into the pond. We saw the wriggling tails of lots of little black tadpoles as they swam about in the shallow, sunlit water. Sadly, the army caused extensive damage during the war years and the 'castle' had to be demolished in 1956.

When Mam visited she often brought us goodies in a wicker picnic basket, and if the weather was fine she would bring out the HMV (His Master's Voice) wind-up gramophone, inside the lid of which was a picture of a small white terrier dog sittting with one ear cocked towards a large horn. She had a pile of twelve-inch, shellac records in paper sleeves. Holding one by the edges with her fingertips she placed it on the turntable, and taking the arm from its cradle she swung it out and carefully lowered the needle onto its edge. After some crackling, we would hear children's songs like *Old Macdonald had a Farm*, *This Old Man* and *Girls and Boys Come out to Play*. Three of the nursery rhymes I recall were Hickory Dickory Dock, Wee Willie Winky and

Lucy Locket. When a record ended I was fascinated by the scratching sounds as the needle swung back and forth in the grooves round the hole in the centre.

Mam loved to read to us and we were told lovely stories about giants, magic carpets that flew through the air and suchlike. With my curiosity aroused, my imagination grew wings and took flight and I sailed away into realms of fantasy. I was scorched by the flame of her enthusiasm and was influenced for life; it was from her and Kitty that I learned the magic of words and acquired those gifts of laughter and quiet listening that are so precious to a growing child. We were given plenty of TLC (tender loving care) and I grew to love the place and the people, feeling warm and secure even when mother and father were not there. They say that absence makes the heart grow fonder and it was true of Mam and Dad. With Dad away in the army most of the time their love had not had chance to fade; it was still as shiny and new as on the day they married and it was obvious to all when they were together.

During these visits we often wore ourselves out running around on our knobbly-kneed, stick-like legs. Leaping about like the newly born foal that had recently been let out to grass, we ran laughing across the meadow playing vigorous games of 'tig' or hide and seek. When I hid in the deep, dark spaces under the drooping branches of the rhodo-dendron shrubs, I could see out but no one could see me. I have fond memories of Mam in her favourite dark blue cotton frock with the white spots playing a kind of pat-a-cake routine on George's hands. She would hold my hands as I put my feet on her and walked up her body and, on reaching her chest, she would swing me over backwards so that both feet landed back on the ground. George would pester for a go, and the performance would be repeated, with lots of giggling, until Mam said, 'I'm worn out and will have to sit down for a bit.' A playground had been set up on the flattened rectangle of packed earth near the house and they pushed us on the swings and the seesaw until they had to rest again.

They set down an old blanket to keep out the dampness of the lush grass and we sat snuggled up cradled in their warmth and loving pres-ence. Sweet-natured, gentle Mam lavished on us all the hugs and kisses that she had saved up since her last visit and those poignant moments are stored in the depths of my psyche never to be forgotten. At times they threaten to burst my heart asunder but the memory of her all-encompassing love never fades. It is like a pale ghost of the past that is greatly treasured and very precious to me. She always spoke softly and quietly from the heart and was awash with tears at the first hint of sentiment. Mam would often tell us exciting stories of battles and miracles from the Bible, which she knew off by heart. We were loved and contented, surrounded by good and caring people and in our secluded valley we were as happy as kings. The gory details of the war mercifully passed us by and we were blissfully unaware that violent battles were about to flare up across the English Channel. We were loved and cared for and that was all that mattered.

On first hearing the mellow, disembodied call of the cuckoo in the distance, Kitty said, 'He is the welcome harbinger of summer.' Nature was coming into her own and the old horseman, Spaven, still a believer in the old country superstitions, showed us the thin hazel twigs, woven into the shape of a cross, which he wore under his shirt. 'They ward off t'witches thar knows,' he said to Dad, before adding, 'If yer turn t'coins in yer pocket yer'll allus 'ave money until t'cuckoo comes agen next yeer.' Dad called him 'that owld gadgie'.

We usually wore short-sleeved smocks that had a pair of pockets in the front, just below waist level to protect our clothes, and these often bulged with all kinds of weird and wondrous items. We picked up many things, such as worms, twigs, leaves, dried-up acorns, conkers, cob nuts, marbles and bits of string. Kitty often said, 'Waste not, want not.' So we took her at her word.

I loved the month of May when there were hardly any biting and stinging insects about. Mam visited us again, coming down with Eric's mam, Winnie. Masses of white mayblossom tipped with pink weighed down the boughs of the hawthorn bushes and, from a distance, it looked as though they were covered in a thick dusting of icing sugar. The rich, heavy scent permeated the warm, still air as wild briar and dog roses blushed pink and white in the burgeoning virescence of the hedgerows. Wild hyacinths were in flower as the tall spikes of foxgloves opened their spotted bells that we called Witch's Thimbles. Beside them tiny green fern fronds were unfurling and the air was full of musical birdsong, which we were coming to recognise. We loved to hear the song of the thrush; the gregarious pipit; the tiny brown tree creepers; the colourful coal tits and the pink-chested chaffinch, and other woodland birds that made up the daily choir. They had paired up and were laying claim to their territories as upright red and white candles of blossom adorned the chestnut trees down the lane.

Kitty took us to a nearby smallholding along the hard-packed earth of the forest paths to see the newborn calfs, which tried to suckle on our fingers. By now, we were becoming increasingly able to recognise our whereabouts by the different shapes and colours of the moss, lichen and algae on certain stones and trees. We were told that the frilly grey lichen on the trunks of fallen trees indicated that the air was very clean. Kitty took great care of us and tried to ensure that we came to no harm but, inevitably, the occasional fall resulted in a grazed elbow or a cut knee. One or other of us would trip over the exposed, raised roots of the spruce trees and the hurt needed to be kissed better, before being washed and smeared with Zam-Buk herbal balm.

On one occasion as we were out walking I tarried, wandering along in a daydream as usual, lagging further and further behind. Something caught my attention and I wandered off the path and into the gloom beneath the closely packed spruce trees. The further into the depths of the forest I ventured, the trees seemed to hold a deeper, more ominous darkness. To a child life is full of curiosity and wonder and I was searching for the red toadstools with the white blotches on them on which the elves and fairies sat. Kitty and Mam had shown us pictures of them when reading Hans Christian Andersen's fairy tales.

The 'other world' was very real to me and I suddenly found myself in a dark, twilight area where a deep chill seemed to emanate from the wild and primitive giants around me. The air was dank and drear as a brooding, menacing stillness reigned and a feeling of melancholy and apprehension crept up on me. The light grew ever dimmer beneath the dark overhanging boughs and I seemed to sense a low and growing, heavily breathing presence. I heard indistinct, stealthy movements; there were eerie echoes and strange whisperings in the air and faint utterances seemed to be coming from behind me. I felt that a dark mystical power was very close and that the aura of latent danger was not of *this* world. My heart was beating fifty to the dozen and chills ran up my spine as I sensed that someone, or something, malignant was very close and watching me. That was it. I froze; petrified with fear; my throat tightened in terror as the horror threatened to stop my breath. I could not shout out or bring myself to turn around – afraid to raise my eyes in case ghastly spectres hovered near.

At that moment, to my vast and utter relief, Kitty found me! Suddenly the voices were gone and a deep hush descended on the forest. It was like the deathly silence that followed the firing of the gamekeeper's gun and you could have heard a pin drop. All of the evil lurking things had fled at Kitty's approach. As she gave me a big hug and a cuddle, she tenderly wiped away the tears that burst forth to stream down my cheeks with the corner of her housecoat. I sobbed uncontrollably; trembling like an aspen on legs that had turned to jelly and they were still rubbery when we rejoined the others. Had the fire gone out at the *Saltergate Inn* letting the devil loose? Was it the voices of lost souls in limbo that I heard; an evil spirit of the woods; the old tramp; the gypsies (who were said to steal and sell children) or just a figment of my highly vivid imagination?

Adults tend to forget the wealth of a child's imagination: they often have the capacity to feel extremes of fear and excitement in response to what adults consider mere trifles. The world of childhood can be a place of frightening fantasy and strange happenings, and to a child unseen forces are still strong and readily accessible. They know the allure of witchcraft and magic and understand the eternal themes of love, truth, power and death, and some are able to *see* things that adults cannot. There are some things that can't be logically explained and, for a while after that terrifying experience, I did not sleep well and had bad dreams, peopled by ghosts, witches, hobgoblins, dryads and evil ogres. On future walks in the 'enchanted forest' I made sure that I stayed close to Kitty and I never wandered off the beaten track alone.

On those late spring mornings the newly risen sun gently warmed and gilded the mellow old stones of the big house. When the blackout blinds were removed and the shutters were opened its rays warmed my bed and formed golden rectangles on the wall. I would lie watching as they crept, almost imperceptibly, across the flowery patterns on the expensive, embossed wallpaper, sedately measuring the relentless passage of time. I remember thinking that, because the sun could move by itself and did not have to be pushed like Eric's tricycle, it must be alive. It seemed to me that it must be intelligent because it wanted to do good things like making us warm and helping things to grow. I *knew* that God must have been controlling it.

Colourful chaffinches twittered as they decorated their nest with bark and lichen after building them from moss, feathers, grass and sheep's wool. As the sunny days lengthened and warmed up, the cows and horses were left out to graze overnight in the fields. In what seemed a never-ending task, little birds flitted back and forth with grubs and worms to repeatedly fill the gaping maws of their tiny, naked offspring. On one of our morning walks, we were upset to find speckled, broken eggshells in lovely pastel shades of grey and blue. Close by were the wrinkly-pink, featherless bodies of two tiny nestlings, their heads with their pale yellow beaks looked far too big for their scraggy necks. The poor things lay broken on the ground having fallen from the nest. We called all newly hatched birds 'gollies'.

The breath of summer was touching the budding trees as the twigs of the ash trees belatedly opened their black leaf buds to put forth fresh, lime-green foliage. These and the red-leaved oaks were usually the last of the trees to do so. Soon, pendulous bunches of tiny single-winged seedcases, which we called keys, would form. The verges beside the lane became crowded with the tall, stemmed umbrellas of white-flowered cow parsley, and Spaven showed us how to dig out the soft white pith from their thick stems to make peashooters. As spring gently eased into early summer, the 'owld gadgie' said, 'Yer must never 'andle yon 'emlocks, or t'deadly nightshade that we call Devil's flowers. Yer see them giant 'ogweeds towerin' above t'others over yonder. Well, they 'ave tiny white 'air-like spines on t'stems that carry poisonous sap. Don't touch 'em, or yer skin'll cum out in 'uge blisters.'

On the following Sunday the mothers came out again and Eric's mother told my Mam that Miss Thorne had written to her again, asking, 'Could you bring him a pair of leather, crêpe-soled sandals as sandshoes are no good on the rough, stony forest roads. Sandals are light and cool and protect the feet. The weather is simply lovely out here and the children are outside a lot of the time. They roam the fields gathering flowers and are as happy as kings. Could you bring Eric some cool summer clothes?' adding, 'He was sick one day after his tea. Possibly the heat had upset him, as he has not ailed otherwise. He is a most intelligent boy and asks hundreds of questions like, Where does lightning come from? Why doesn't it strike trees? Why does God make the sun shine? and so on.'

Even in those austere times, hard-pressed working-class mothers, like ours, tried to maintain the old traditions. Although she was finding it hard to make ends meet, Mam still managed to bring us at least one item of new clothing at this time. It was a long-established Yorkshire custom to wear something new, and preferably white, in honour of Whitsuntide and that Monday, as the dreaming valley lay warm, calm and hushed, was to be no exception. Mam brought George and me a new white shirt. The sun beat down from a blue and cloudless sky that formed a perfect backdrop to the vivid, green foliage of the trees. The stillness and beauty of the place were overwhelming and on days like that it was hard to believe that there was a war on.

In the sunny dining room the windows were wide open and Miss Thorne had placed bunches of yellow-flowering broom in there. Yet another Whitsuntide custom in these parts, it was believed to bring good luck. We were served delicious roast lamb with freshly picked home-grown vegetables and the first, sweet-tasting, new potatoes of the year, all smothered in rich, brown gravy. This was followed by thick and steaming, creamy custard poured over a slice of hot, tangy, 'goose-gog' pie that was two inches deep. 'I have used only freshly picked, early fruits and have baked it specially for you little ones, so be good bairns and eat it all up,' Dinner Lady said. She maintained that gooseberries were good for the liver and stomach.

5

Grove House

By late May, the rhododendron shrubs were coming into full flower beside the forest tracks, and the mauve and pink blooms were the size of my face. It had been decided that Sutherland Lodge, being so close to the newly opened army camp, might become a target for enemy aircraft. It was also too far off the beaten track making it difficult for our relatives to visit. As Mam had remarked, 'It's a beautiful spot but it's too out of the way.' Plans were made to move us out.

On a fine, sunny day Robinson's motor coach and a pantechnicon arrived and took everything and everyone to the newly set-up nursery school at Grove House. This was about three miles east as the crow flies, but seventeen miles by coach along the winding country roads. Our journey took us south along forest tracks and narrow lanes to the main Pickering road. From there we travelled up the A169 Whitby road as far as the Lockton turn-off, where a narrow road dropped down from the wide sweep of the moors, descending into a valley and crossed a narrow stone bridge beside an old watermill. The coach then climbed the steep hill into the isolated hamlet of Levisham with its quaint stone houses, farms and wide grass verges.

From here we travelled along a narrow sunken lane between high earthen banks topped with thorn hedgerows and dry-stone walls, before traversing an open, unfenced grassy area where cattle grazed. Here the road swung sharply to the left and down a steep incline, becoming a leafy lane that emerged at a little railway station. We had passed this spot on the train eight months earlier. Grove House stood about a hundred yards to the east of the level crossing. It was tucked away in a beautiful wooded valley on the southern edge of the rugged North Yorkshire Moors. One elderly local, when asked, 'Why was the station built so far from the village?', replied with laconic country logic, 'Ah suppose they wanted it close t' t'railway line.'

The large, stone-built house was said to have been converted from an old farmhouse around the year 1856, the work being done on the orders of the Reverend Robert Skelton who was the Rector of Levisham and the Vicar of Rosedale. The house was built with locally quarried, golden sandstone, which had become blackened by the smoke from the steam trains that had passed close by for more than a century. The reverend gentleman had been obliged to sell his former residence, Levisham Hall, and most of his local properties to pay off his debts on becoming bankrupt. James Walker, an entrepreneur from Leeds, bought his former estate and by 1859 he, his wife and their six children were in residence at the Hall.

By 1881 Grove House had become the home of Robert Hansell, a local iron ore proprietor from Rosedale, who was married to Hannah, the daughter of the Reverend Skelton. At the time of the 1891 census the house was unoccupied, standing silent and sadly neglected. After it was reoccupied, a large two-storey extension was added at the eastern side and, at a later date, a female member of the Rowntrees of York bought it and used it as an occasional holiday home.

The gravelled lane crossed the railway line close to a brick signal box and the station buildings could be clearly seen from the house, as there were no trees to block the view at that time and we were able to watch the steam trains coming and going. There were two old, semi-detached, stone cottages almost opposite the booking office, which were set back behind small front gardens on the far side of the line. Jack Pickering, the junior signalman, lived in one of them, and a short distance north of his signal cabin there was another narrow, gated level crossing linking two farm tracks.

On arrival we followed the spare and sprightly figure of Miss Thorne from the coach, which had pulled up under the luxuriant, green foliage of a towering beech tree. Kitty held open the heavy, five-barred gate and we skipped up the gravelled drive that was edged with neatly trimmed lawns and flowerbeds. A lovely, variegated holly shrub, with white-edged leaves, stood on the lawn near the station goods yard. In the borders the last few spikes of grey-green leaved, purple-flowered

honesty were going over and flat, round, green seedcases were forming. In time these would become large and opaque and we called them
silver pennies. In the borders tulips and primulas were still in flower.

Grove House, a solid, thick-walled, seven-bedroomed residence
within twelve acres of gardens and shrubbery, nestled in the lee of a
steep wooded hillside deep in the valley amidst the peace and quiet of
lovely countryside. It was a wonderful old Victorian gentleman's house
and its grandeur and scale was in stark contrast with our working-class
house that could have fitted into one corner of it. There were only
fourteen children – aged from two to six years – in the nursery when
the war started, but that number had grown to twenty-four as the
bombing raids on Middlesbrough had increased.

Our little band of infants and toddlers entered the house through
an oak door that led into a square, stone-built porch with a crenellated
parapet. The side windows had wooden shutters on the outside and
above the inner door was a rectangular stained-glass window. When
the sun shone it cast red and orange-coloured patterns onto the plush
carpet below the intricately wrought-iron chandelier that hung over
the long corridor. Passing dark brown wainscoting, we came to the
foot of the wide staircase with its intricately carved newel post. Its risers
and treads were thickly carpeted and the banisters were made of pitch
pine. Turning right we passed through a finely carved, panelled door
into a large private lounge, which was to become our play room.

The long room had two wide, large-paned sash windows with wood-
panelled reveals. The thick walls were wood-panelled and the windows
looked out onto a wide, paved verandah with a glass roof that was supported on square wooden posts. It formed an open-sided portico and
French doors led on to it. On the far side four stone steps led down
to a gravelled area, beyond which were more well-tended lawns and
colourful flowerbeds. The large, square windows were not blast-taped
as they had blackout screens and sturdy wooden shutters to protect us
from the battering rain and howling gales. Carved, forward-facing lion
heads adorned the top corners of the fluted architraves of the windows.
Apparently, lions' heads featured prominently on the Rowntree family
crest. The high-ceilinged room had beautifully moulded medallions
and cornices, and on the south wall was a wide, stone chimneybreast
with a magnificent marble fireplace built to hold a blazing log fire. In
front of it was a wire-mesh fireguard to ensure that we did not come
to any harm.

Behind the play room lay the dining room, which also had a fine but smaller fireplace. A doorway led from it into a wide, stone-built, glass-windowed porch that faced south onto the grassy garden at the rear of the house. Ten yards away from the porch was a smooth-barked Locust tree, also known as Silver Chain or White Laburnum – a tree of light and graceful proportions which had long slender branches, and two feet up from its base it forked and its leaning trunk made it easy for agile youngsters such as us to climb it. It was just one of the many exotic and beautiful ornamental trees and shrubs in the spacious surroundings of the grand old house that we were to come to know every inch of. Some were rare species brought from foreign lands by wealthy owners, which was apparently the fashionable thing to do in Victorian times.

To the left of the front hallway was a large cloakroom, and behind it lay a stone-flagged kitchen with low beams that had large metal hooks in them. In the centre stood a heavy wooden table scrubbed almost white, and a deep, vitreous china sink stood under the blast-taped window of the scullery next door. It was a much smaller kitchen than the one at Sutherland Lodge but this time we had the whole house to ourselves. Behind the kitchen there was a large larder that kept the food cool.

The grand staircase had a gracefully curving balustrade and there were beautiful-stained glass windows above the landing halfway up. At the top there was a large bathroom and our metal-framed beds had been set up in the dormitory. Five large bedrooms, in which the nursery staff were to sleep, led off a long corridor. The rooms had a small wrought-iron, black-leaded fireplace with a mantle-shelf supported on delicately fluted, wooden columns, and there was a fender with a brass rail around each hearth. The bedrooms were directly above the kitchen and larder and their small-paned windows were all blast-taped.

At the southern end of the garden there was an overgrown pond, where we saw white-billed coots that dived and stayed under the water for so long that we thought they must have drowned. We were not allowed down there on our own but Kitty took us to see the small brown, chestnut-cheeked little grebes, commonly called dabchicks, with the female carrying three fluffy chicks on her back. She had a small whitish patch on each cheek where the beak joined it and her nest actually floated on the water amongst the reeds. There were small furtive waterhens with white-streaked flanks and red beaks tipped with yellow that looked as if they were wearing red garters on their green legs. They are, more correctly, called moorhens and we watched them as they dived for food. Emerging mayflies performed their strange up-and-down dance above the placid, pearly sheen of the water, and hundreds of gnats formed smoky clouds. A long rustic fence separated the garden from the station goods yard. The wooded slopes above the house were clothed in a mixture of conifers and deciduous trees.

The large, three-bedroom, stone-built station house stood just south of the pair of cottages and its gable end abutted the northbound platform. The door of the paved yard at the back of the house led directly onto this 'up' platform. Near it was a cast-iron, Rowntree's one penny chocolate dispensing machine and close by stood a bench. The gable end of the house had a clock let into it at about shoulder height. It had a round, white dial faced with black Roman numerals. Late tulips were in flower in its little front garden where the door to the kitchen was set within a rectangular stone porch. The front windows overlooked the fields beside the railway line.

The kind and good-natured senior signalman, Mr Walter Artley, lived here, and on rising his first job was to wind up the platform clock. A door from the first sitting room led into the kitchen where a wooden clothes maiden, that was raised and lowered by means of cords and pulleys, hung from the ceiling above a gleaming black-leaded fire range.

The stairs led from the kitchen to the bedrooms where ceramic pitchers and ewers were used for washing. Walter lived here with his wife and their four children, aged from two to twelve years old. Mrs Artley, a friendly and caring lady, played the organ in Levisham Chapel-of-Ease every Sunday, and also played for the services held in the tiny valley church in the summer months.

There was a neatly cultivated flower and vegetable garden behind the station house, and it had an outside brick coalhouse and a privy with a flush toilet. A narrow beck ran past the bottom of their long garden before it swung west to drain into Pickering Beck. In dry, calm weather the beck could be heard babbling quietly over the water-worn pebbles of its stony bed. The Artleys kept a few black-faced Masham sheep and we would often hear the lowing of their black and brown Holstein cows as they grazed in the meadow. The smelly cow byre and the stables were situated in a range of wooden buildings at the far end of the field. The excess milk was carried across to Grove House in two-gallon, white-enamelled jugs to be sold to Dinner Lady.

On balmy early summer evenings we could hear Mrs Artley calling the cows in, as sound carried a long way in the quietness of that deep valley. The animals would amble along with their distended udders leaking milk and after we got to know her eldest daughter Monica, she would occasionally take us into the warm, cosy atmosphere of the byre. We liked to watch Mrs Artley as she sat on a three-legged stool with her head resting against the cow's side calmly milking them by hand. The milk from the limpid-eyed cows would squirt noisily into the white-enamelled pails. The cows seemed like huge beasts to us but they had a nice warm, sweet smell close up. Occasionally, as a special treat, we would be given a glass of the warm, creamy milk, which was now at its richest and most plentiful as the meadow grass was lush and green. Mrs Artley used to separate the lumpy curds from the thin watery whey to make cheese in an old contraption that had a wooden barrel fixed to a cast-iron wheel. She rotated it by turning the handle on the side and the whey was given to the pigs.

The stables housed Charlie, their loveable little black pony; Daisy, their roan horse, and her foal. They called the partition between their stalls the skelbeast, and the cow byre was known as the shippon – terms that lingered from a bygone age. They also kept a few clucking and scratching hens and reared a couple of pigs that were killed at Christmas to supply the family with sufficient ham and bacon for the year to come. Oil lamps were used to light the place and the small-paned windows were criss-crossed with sticky blast-tape like the railway cottages.

Levisham village was one and a half miles away up the steep gravelled lane, which – during high summer when the stones were dry and sunlit – became a dazzling white ribbon. The village could be reached by a shorter but steeper route as a rutted, earthen footpath led off the lane just above Grove House, passing behind the range of stone outbuildings that housed the electric generator and stored coal, garden tools and suchlike. It continued eastward before swinging left to climb steeply through mixed woodland and hazel shrubs. It emerged into open fields halfway up the hillside and led steeply up to a barn. It then passed a wooden bench, erected to celebrate the Coronation of King George VI three years earlier. From here there was an excellent view of Newtondale, the railway line running through it and Newton village perched on the opposite hilltop. The path continued before emerging on a lane that led to Levisham Chapel-of-Ease. The 'squire' of the manor was a Mr Baldwin, the co-founder of the Paton and Baldwin wool manufacturing and knitting pattern empire, a firm that was a household name at that time. He had lived in Levisham Hall with his family for the last sixteen years.

The Hall was actually little more than a large, three-storey cottage with a castellated stone porch and double bay windows. It was full of quaint nooks and tiny rooms and its commanding position gave it fine views of the Lockton valley and the countryside to the south. Around the turn of the century, the wife of the future Lord Baden-Powell had hired the Hall for an extended holiday with her young family while her husband Robert, a cavalry officer, was fighting in the Boer War. He, of course, became famed for his founding of the Boy Scout movement in 1908 and the Girl Guides two years later.

On those glorious summer mornings the golden light of the sun, as it rose over the high ridge to the east, lit up the dark fringe of trees on the opposite hillside turning them a bright green. The dawn of a new day was the signal for choirs of birds to break into gloriously cascading waves of song. While the big house was still immersed in half-light and sombre shadows, we were roused, washed and dressed. The strength-ening power of the ascending sun slowly burnt off the dew on the meadow and her rays dissipated the mists from the valley, as we sat down to breakfast. This usually consisted of thick, steaming porridge, made with Scott's Porridge Oats, that had a dollop of jam or treacle on it. We then filled up on thickly buttered toast and marmalade. Every morning, after breakfast, Kitty sat the younger children on a row of little ceramic chamber potties that we called pos (pronounced pose) or jerries. They sat outside on the verandah if the weather was dry and warm, but if it was cold or wet they would be brought inside until they had done their 'duty', leaving the windows and doors open because of the smell. We older children were able to go to the toilet by ourselves. The large dormitory had a polished wooden floor and an elegant tiled fireplace and it was in here that most of the younger children slept.

The older ones, including myself, were allowed to stay up a little later than the rest as we slept in the play room. At midday we had a hot savoury meal with plenty of potatoes and vegetables depending on the season of the year, as there were no freezers to keep food fresh in those days. A sweet of sago, tapioca (that we called frogspawn), rice pudding, jam roly-poly or plum duff followed. After our meal we were laid in our little beds with the window shutters closed and this was our regular nap of an hour or so to allow our food to digest. In the half-light the ugly leonine faces above the windows frightened me and I hid my head under the bedclothes. If we were naughty and refused to lie down, or if Eric and I disturbed the other children by talking, we were made to stand in the corner with our faces to the wall. We were often told off but were never smacked. After our nap we would sometimes be taken for a walk along the path that started not far from the kitchen door.

Pretending to be soldiers or airmen, we chattered and babbled on. Aeroplanes were all the rage at that time and we zoomed about with our arms outspread dodging round the adults. We no doubt drove them mad making aeroplane noises as we bombed and killed hundreds of nasty Jerries in our imagination. My three-year-old brother George was quite content watching a snail pushing out one feeler at a time as it emerged from its shell, or in pushing the large, fluffy white toy Scottie dog along. With its short fur and stubby upright tail, it was mounted on a steel framework that had four rubber-tyred tin wheels. It had a tubular steel handle with which to trundle it along and our George really loved it. Eric preferred to pedal around on the flat-seated tricycle that had replaced the one wrecked at Sutherland Lodge.

In the evenings, tired out and grimy but well fed, we were put in the magnificent antique bath that had bright, shiny copper taps and beautiful polished mahogany side panels. It could comfortably accommodate three adults within its massive tub, but the staff had to go sparingly on the amount of water they used, otherwise we might have drowned in it. At home the anodised tub had been placed in front of the kitchen fire and it took several pans and kettles of boiling water to fill it. Here we had scalding hot water at just the turn of a tap and it was still a great novelty to us; we had never seen such luxury, even at Sutherland Lodge! Amid great clouds of steam four or five of us would splash about in it and, with our little naked bodies glowing pink and warm, Kitty would dry us. I was kept snug and warm wrapped in a fluffy white towel and she gave me lots of hugs and I loved her very much. We would have done anything for her. She was pure of heart and would never dream of hurting anybody's feelings; in fact, there was not a hint of deceit in her make-up.

We knelt by our beds every night to say the prayers that Kitty had taught us, such as, ' As I lay me down to sleep, I ask thee Lord my soul to keep, If I should die before I wake, I ask thee Lord my soul to take! Amen' and 'Gentle Jesus meek and mild, Look upon a little child, Pity my complicity, Come to me when I die. Amen.' After that we were tucked into our beds, scarcely aware that there was a war on outside our cosy, sheltered world. At times, as I lay tucked up in bed, I could hear the three harsh screaming barks of a dog fox and the quietness was sometimes rudely shattered by the painful death cries of some small animal in the woods. When woken by the wind as it rattled the wooden shutters during heavy rainstorms, I would lay in the darkened room listening to the sounds of the rushing water in the flooded beck. In dry weather water just trickled down the runnel beside the lane that led up to Levisham village, but at times like this, it became a gushing torrent. Gusts of wind would buffet the sturdy old house as they howled round it like the spirits in hell. As the thunder rumbled and growled and the lightning flashed I would hide under the bed covers frightened but enthralled by the awesome power of nature. Kitty got us to count the seconds between the flash and the thunder when we were unable to sleep and this helped to take our minds off it for a while. She said, 'You can tell by the time between them whether it is moving away or not.'

We would get quite excited when we were told that 'the parents are coming out to visit the bairns'. We would sit and wait expectantly in the roofed shelter or on the seat of the bench on the station platform, and listen eagerly for the first faint train whistle to come from the quiet remoteness of the Newtondale Gorge. In the goods yard there was a big warehouse where coal for the trains was stored, but ours was delivered in a lorry that came from Pickering. Nearby was a small wooden hut, with a stovepipe chimney sticking up from its sloping roof in which paraffin and oil were stored for use in the lamps on the platform, in the station house and in the booking office.

We chatted and fidgeted as we impatiently waited. It was so still and quiet that we could hear the Artley's sheep as they ripped up and chomped on the tussocks of grass. Behind us the hundreds of colourful roses – that grew in profusion by the diagonally sloping slats of the fence – scented the air. The flowerbeds were edged with white-painted stones and the hanging baskets and tubs on the platforms were well tended and bright. In recent years, Mr Artley had won first prize in the annual Best Kept Railway competition on a number of occasions. We became excited on hearing a faraway whistle and feeling a slight vibration under our feet. Puffing sounds grew louder and the shiny-black steam train appeared round the bend in clouds of black smoke and hissing white steam.

Our tremulous excitement increased as the great engine rumbled to a halt. The heavy doors slammed back and the parents and relatives stepped down onto the platform. Mam was there with Dad in his civvy clothes, which meant that he had a week's leave. I raced towards them to be scooped up into Mam's loving arms and she hugged me ever so tight and smothered me in loving kisses. George was still in the garden with Kitty, as he was too young to be wandering about on the platform. I did not understood why there were tears running down Mam's cheeks when we were so happy.

It was a warm sunny day at the beginning of June and we played football with Dad in the field. When he took off his jacket and rolled up his sleeves we were reminded of his army service as a young man. His strong, muscular, sunburnt arms, with their haze of fine fair hairs, were covered in colourful red, black and blue tattoos. On one arm there was a tattoo of his army badge, on the other there was a naked woman with a snake wrapped around her that extended from the back of his hand to his elbow, and when he clenched and unclenched his fist it looked as though she was dancing. After working up a good sweat he took his shirt off, unveiling the great spread eagle tattooed across his chest. It looked as though it was flying when he tensed and relaxed his pectoral muscles.

He told us fascinating stories about his sea voyages to foreign lands where he had seen dolphins and flying fish, and he talked of his army service in China, Egypt and India, saying, 'In India we had servants and lived like gentlemen. The charwallahs made and served us tea and punkahwallahs cooled us with fans made from palm fronds. The atmosphere was very dry and hot. Darzis made us new clothes and dhobiwallahs did our laundry, washing our clothes in the river in which huge venomous snakes could be seen swimming.' He told us that 'there were numerous beggars in dhotis [loincloths] and the sacred cows wandered about the streets wearing garlands of flowers round their necks'. He showed us pictures of some of the animals he had seen, such as elephants, Bengal tigers, monkeys, peacocks and hyenas. 'July was the rainy season,' he continued. 'It was heaviest in the evenings when it really lashed down and it went on for weeks – often with spectacular displays of lightning. At other times the blazing sun bleached our hair and our uniforms as the bullock cart drivers took us past banana plantations and beneath coconut palms and we paid them in rupees and annas.' He told us about the Red Fort in Delhi and the

Black Hole of Calcutta; he had seen so many wonderful exotic things that we could only dream about.

After a while we grew tired of sitting and were eager to run about again, and Dad told us how the Indians had played them at football in their bare feet on rough sand and gravel pitches. He dribbled a rubber ball around us pretending to be the new blonde-haired Middlesbrough football sensation, Wilf Mannion, and I was supposed to be George Hardwick, the brilliant left full back with the film star good looks reminiscent of Clark Gable. A local lad, just like Mannion, he was to captain the England team after the war. Before the war, Dad had been among the cheering crowd at Ayresome Park football ground when twenty-year-old Mannion had scored four goals for the 'Boro' in a dazzling exhibition of his footballing skills. The Boro were in the top division of the Football League and on a bright sunny day two weeks before the Christmas of 1938, Dad had seen them thrash the tangerine-shirted Blackpool team 9-2. He had been there when they had recently beaten Portsmouth 8-2 when Mannion had scored a brilliant hat trick. He was Dad's hero.

Soon afterwards, the mayblossom faded and fell and the elders produced their pinky-white curds. Blatant, blood-red blotches of wild poppy splashed the lush greenery of the roadside verges, contrasting sharply with the pallid umbels of the hedge parsley. The air on that sultry afternoon became oppressive as dark, cumulus clouds massed and heaved up behind the western hillside. The light faded and ragged rain clouds raced overhead as the wind rose. As the storm increased in fury, the wind shrieked and howled like a multitude of lost souls, and the tops of the trees thrashed about wildly as the rain clattered down in stair rods onto the portico roof. The beck that was normally just a trickle became a deep raging torrent and rainwater dripped incessantly from the eaves until, suddenly, the violence of the summer storm abated as quickly as it had arisen.

On that unusually dull and chilly summer day Mam came to visit us again, but Dad was not with her as all leave had been cancelled. She was wearing her dark-blue, narrow brimmed hat, her favourite light blue, white-spotted frock and her navy-blue coat, but I sensed a deep sadness and sorrow in her, and a whole range of emotions seemed to flit across her honest open face. The smile that usually lit it up was missing this time and she looked as pale and melancholy as the clouded, battleship-grey sky. In the dim half-light of the hallway I could see that she was close to tears, which made me feel sad in return. We were not to know that she had just learned that her younger brother, Private John Bradford, was in the retreat to the French coast. His battalion was fighting a rearguard action with their backs to the sea as thousands of French, British and Allied troops were surrounded by the Germans and trapped on the beaches near Dunkirk. Some sought refuge in the high, bone-coloured sand dunes that rimmed the beaches in which even marram grass struggled to survive.

I was to learn later that the German army had smashed its way through neutral Holland and Belgium in just four days, and in the near rout towns and villages had become flaming ruins. Major General Erwin Rommel, in command of the 7th Panzer Division, had broken through the last of the French defences and turned back an Anglo-French coun-ter-attack at Arras in which Uncle John had been involved. Rommel's thrust to the Somme had divided the BEF from the French forces to the south. The *Wehrmacht* had swept across northern France driving the BEF before them, before thrusting north towards the coast. Britain's 'invincible army' was in full flight, caught in a pincer movement. The whole front crumbled, and the Belgian government capitulated.

As the Germans advanced in persistent drizzle towards the flat and marshy coastal plains, Uncle John was among the troops vainly strug-gling against overwhelming odds to hold the defensive perimeter line on the canal that ran from Burgues, through Furnes to the Nieuport area to the east of Dunkirk. The name must have reminded him of the Newport area of Middlesbrough where he had grown up and he must have wished that he was back there.

Later he told Gran of the long queues of soldiers, wearing great-coats or dripping groundsheets, on the crowded beaches as the rain was driven on by a cold northerly wind. Shivering with cold and fear they waited patiently for their turn to be taken off. The canals and roads were choked with wrecked lorries and the fields flooded as Luftwaffe bombs breached the dykes. Abandoned harrows, rakes and spades spoke of a more peaceful time.

Winston Churchill then gave the go-ahead for a massive rescue bid. More than 100,000 soldiers were quickly taken onto ships at Dunkirk harbour and, providentially for a time, they were hidden under a dense bank of fog. The men waded shoulder deep into the sea to meet the flotilla of small boats that had made the parlous Channel crossing to bring men directly home, or to ferry them to the waiting ships. Screaming, crank-winged Junkers 87s, known as Stukas, swept down like dark, howling birds of prey to strafe and bomb the waiting ships, the small boats and the long orderly zigzag lines of soldiers. Dazed and wounded men sat or lay on the open beach crying out for water or medical attention. It was pure mayhem. The RAF was conspicuous by its absence having lost half of its obsolete aircraft within the first forty-eight hours. It was a sad tale of heroic failure. Broken bodies littered the beaches like squashed fruit and the sweet, cloying, gut-wrenching stench of putrefaction was everywhere. The tides ran red and black with blood and oil as hundreds of khaki-clad bodies floated face down in the filthy water.

Gran and her daughters, who had seen the bloodstained stretchers on the cinema newsreels, were relieved to learn that John was safe. He had been among the last to get away. Totally worn out he had curled up on the deck of the ship under his greatcoat, collapsing into a sleep of utter exhaustion for the whole trip. He was in a sorry state and the passage home became just a hazy memory. On arrival back in Britain he was hungry and unshaven and sported a week's growth of stubble. Just twenty-one years old, he was unspeakably weary with eyes that were red-rimmed and bloodshot. When he disembarked under the grey barrage balloons at Dover he was half-starved, with his sodden uniform ripped and filthy. They were beaten but unconquered in spirit as they waited to be sent home on much-needed leave.

All told, nearly 350,000 British, French, Belgian and Polish troops were brought out and the *Daily Mirror* banner headlines called the whole evacuation 'Bloody Marvellous'. By some miracle, most of the army had been saved to fight another day.

Many scheduled trains were cancelled in order to get the men away from the coast and Uncle John was given a blank postcard on which to write his Christian name, home address and 'Am safe'. On receiving it Gran was over the moon. John was sent to a rest camp for a couple of days to be re-equipped and to recuperate a little before being given a seventy-two-hour leave pass. Once home his mother and three sisters greeted him with tears of joy and relief. He slept long and late and soon made up for his recent lack of food. People bought him beer in the local pub and the returning heroes were allowed into dances and cinemas without paying. On visiting Archie, Gran said, 'I was so worried when John was sent abroad but he has experienced the utter madness of war at first hand.'

He now knew the horror and pity of seeing friends killed in combat, and had gazed repeatedly on the repulsive face of death. He had left home little more than a boy but had returned a man. On leave he refused to talk about it saying only that it was too close and too painful to think about. He just wanted to blot out of his mind the dull, stupid expression he had seen on the faces of the dead, and it would be some time before he laughed out loud again.

The ranks of Uncle John's battalion had been sorely depleted by the debacle in France, and John was promoted to Corporal. The Green Howards were based at Richmond in North Yorkshire, but he, and hundreds of other men from the defeated army, were retrained and soon afterwards posted to Blandford in Dorset, becoming part of the 50th Northumbrian Division. They had learned some harsh lessons in France and here they continued to hone their new skills. The battalion was made to work hard and the men were brought to a high state of fitness. The locals became accustomed to the sound of their heavy, steel-shod boots crashing down onto the metalled roads. Carrying heavy packs they manoeuvred and streamed over tough assault courses; they dug trenches, hacking into the hard earth with their heart-shaped trenching tools.

We saw troop trains passing through Levisham station crammed with grim-faced soldiers, hollow-eyed from lack of sleep, many of them with bandaged heads or their arms in slings. These, like our Uncle John, were the lucky ones and they waved to us from the carriage. The humiliating retreat to and from Dunkirk had been an unmitigated disaster. England had not been so vulnerable since the Napoleonic Wars and the government came perilously close to caving in with many people feeling that the war was all but lost. The country was at rock bottom and now stood alone against the might of the all-conquering Germans. In mid-June German troops marched up the Champs Élysées, and a bloody battle on English soil could quite easily have been next as England was now within easy striking distance of the Luftwaffe. In a stirring speech Winston Churchill said, 'Let us brace ourselves to our duty …'

At Grove House time passed peacefully and the long hot, blazing summer days were followed by short sweaty nights. We always seemed to have long, hot summers in those early war years and we played in the sunshine blissfully unaware of what was taking place across the English Channel. One day, as we were playing out on the daisy-covered lawn vainly attempting to catch grasshoppers, a German Dornier bomber roared by very low overhead. It was black and huge and seemed to be following the railway line northwards. The sudden ear-splitting roar shocked and frightened us; it was there and gone in no time, leaving the air pulsating, before we had time to realise what had happened. We were terrified and in a panic and crying our eyes out as Kitty hurried us – a little too late – into the dubious safety of the day-room.

6

Salad Days

Balmy, sunlit days followed one upon the other and we made chains from the daisies scattered across the neatly trimmed lawns. Bees buzzed busily working tirelessly as they went from flower to flower to make sweet golden honey. Kitty told us, 'a bee has to visit thousands of flowers to make just one spoonful of honey.' Colourful butterflies fluttered by or basked in the sun as pale-blue damselflies with long thin bodies whizzed about on shimmering translucent wings. On the horse chestnut tree, the green, spiky seedcases were starting to fill out and bunches of tiny green berries had succeeded the great white curds of the elder-blossom. In the verdant tranquillity of that sequestered, sylvan setting it was hard to believe there was a war on.

On certain mornings our grey-haired gardener-handyman, who wore a flat cap, waistcoat, green corduroy trousers held up by a brass-buckled leather belt and heavy boots, was fuming after finding the lawns covered in freshly excavated molehills. He called the moles nasty mouldiwarps; the Artley's cows were kine, neats or oxen; rabbits were coneys and wood pigeons were cushats. The speech patterns of more than a hundred years back were alive and well in him; he was a throwback to an earlier way of life that was fast disappearing.

We would often glimpse colourful birds and sometimes hear the faint hollow knockings of woodpeckers in the woods. In the meadow we picked the wild flowers that grew in abundance and enjoyed the summer scents of newly mown rye grass and foxtails. We held buttercups under each other's chins believing that if they reflected the yellow of the petals it indicated that that person liked butter. We were delighted when we saw baby rabbits with their bobbing white scuts from the play room windows. They hopped and bounced contentedly across the grass on their soft padded feet, but made a dash for cover if anyone approached.

Above a thickly wooded area beside the lane up to Levisham there was a south-facing grassy bank that was warmed by the sun in the afternoon and well into the long summer evenings. On the other side of the road was a gulley, known locally as a 'griff'. The stunted silver birch and scrub oaks struggled to grow on it and did not cast much shade, making it ideal for the adders that thrived there. The old gardener called them northern vipers, adding, 'Snakes won't rest under an ash tree or on its leaves. It 'as magical properties and an adder can be killed by a single blow from an ash stick.' He always kept an ash walking stick with him and he told us that, 'Snakes are cold-blooded reptiles and can only raise their body temperature by getting 'eat directly from t'sun or by absorbing it from sun-warmed surfaces.'

The area was known locally as Adder Bank and Miss Thorne had sternly warned us never to go up there. However, if no one was watching we would sometimes skip up the lane and across to a small tree by the side of the road that was easy to climb. From our perch we would watch the snakes basking in the hot afternoon sunshine. One day, when Kitty wasn't looking, we sneaked out through the small wicket gate near the goods yard as we had seen some adders – now in their bright summer colours – near the railway crossing. They lay on the warm stones between the railway sleepers and we dared one another to jump from one heavy wooden sleeper to the next. In our ignorance and innocence we did not see the danger. Jack Pickering, on spotting us from the high window of the signal cabin, shouted, 'Hey, you kids, get off that line!' and Kitty came running out to us. We shouted and yelped in sudden fear when a snake, that had horrible reddish-brown eyes with a thin vertical slit for a pupil, reared up baring its fangs as we leapt over it.

Miss Thorne told us later, 'They are the only snakes in Britain that have a poisonous bite, but fortunately this is rarely fatal to humans.' Whenever we found one of their colourless, discarded skins we put it in our smock pockets along with our other 'treasures'. One day, on hearing a tiny piercing scream and seeing the back legs of a frog hanging from the wide mouth of one of the flat-headed adders, I hit it with a stick and the frog made its escape. Although they are reptiles, we knew that they gave birth to live young in the autumn. We had seen the young ones from our perch up in the tree. In the cooler days of cloud and rain they became sluggish and slow moving, which made them easy meat for foxes, hawks and other birds of prey.

The local farmhands, in their thick corduroy trousers, sweated in the enervating heat as they led their horse and wagon down the steep 1 in 5 gradient to the station. They had their shirtsleeves rolled up showing their bulging biceps. The heavy, wooden wagon was filled to the top with rolled-up fleeces. We had watched the Artley's black-faced Masham sheep being dipped. Gangs of men travelled from farm to farm to carry out the shearing. Grabbing and unceremoniously upending the sheep, they used metal-bladed hand clippers to remove the greasy, matted fleeces in no time. 'It's a soap-like substance called lanolin that makes their wool so greasy,' Kitty told us. Afterwards they looked more like skinny goats than sheep and we laughed at them; they seemed so small and funny without their woolly coats. Their thin necks and near-naked pink skin was nicked and bleeding in places.

Soon afterwards we were taken to a local farm to see a Large White Yorkshire sow that had recently farrowed. She had to lie down very carefully as there were eleven tiny pink piglets climbing over each other to nuzzle at the double row of teats on her fat underbelly. After weaning, ten of them were taken away by the men from the Ministry.

In the heat and glare of late June the earthen paths became hard, dry and dusty and the new mown hay lay in thick, yellowish-green swathes that slowly faded in colour as it dried out on the shorn and baking fields. The waist-high hay had been mown down in long, rhythmic sweeps of the scythes, held in the strong hands of the sweating and cheerfully singing farmhands. In their occasional breaks they would whet (sharpen) the long, curving, cutting edges using a coarse stone. From time to time, wielding two-pronged pitchforks, they tossed and turned it and left it to dry. This ancient, tried-and-tested method was known as tedding. Soon afterwards, to our delight, the clover, vetch and trefoil scented hay was gathered up into ridges (known as windrows) by men using light and beautifully crafted wooden hay-rakes. The windrows that covered the hillside slowly changed from green to golden brown in the unrelenting sunshine that burned down day after day. We thought that the ridges of soft, sweet-scented hay had been put there especially for us to roll around and play in.

Shortly afterwards, in the sultry heat, the summer-scented ridges were raked in and piled up to form haycocks in which we made dens until they were carted away by the farmhands. The aroma of rowans, sometimes called mountain ash, scented the air as they were in full blossom at that time of year. The great, placid cart-horses sweated in the shafts of the wagons as they plodded back and forth between the hayfields and the stackyards with their mighty haunches rippling and shining in the summer sun. Sweating, pitchfork-wielding farmhands tossed the hay onto large open wagons. The great, wooden-spoked wheels, with their iron-rimmed tyres, rumbled and crunched over the stones embedded in the hard-packed earth as they wended their way up to Levisham village between high earthen banks that were topped by dry-stone walls or quickthorn hedges. These ancient sunken lanes were known locally as holloways. The men and the horses were glad to get out of the blazing sun into the welcome shade of the tree-embowered lane, where shafts of sunlight struck through breaks in the luxuriant canopies to turn the fern fronds a brighter green.

The hay gradually filled up the barns and was used as fodder over the winter months with the excess being made into large gable-ended hayricks in the stackyard. These were built and thatched with great care and pride to be looked at and enjoyed; an art passed down through generations of fine craftsmen. This protected them from future onslaughts of wind and rain. We found hay everywhere; bits of it littered the lanes and the verges and it was tangled in the hedgerows for weeks.

In midsummer, when the sun shone on both sides of the hedge, we cast short shadows and this now occurred at around two o'clock due to the double summertime that was now in force. I thought that the shadows were inside us and that the sun made them fall onto the ground. Occasionally I was allowed to play with the Artley children on the swing that they had set up in their field, and I enjoyed being taken up onto the high, almost treeless moors well away from the army's training areas. We would help Mrs Artley to pick the small wild strawberries, and at a later date, the ripe and juicy bilberries. The latter were covered in a grey powdering of yeast and, after they had grown to purple ripeness on the low, ground-hugging plants, they turned our tongues and fingers blue. Later, we picked the wild, hairy 'goosegogs' (gooseberries), with which Dinner Lady used to bake delicious steaming hot pies.

The airy vastness of the high moors could be beautiful or utterly bleak. Up there in the bracing air, the great enveloping silence was occasionally broken by the plaintive bleating of the hardy Swaledale sheep. At other times it was the haunting, pitiful call of the shy and wary curlew, with its long downward-curving beak, that we heard. It was hard to see them in their camouflaged plumage, even when they were close by, as they were barely visible against the russet-brown of last year's dried-up bracken. They seemed to prefer the marshy areas of the moors. The ling was springy beneath our feet and the twisted woody stems of the old heather had a dry, dusty smell. I chased after the green, chirruping grasshoppers that were easily alarmed and leapt away in a long curving flight. Occasionally, the sudden clattering explosion of a red grouse would startle us as it sprang up with whirring wings from right under our feet. The male bird, about the size of a small chicken, had dark reddish plumage with a bright red wattle over its eyes and white leg feathers. To me its call sounded like 'Go back! Go back.' Scattered over the moors we saw large ancient standing stones and cairns that were composed of heaped-up stones. There were heaps of piled-up peat turfs, some as tall as six feet, that the diggers had left to dry out as the use of peat as a winter fuel was quite common. There were tangled patches of dead bracken everywhere and amongst it the newly emerging shoots were just starting to unfurl looking like small, brilliant green question marks.

The Artleys owned two defunct, but clean, furnished railway carriages that were kept in the goods yard sidings, and their paying guests sometimes came with us. We called them the camping carriages and the family had been renting them out since before the war. They also provided bed and breakfast and an upstairs bathroom in the station house at a rate of six shillings a week, and at times the house was so full that the family had to sleep in the wash house at the bottom of their yard. Many guests came back year after year to enjoy their hospitality and wholesome fare and some became family friends. They came here to escape from the anxiety of the war-threatened towns and cities for a little while. Here they could walk and enjoy the soothing peace and tranquillity of the deep forests and could relax in the glory of the open moors and the quietness of the countryside. It was an enchanted place, unspoilt by man. Some got lost when the weather suddenly turned hostile and only the hardy Moor Jocks (sheep) were able to endure the harsh conditions. The Artley children used to come in to the nursery school where they played with us for hours on end. Clifford was closer to our George's age than the other three.

The Dog Days begin when the Dog Star, Sirius, the brightest star in the heavens, rises and sets. The Romans believed that dogs went mad at that time of the year and the old gardener said to Kitty, 'tell 'em not to touch t'dog roses in t'edgerows as they're 'armful. If they were to put their fingers on their eyes or ears afterwards they could go blind or get an earache,' adding sagely, 'when t'Dog Days be clear t'will be fine all t'yeer', and that year they had been and it was.

Eric and I were forever asking questions about the environment around us. We had become watchers of the natural world and we were learning the names of the animals, the trees and the plants by observation. As day succeeded day and week followed week I was becoming more aware of the power and order of nature and the law of kill and be killed. At times I got things mixed up, as children do. In the morning I would watch the sunlight creeping down the hillside and it seemed to me that it was pushing the shadows ahead of it: I thought that it was shoving the darkness into the ground in the valley bottom. Later, as it set in the west, the shadows came up again, stealing away the colours and filling the air with darkness and that made it night. To my childish reasoning that was why it was dark under the ground all the time. Many of these early observations of nature were to stay with me, and the lessons learned were to have a profound influence on the course of my life.

After Kitty moved to Grove House, Alan would cycle over to Newton-on-Rawcliffe, where he left his bike and walked down the steep path. Even when she could not see him she knew he was coming as he whistled loudly everywhere he went. Whenever she was with him she was radiant and her face lit up with pleasure. If the weather was fine and sunny he often took her for long, loitering walks and they would sit in the quiet of sun-drenched glades or linger in the dappled shade of the wild woods. Here they walked arm-in-arm, quietly talking as only lovers can and, with no one there to see them, they would gaze into each other's eyes and share a kiss or two. Their liking became a fondness that blossomed into full-blown love – a love that was to transform their lives and bring them joy and happiness.

Warm-hearted Kitty tried so hard to make up for the maternal love that she knew was missing from our young lives: she seemed to instinctively sense how important it was that someone should love and care for us. She had experienced the emotional pain on being put into a home as a child; maybe she too had lain awake at night afraid of the dark and its secrets; maybe she had once yearned for a parent to hug and cuddle her and kiss away the dark forebodings. She was so kind-hearted; there was not a malicious thought in her.

Sometimes, if the weather was kind, she took us up the track that started close to a tall railway signal post on the other side of the railway line. After a short, flat stretch of grass-seamed track we crossed the little footbridge that spanned the shallow waters of the boulder-strewn Pickering Beck. Its white-painted handrails reflected the glare of the sun and as we peered into the clear water gurgling over the smooth stones it threw off scintillating and shifting darts of light. Below the surface the fast-flowing stream shook its long, green tresses of waterweed. Ugly flatheads and spiny sticklebacks darted about on the bottom but we left them for another day. The stony path gradually became a narrow hard-packed earthen track that climbed the steep hillside. It became very muddy after rain and near the crest there was a hairpin bend. The path came out on a hedge-lined lane that led into the pretty village of Newton-on-Rawcliffe that stood 300 feet above the railway line.

In the middle of the village was a large grassy green close to the *White Swan* public house. We walked down to the duck pond that was close to the road and had a raised grassy bank; the sun twinkling on its wind-ruffled surface fascinated me. A little further down was another small pond, the two being separated by a muddy farm track down which the local farmers brought their cattle during droughts. This track was often churned up into an ankle-deep morass in wet spells. We liked to see the ducks preening and upending; cutting themselves in half and turning the water murky with their dabbling. We fed them bits of stale bread and were delighted to see the flotilla of fluffy ducklings that paddled like mad in their mother's wake sending widening ripples across the sun-glinting surface.

We were happily enjoying the warmth of the sun and the peaceful village scene when we suddenly became aware of a wild and strange-looking boy staring at us intently from the other side of the road. He had long, filthy, matted hair that hung down to his shoulders and was wearing dirty, ragged clothes. Kitty told us that he lived with his parents in a shack in the woods, adding, 'he never mixes with or speaks to anyone. The family are reclusive and probably of gypsy stock.' Feeling scared and uncomfortable we asked her to take us back to Grove House.

We hurried to the top of the path, and as we set off down to the railway in the valley we kept looking back to make sure that the wild boy was not following us. The view from the top was magnificent; far below Grove House looked as if it was floating in a sea of bright green foliage, with the tree canopies on the steep slopes above the house at their full and luxuriant best. We were glad to get back down that day. Sometimes the Vicar of Newton-on-Rawcliffe used the same steep path when he came to conduct short prayer services for us. The Reverend Tibbit, the middle-aged vicar of the church of St John, was an eccentric bachelor. His hurrying cloaked figure could sometimes be seen followed (at a safe distance) by groups of local children who pursued him, insolently shouting, 'Tib, Tib, Tib, Tib!' He completely ignored them, abstractedly muttering, 'Boys will be boys.'

Kitty occasionally took some of us older children for a longer walk taking ham salads, meat pies, biscuits and pop prepared and packed up for us by Dinner Lady. One day she took us on a walk through the woods and up to Levisham village on the path that came out near the duck pond. We spent some time in the Chapel-of-Ease and found the little wooden mouse that was carved on the cover of the baptismal font. It was the trademark of Robert Thompson, the carpenter from Kilburn. As we noisily emerged, we disturbed the rooks nesting in the tall pine trees and their raucous cries added to our irreverent din. A farmhand was guiding a herd of cows up the main street with a stick and we took care not to stand in the wet cow claps. Eric trod in one and we made sure that we stayed upwind of him for a while.

We saw a number of deaf and dumb children who had also been evacuated here from Middlesbrough. They were pupils at the special school set up in the old village schoolroom that had closed when the war started. It stood just across the lane from the Chapel-of-Ease and next to the big house that had once been the village inn. The old inn, actually two houses made into one, was now a guest house. It stood by the village green, where the main road divided, and it was packed with paying guests at this time of the year. Most of them had had to make the long climb up from the station, their train usually being met by a young lad who lugged their cases up the steep hill for them. It was so popular that seven huts containing beds had been erected behind it.

The present incumbent, the Reverend Frederick Newby Kent, had only been here for six months, and he was often seen tinkering with, or roaring about the lanes, on his beloved Francis Barnett motorbike. We hopped and skipped down the steep lane, with its 1 in 4 incline, that descended through the woods to the bracken-clad slopes of Levisham Beck, which had its source – a mere trickle – in the bosom of the moors in the Hole of Horcum.

The waters of the tiny, fast-flowing stream leapt, fell, and leapt again between its steep banks. It gushed over coruscating waterfalls, which held small rainbows in their spray. The crystal clear waters then bounded and tumbled ever downwards before splashing and gurgling past the picturesque water mill that stood beside the old stone bridge. The mill had once been the property of the Reverend Skelton and there was a deep rock pool where fat trout with dark markings along their sides basked – until we disturbed them. Lower down, the brook flowed less rapidly as it levelled out, and beside it tall clumps of bright green ferns grew in abundance. The stream, with its grassy banks kept close-cropped by the wandering Masham sheep, flowed through the quiet isolation of the lovely Levisham-Lockton valley before emptying itself into Pickering Beck.

We trooped along with jam jars and fine-mesh nets on the end of canes as the birds twittered and powerful scents of flowering honey-suckle and wild garlic assailed our nostrils. We attempted to catch the red-breasted sticklebacks, while the spiny-backed bullheads, which we called flatheads, zigzagged about erratically. We left a muddy cloud when we lifted the stones from the bed of the stream. Wary of the ugly, bewhiskered, stone loaches we left them well alone. We had a picnic on the soft velvety grass, with juice dripping from our chins as we bit into luscious, shiny-red tomatoes that the gardener called love apples. Kitty poured sparkling lemonade from glass bottles that had a thick wire contraption, to which stoppers made of white pot were fixed. We ran and frolicked in the warmth of the sun that beat down from a clear blue sky. The grassy banks and the bracken-clad slopes were a vivid green and the clear waters sparkled in the sunlight. Salad days indeed!

The picturesque little church of St Mary was reached by means of a steep track that led off from the Levisham–Lockton road. It stood within its crowded churchyard and the summer sun showed up the crusty grey lichen on the gravestones. The small square tower had been built at its western end. It was now tucked away in the verdant folds of this green and pleasant vale, but in times long past, it had stood close to the old Whitby to Pickering road. It had been called Sleights Road on old maps but it was now little more than a narrow bridle track that led down to Farwath. We entered the church through a small stone porch and Kitty pointed out some intricately carved Anglo-Saxon remnants embedded in its walls. Once inside, our high-pitched voices were thrown back as hollow-sounding, spooky echoes that agitated the dust motes and it felt as if we had stepped into a past age; a time before our time; and we suddenly became subdued and quiet. It seemed as though the past was trapped within its ancient walls where a deep and timeless silence reigned. We were reluctant to disturb the reverent hush of the long years and the shadows in the corners seemed to waver and stir. It was hot and sunny outside but it felt dank and chill in there.

On the floor of the chancel there was a very old grave slab with what looked like a crusader's sword incised upon it; its history was a mystery lost in the mists of time. The Skelton family vault stood within the brass altar rails where the two Roberts, father and son, had been rectors. They had moved into the Hall soon after it was built in 1792 and had extensively rebuilt the church to the glory of God in the year 1802. Their memorial hatchments could be seen on the stout stone walls on either side of the rounded Saxon arch that separated the nave from the chancel and altar. We were glad to get out of the gloom of that dusty old place and, emerging into the balmy air, we were dazzled by the sun's blinding rays. Bees buzzed busily, green grasshoppers chirred cheerfully, jumping away as we tried in vain to catch them as the scent of wild flowers filled the air.

Full of exuberance and the joy of life we skipped and raced around on the yielding springy turf. On such brilliant and heavenly summer days as these we seemed to be imbued with endless vitality. In the fields next to the station the farmhands followed the flailing wooden blades that pushed the heads of corn into the horse-drawn cutter and self-binder. The scene was reminiscent of gulls flocking behind a paddle steamer as the reaper-binder swept through a sea of golden corn leaving a swath of stubble in its wake. As the twine-bound sheaves were thrown out at regular intervals, they were propped up against each other to form pyramid-shaped stooks that allowed the air to circulate.

The days were long and lovely and I experienced moments of dreamlike rapture and a quickening of the senses. I was enjoying a free and open way of life and seeing the natural world at close quarters was giving me some conception of the interdependence of all living things. We were so lucky to be growing up in such idyllic surroundings and my soul was nourished and lifted by it. Although unaware of it, I was getting some inkling of the kindredness and balance of all natural things and experiencing the full gamut of emotions, from love, joy and wonder to fear, guilt and helplessness. I was starting to appreciate the sheer godlike beauty, power and majesty of nature and to realise that I was just a tiny part in the great interlocking pattern of things. I watched and learned as the days came and went, and the harsh realities of the war scarcely touched us in our sheltered world.

We heard the tinny clatter of gunfire more and more often. Once the army training camp became established at Keldy Castle the peace and quiet of the Newtondale valley was never quite the same, as soldiers charged around in battledress taking part in military exercises and mock battles. They were being trained for combat prior to being posted to one of the war zones, and we often saw soldiers crouched and running with their rifles in the trail position with their silhouettes clearly outlined against the skyline. The distant machine-gun fire from up on the moors sounded like tearing cloth and we felt the earth-shaking crump of the shells against our eardrums. They sent up plumes of black smoke that drifted away on the wind, and the deep thud of the powerful guns was accompanied by the metallic clattering of caterpillar tracks. Tanks, heavy-armoured vehicles and Bren gun carriers rattling by added to the general cacophony.

The sudden roar of a train as it thundered through drowned it all out and we would sometimes come across soldiers in woollen hats, their faces blackened with burnt cork. They held their rifles in front of them as they crawled across the fields on their elbows and sometimes we would see them lying on their bellies under the hedgerows with their Enfield .303 rifles poking through the gaps. As our little column passed we tried to keep in step as the soldiers did, and Kitty said, 'You must never pick anything up, especially shrapnel and spent bullets, no matter how interesting it might seem.' It all seemed so exciting to us.

Before the army arrived most of the country sounds had emanated from the birds and the farm animals, although, at harvest time, the chugging of the steam traction engine and the slapping belt of the threshing machine could be heard as they were taken from farm to farm in rotation. The placid, lumbering cart-horses had clip-clopped along these quiet lanes for generations, and the magnificent draught animals trundled their loaded wagons down to the station and carted goods up from it and we would hear the ponderous rumbling of their heavy, metal-shod wheels. The contrast between the military din and the soothing, age-old country sounds was stark but in the evenings the peace and quiet returned.

Mam came to visit us again without Dad as the threat of invasion was very real and all leave had been cancelled. She told us that in mid-

August large numbers of German planes based in Scandinavia had crossed the north-east coast to bomb our airfields. The sirens sounded night after night and she had spent most of her time in the underground shelters on The Common where people made tea, had singsongs, and played cards to pass the time. Dad got a forty-eight hour pass and told her that he had been kept really busy firing at the German bombers. He said, 'You should have seen the strings of red and orange flak as it snaked up into the night sky. It was an awe-inspiring sight and sometimes it formed an S-shape as we swung our long gun barrels round. Even if we didn't hit the blighters it made them fly higher making their bombing less accurate.'

One Sunday, the Artley family was walking down the lane from Levisham on their way back from church, when a young soldier suddenly jumped out from behind a bush and alarmed them. Pointing his rifle at them, he belligerently shouted, 'Halt! Who goes there? Friend or foe? Advance and be recognised.' His gleaming, double-edged bayonet was fixed to the business end of his rifle leaving the empty, canvas frog dangling from his webbing belt. When they explained that they lived at the railway station he looked a bit sheepish and allowed them to continue. It seems he had only recently been posted to the area and was a little overenthusiastic. Kitty and Rosemary sometimes got bored on going all day without seeing anyone, so to break the monotony they used to pop over to the station house sitting room for a chat with the Artleys. Here they could share in the latest gossip over a nice cup of tea and listen to the latest war bulletins on their mahogany-encased wireless set.

We saw troop trains crammed with soldiers that clattered through without stopping as sparks flew from the wheels and the acrid smell of oil on hot iron hung in the air. The men leaned out of the carriage windows waving and shouting to us but what they said was blown away on the wind and drowned out by the train's roaring passage. We stood by the maroon and cream waiting room and vigorously waved back. Quite often the trains were hauling weapons and ammunition wagons, as apparently there were ammunition dumps located somewhere further up the line. When the tarpaulin covers of the clanking, flat-backed trucks blew back we sometimes caught a glimpse of a camouflaged tank or the protruding muzzle of a huge gun. Posters on the notice boards asked everyone to 'Be like dad and keep mum', while others warned that 'Careless talk costs lives', 'Keep it under your hat' or 'The walls have ears' which I never understood. In my mind I saw walls literally with ears sticking out of them. There was, at that time, a fear of imminent invasion as the victorious Germans now occupied the defeated countries on the other side of the Channel; nevertheless, we felt safe and secure here with all the soldiers and weapons around.

On our walks with Kitty during the nutting time of late summer and early autumn, the days were still warm and we crunched over the thick carpets of dark brown, bristly-cased beech mast that lay beneath the trees on the hillside. The nuts are only produced in large quantities during hot, dry summers and the deer (which we glimpsed from time to time), the squirrels, the blackbirds, the pheasants, the dormice and the badgers loved them. In the damper areas the boughs of the hazel shrubs were heavy with clusters of green-frilled cobnuts and the pockets of our smocks bulged as we crammed in as many as possible. The old gardener-handyman called them filberts. In the background we could hear the faint tinkling of trickling rills and the woods echoed to the knocking sounds of the tiny, stubby nuthatches. When collecting the nuts they take them to a convenient crevice, like those in the deeply fissured bark of the pine and oak trees, and wedge them in; they then proceed to hammer away at them with their small, straight beaks until the shell cracks and they can reach the kernel. Kitty said, 'In Celtic times, the hazel was known as the tree of knowledge and its nuts were said to be the ultimate receptacles of wisdom.' Maybe we were gaining in wisdom, for we ate plenty of them.

As the lush fruitfulness of autumn crept on, the weather turned chilly, and thick, shifting mists often blotted out the hillsides. Locally, the potatoes and the harvest had been safely gathered in and the corn stubble had turned from burnished gold to a dull grey. Before the war it had been burned and the ashes had helped to enrich the soil, but now it had to be ploughed in due to the blackout regulations. Flocks of screaming gulls followed the team of horses, looking on from a distance, like tiny scraps of white paper blowing about in the wind. In the low autumn sunlight, the leaves of the deciduous trees stood out in various tints of gold, yellow, red and brown, contrasting sharply with the dark leaves of the evergreens. We saw red squirrels racing back and forth hastily gathering up the nuts before scurrying away to hide them before the winter set in.

On certain days the valley was shrouded in thick white swirling fog which lingered all day, and there was frost on the grass in the early mornings as the year moved inexorably on. The ripe crab apples, sloes and blackberries were picked and Dinner Lady used them to make delicious jams and jellies in huge bubbling, steaming pans. Eric and I, by this time, were having lessons with Miss Thorne as, by rights, we should have been starting school. We played with water, plasticine and sand, not realising that we were learning the basics of volume and measurement. Miss Thorne poured equal quantities of water into a short wide glass and a tall thin glass, saying, 'Which glass has the most water in it?' We both thought that the tall glass held more than the other one as we were still too young to understand conservation of volume. She said, 'The mind is a treasure house that should be kept well stocked and once knowledge is safely stored the world can never take it away.'

In early autumn, a ten-year-old girl called Anne-Marie Calvert had entered our lives. She had been evacuated to Levisham village with her mother and her brother Richard after their house was damaged in a raid on York in early August. The anxiety and worry caused her mother to bring her and her brother to this relatively safe, secluded spot.

One day as dew lay on the grass, Anne-Marie came along the lane beside the nursery school. Seeing George and me playing close to the gate, she came in and said, 'Mother has made a lovely stew with lots of fresh vegetables from our garden. Would you like to come over and try some?' Being a growing lad and always hungry, I didn't take much persuading. The stew was simmering away in a black pot that looked to me like a witch's cauldron, and there was an iron bar fixed to the wall, which was hinged and could be swung out over the open fire. It was called a 'reckon' in these parts and the stew pot was suspended from it. 'Sit yerself down luv,' Mrs Calvert said, as she ladled out the stew. It was delicious but there were lots of tiny bones in it as it was wood pigeon stew. On the stone-flagged floor of the kitchen lay several peg rugs, which the family had made from strips of old clothing that they pushed through a piece of hessian sacking with a wooden prodder; my favourite rug had the shape of a Spitfire worked into it. A glass-shaded paraffin lamp hung from a hook in the ceiling.

Anne-Marie said, 'When the soldiers are down by the beck training they sometimes come to the kitchen and say "Any chance of a drop of tea missus?" They bring their tin mugs and Mum fills them up but if their sergeant appears they quickly chuck it away.'

We would sometimes see her near Grove House picking bunches of wild flowers to take to school. Each day, when the mail train came through, the incoming mailbag was passed out to Mr Artley or Jack Pickering who, between them, worked half a day on and half a day off. The bag of outgoing mail was collected from the platform by the guard. Jack worked the signals and issued the tickets and whenever a train came through he would collect a large metal hoop, beneath which hung a leather pouch containing the tablet. The train driver would lean out and place this hoop over the arm of the man on duty, and this important safety procedure ensured that no two trains could be on our stretch of line at the same time. The tablet was then placed into a device in the signal box, which caused the signals to change, thus reducing the chances of an accident. The tablet was replaced when the next train came through.

The busiest day was Monday, when Mr Artley scuttled here and there in his shiny-peaked black cap and black waistcoat, regularly pulling out his large Hunter watch on its gold chain to check that everything was on time and running smoothly. The platform was all hustle and bustle as it was market day in Pickering and there were large numbers of local people going there. The farmhands and the women of Levisham and the various outlying farmsteads eagerly looked forward to these weekly shopping trips into town.

When he was not too busy, Jack would sometimes get a few of us older children together and take us into the signal box, saying, 'Yer can 'elp me ter change t'points if yer like.' As he pulled back one of the ten shiny metal levers, we 'helped' by holding on to it with him. We loved to look out of the windows as a great hissing black steam train thundered past making the box tremble under our feet.

One Monday Kitty took a few of us on the six-mile journey to Pickering and Eric and I were delighted to be part of this special treat. The track south of Levisham station beyond the two tall signal posts became single track, and it ran straight as far as the hamlet of Farwath. After that it was all bends with the line crossing and re-crossing the beck as it passed the lovely mixed woodland that clothed the steep slopes on either side.

At that time steam trains still ran from Pickering to all four cardinal points of the compass. Kitty had handed over our tickets to be clicked by a man in a black uniform and took us out of the station. We joined the hustle and bustle of the crowds in the market place that milled around under the brightly striped awnings of the stalls, gazing in wonder at the clothes, crockery, vegetables and sundry items that could still be bought in spite of the increasing shortages. We stayed close to Kitty as she moved amid the myriad sights and smells, including odours of wet fish fresh from Whitby. It was a new and exciting experience and we stared in wonder at the hundreds of brightly coloured goodies on display. Many of the little shops lining the street had tiny, old-world, glass-bottle windowpanes that distorted the things on the other side.

At the top end of the market stood The Vaults where we had our hair cut. Nearby stood an old antique shop that had once been a cinema, where a strange box-like structure hung out over the pavement; apparently this had been part of the projectionist's room. There was a row of old railway cottages; a tobacconist's hut and some wooden benches under a low stone wall where we sat and rested for a while.

We were taken to see a Punch and Judy show and, although a bit shocked and frightened, we were fascinated and totally absorbed at the same time. The actions of the hook-nosed, long-chinned, hunchbacked Mr Punch were dreadful. He murdered his baby by banging its head on the walls and floor because it cried; he then bludgeoned his wife to death when she disapproved and he hurled their bodies out of the window. The policeman put him in jail and he was sentenced to death by hanging, but he throttled the hangman with his own noose and escaped. The show gave us a glimpse of a cruel and savage time in England's history, but, on reflection, was it any worse than what was happening in war-torn Europe? Brutal Nazis were slaughtering weak and vulnerable people on a vast scale, and like Mr Punch they seemed to have thrown all decent human values out of the window.

We were then taken for tea in a café near the old Memorial Hall and had pikelets thickly spread with real, deep yellow, farm-produced butter. A year later the café was to become one of the many British restaurants that the government was setting up all over the country. Churchill had suggested setting up these canteen-like communal feeding centres during the Blitz so that nutritious, three-course meals would be available for under a shilling. They were to be non-profit making and were to be staffed by the WVS who would produce nourishing meals from non-rationed foods. With the pootering tunes of a nearby steam organ still ringing in our ears, we were treated to scrumptious curd tarts; then tired out but happy we boarded the train to return to the warm, loving atmosphere of Grove House. It was crowded with heavily laden country dwellers heading back after a good day out.

On a warm October day of hazy sunshine, an elderly gentleman from The Settlement led us out onto the verandah by the play room to have our photographs taken. The picture was made into a postcard and sent to all the parents and I still treasure that fading black and white picture.

Soon afterwards we were gathered together and sat cross-legged around the wooden-cased wireless set in the dining room. We knew that it must be for something special. We were to hear the fourteen-year-old Princess Elizabeth make her debut broadcast in which she said to all evacuees, 'my sister Margaret Rose and I feel so much for you, as we know from experience what it means to be away from those we love most. To you living in new surroundings we send a message of true sympathy ...' The bombing of London went on continuously for fifty-seven days and Buckingham Palace had been bombed twice in the five weeks prior to the broadcast but, luckily, the Royal Family had been staying at Windsor Castle overnight. These tragic events did not really register with us at the time as our age and lack of understanding must have protected us. To us the war seemed very exciting.

A few days later, as the days grew cooler and the nights were drawing in, Kitty celebrated her twenty-first birthday; an important 'coming of age' occasion in those days. At twenty-one a person was deemed to be an adult and no longer subject to parental control. As the remains of the day gave way to dusk, a small party was held in the cosy warmth and brightness of the dining room. We were already warmly tucked up in our beds and a fire burned brightly in the grate as a nice get together of Kitty's friends took place. Alan Brown, her fiancé, had been brought over on the motorbike of a friend. Generally his fingers were intertwined with Kitty's or he had his arm around her waist. Tommy Gibson, the jolly farmer from Cropton, was there and it was said that he was keen on the attractive Rosemary Waters. The constantly smiling and cheerful Artleys came over from the station house to join the party.

Plainly wrapped presents (patterned paper was very scarce by then) were brought and given, and Mrs Ruonne had baked Kitty a big, two-layered sponge cake with damson jam in the middle. She had iced it, put candles on it and decorated it with a '21' and the 'key of the door'. They enjoyed open sandwiches made with crusty farmhouse bread topped with tasty egg, ham, corned beef or cheese, followed by home-made fairy cakes, cream slices and, as a special treat, a sherry trifle. The room resounded with laughter and happy voices as they exchanged light-hearted anecdotes. Later they gathered round the piano to sing the popular songs of the time. To break the ice a few glasses of port and sherry were drunk while the men had beer. Kitty was young, in love and very happy.

At the end of the month, as nature's mighty pulse began to slow, we could see the vapour from each other's breath hanging like mist on the icy air. There were cold north-easterly winds that made the dry, crinkly, brown leaves that still clung to the beech tree by the gate rattle and fall. The sycamore trees lost the glory of their crimson, russet and golden foliage and there were early morning frosts. The lawns were covered in damp frozen leaves and there was a thin smattering of double-winged sycamore seeds that we called helicopters. It was a time of dampness and decay, and writhing wraith-like mists rolled down the hillsides to gather in the dells and hollows, making the thick brown layer of leaf mould soggy underfoot. The mists muffled our footfalls as we walked in the depths of the dark, dank, dripping woods. The horses had been taken into the shelter of their dry, straw-littered stables to sleep at night and were relishing their first feedings of nutritious, summer hay, as there was no grazing to be had.

In November the men from the Ministry called to inspect the stock and the Artleys had to hide their second pig in the privy down the yard until they left. The law only allowed people to keep one pig for their personal use; any other pigs were supposed to be sold (cheaply) to the Ministry of Food and the piglets had to be fattened up beforehand. Most of the carcass of the second pig was bought by Miss Thorne and the salted and muslin-covered hams and flitches, which were hung from the hooks in the kitchen, kept us supplied for weeks on end.

As the long sleep of winter began, thick, dank fogs shrouded the big house turning the shrubbery and trees into looming, vaguely threatening spectres. To me they were hazy and amorphous, shape-shifting phantoms of the woods just like the misty wraiths that dwelt at the periphery of my vision, which always – on turning to see them – moved rapidly away. Or was it only the creeping, grey fog playing tricks on my young impressionable mind again? As an extra precaution at bedtime I knelt to pray fervently, asking the good Lord to 'Please, protect Mam, Dad, our George and me from ghosts, evil spirits and things that go bump in the night.' I then curled up under the covers hiding from the unspeakable terrors that lurked in the vast and frigid darkness.

At night an intense blackness now covered the land, as the blackout here was almost total. The edges of the station platforms had been painted white to make passengers aware of the dangerous drop down to the track. The platform paraffin lamps were lit for short periods of time, only whenever a train was due to stop, and the glass panes had been painted black, except for a small square in the bottom corner. This allowed just enough faint light to be shed downwards onto the flagstones and these were known as glimmer lights. One dark and cloudy late afternoon in November, after the sun had set behind the western ridge, Anne-Marie and her brother were returning from school in York when the train, for some unknown reason, stopped a little way out from the station. Richard, thinking they had arrived, opened the door in the total darkness and stepped out, falling on to the cinders beside the track. He was badly grazed, but thankfully no bones were broken.

On an earlier occasion he had managed to catch a small adder, which he had put into an empty milk bottle to take to school. When they boarded the train the carriage had quickly emptied and they had it all to themselves. It was Richard who showed us how to put halfpennies on the line to be squashed flat by the train wheels and, being very young and gullible, we thought that this made them into pennies. We tried to use them in the chocolate vending machine and were disappointed when no chocolate came out.

December came in with icy winds, frosts and snow, and with the dark cold nights now twice as long as the days, the shutters were closed and the blackout curtains were put in place long before teatime. As a special treat we were taken on Mr Brown's coach to a Christmas concert at Cropton village hall. Six months earlier, a lady had formed a club for the local youngsters and evacuees from Middlesbrough; they put on a show, which was a great success and we thoroughly enjoyed it.

In the days leading up to Christmas, Santa Claus was never far from our minds and our excitement increased, with much of the joy being in the anticipation. We helped to cut and paint strips of paper in bright colours and, linking them together, we made chains which were hung in loops across the play room and dining room. We had saved up all our silver foil wrappers, from which we made tree decorations, and we thought they looked as good as the bought ones. Our attempts at painting Father Christmas with his reindeers and sleigh were pinned up on the walls, and the gardener brought in sprigs of red-berried holly, along with ivy and mistletoe, which grew as a parasite on the bark of the local oak and apple trees. The Christmas tree, which was set up in the corner, had a fairy on the top of it and was decorated with lots of our glittering home-made baubles and tinsel. Cotton wool was laid on the branches to represent snow and we had hung some of the long, pendulous, light-brown spruce tree cones on them.

We were so excited as we emptied our bulging stocking onto our beds on Christmas morning. People did not have quite the same quantity or quality of food as they had the previous year as the shipping losses were really starting to bite, but the government had allowed us a few extra rations over the Christmas period. Even so, Dinner Lady still managed to cook us a lovely Christmas dinner of roast chicken with bacon, sausagemeat and herb stuffing; crispy roast potatoes; fresh vegetables and rich steaming gravy. This was followed by plum pudding with lashings of hot custard. Later, after a short nap, games and a tea party, with paste sandwiches, mince pies, cakes, jelly and custard, was held. The Calvert and the Artley children came over and, wearing paper hats, we laughed, giggled, and thoroughly enjoyed the party. We excitedly pulled Christmas crackers but I never did understand the jokes that were printed on the slips of paper inside. Father Christmas came with a sack full of lovely presents. We sniggered behind our hands when we saw him kissing Kitty under the mistletoe.

Alan and Kitty were married at St Gregory's Church, Cropton, the following month, and Alan's friend Lloyd Thorpe was their best man. They lived with Alan's parents in the bungalow in the forest until they moved to nearby Kirby Misperton. Kitty and Alan continued to live at Peep o' Day Bungalow for a further three years, by which time he was driving lorry loads of logs from the forest to Pickering station.

Although we were far from home, Christmas still managed to weave its magic spell, and many of our presents were the result of a year's hard work by the dedicated ladies of the local WI. On Boxing Day several parents came to share the festive season with their children and I was flabbergasted when Mrs Robson gave her daughters, Nancy and Sylvia, a lovely, yellow banana each. It soon went out of my mind when Mam brought me a bus conductor's outfit, with a flat, peaked cap and a ticket machine that went 'ding' when the little lever at the side was pressed. In those short, dim days, as the year was fleeing fast, there were shortages of just about everything.

7

The Land of Lost Content

In January, the snow that lay six inches deep around Grove House muffled our footfalls, and round about us the drifts had created a magical and fantastic scene. Snow was piled up against the house by the strong, bitterly cold north-easterly winds and the hedges and the rhododendron shrubs were transformed into great white mounds and humps. We caught a glimpse of the white rump of a fleeing roe deer near the pond, which hunger had brought down from the forest in search of food. Being very wary animals they try to avoid human contact, and if they detect even the slightest scent of a person they cough to warn the rest of the herd who spring into flight and dash for cover. Strange birds and other small, hungry creatures came into the gardens leaving tiny prints in the virgin snow. Snow thickly blanketed the lawns and the drive and we competed with each other to see who could leave the most footprints in it.

We helped (or hindered?) the nursery assistants in building a snowman. The snow was brittle – not too wet – and therefore ideal for making snowmen and snowballs, and it creaked as we rolled it into large balls to make the body parts. We patted and moulded him into shape using coal for his eyes and buttons, and a carrot for his nose. Sticking a pipe in his mouth, Kitty tied one of the gardener's old mufflers round his neck and put a flat cloth cap on his head. The stillness of the dozing valley was rudely torn apart and the naked woods echoed to our shouts and laughter as snow lay heavy on the leaves and boughs of the spruce trees. We happily raced and jumped about in the thick drifts and had snowball fights. The Stancliffe girls were away from home, so

Jack Pickering brought their sledge from the outbuilding where it had been stored all year. Sitting one of us in front of him, he took us on hectic, scary flights with the sledge going pell-mell down the steep snow-covered lane until he dug his heels in and skidded to a halt on the level bit just before the railway crossing. We squealed with delight. Later we sucked on the long icicles that we had snapped off the portico eaves and ran about in our wellies until our legs began to hurt above our socks that had slipped down. The wet tops had chafed the skin making a red ring that was very sore and when we were taken in to the play room, red-cheeked and blue-nosed, the caring nursery assistants smeared our legs with soothing Vaseline or Snowfire ointment.

Eric and I, along with a few of the other five-year-olds, had been having lessons with Miss Thorne, but she was not a fully certified teacher; therefore, steps were being taken for us to start our formal education. Arrangements were made for Eric to be billeted with a Mr Wilson Sleightholme up in Newton village. I was not to see Eric again, except for a brief spell soon after the war, and it was to be a further fifty-odd years before we came into contact with each other again.

I loved it at Grove House where I was secure and cared for by trustworthy, kind and loving people and it seemed a truly magical place to me. In the smoke and chemical-laden atmosphere of Middlesbrough I was often unwell and seemed to get every childhood illness going. Here, in the sylvan beauty and tranquillity of this secluded wooded valley, I was flourishing and growing tall and straight, like the surrounding spruce trees. Fresh air and exercise were honing my appetite and I was filling out. Living a tranquil, simple and wholesome life, I was happy and the world seemed to be a lovely place, but, in my blissful innocence, I was unaware that great changes were being planned and these were soon to change my cosy, cosseted little world forever.

In early February Mam came to visit us and she told me that my Uncle Archie, now a tall handsome fifteen-year-old, was back home and had started work washing and filling milk bottles. A few months later he began his apprenticeship as a steel plater in the Bridge Yard that was part of the sprawling Britannia steelworks. The firm was justifiably proud of having built the Newport (Tees) Bridge, as well as the world-famous bridge that spanned Sydney Harbour, which was the largest and heaviest arch bridge in the world at that time.

It seems that arrangements had been made for me to replace him. I had been allowed to stay on as my younger brother was still here but

Mam wanted me to go to the same billet as her sister's son. I was rather apprehensive of what was in store for me and hated the thought of having to leave, as I had loved it so much at Sutherland Lodge and here. However, Mam assured me that it would be nice to have Jimmy to play with and she assured me that he would look after me and I would like it. Mam came through to take me to my new home but George was to stay on.

The day I left Grove House for the last time was a sad, sad day for me. I cried as if my heart was broken (and maybe it was) and there were tears in the eyes of the nursery assistants. My favourite grown-up, apart from Mam and Dad, was Kitty who was now married to Alan, becoming Mrs Catherine Brown. She had given up her job and they were both living happily at Peep-o Day Bungalow. My little brother George, and several of my young friends, had come to see me off; they were all loved and so precious to me, and most of them were sobbing openly. I tried to speak to them as I sensed that I would never see them again, but my heart was too full and I could not get the words out. I never forgot Kitty who had shared her love and knowledge with us and I will owe her a debt of gratitude until the day I die.

All too soon the train, with a great steel snowplough fixed to the front, pulled in at the platform. On that dismal day under a sullen sky loaded with yet more snow to come, the final kisses, hugs and best wishes were exchanged before Mam and I mounted the high wooden step of the railway carriage. It was a bitter wrench and such a sorrowful parting! My whole being was suffused with an overwhelming love for that place and its kind and caring people, and I grieved for all that I was to leave behind. I still think back to those wonderful times where I had lived and played so happily. It was truly a haven of peace and love. To this day memories of those days well up from the depths of my soul, like milk coming to the boil, and they will live in my heart forever. I am filled with a glow of gratitude and pleasure when I think of those sweet, much-treasured times. It was my Elysium; a place that overflowed with tenderness and kindness.

As I set off for pastures new a chapter in my short life closed and a new leaf was about to be turned. The great steam locomotive slowly huffed and puffed its way out of the station and I gazed at the small group that stood huddled together, waving until they were out of sight. I snuggled up into the warmth of Mam's body feeling sad but secure within her loving arms. She held my tiny hand while I lay my head against her bosom and she hugged and kissed me, holding me ever so close calling me her precious little lost lamb. I looked through tear-blurred eyes on the beauty of my secluded valley for the last time. It had been a safe haven from the storms of life and I had been so happy there. The dark green of the pine and spruce trees and the bare limbs of the deciduous trees stood out starkly against the brilliant whiteness of the snow, and involuntary sobs racked my slender frame as I realised that I would never see it again. There was an empty ache in my heart as fond memories of the happy times spent there rose up and I think the following verse expresses perfectly my sentiments at that sad time:

> *That is the land of lost content,*
> *I see it shining plain,*
> *The happy highways where I went*
> *And cannot come again.*
> A.E.Houseman (1859–1936)

Children are very resilient and soon bounce back, and by the time we reached Pickering I was my usual pestering and attention-seeking self again. My normal ebullience returned and I was forever asking, 'Can I (this)?' and 'Can I (that)?' As we had to change trains here, we had a mug of strong, stewed tea and a hard rock cake in the refreshment room, as a bitterly cold, piercing wind blew along the covered platform. Mam bought some Liquorice Allsorts, one of my favourite sweets, for the journey and suggested that we should sit for a little while by the warmth of the open fire in the Ladies waiting room.

Eventually, we clambered onto the train for Malton, which steamed through the tiny, quaintly named Marishes Road station, as thick flurries of snow blurred the telegraph poles that raced past the carriage windows. After a flat, six-mile journey south, the track linked up with the main Scarborough to York line at Rillington where the line turned west through the Derwent valley. In the wan winter sunshine the meandering river, which was seldom out of sight, looked like a silver serpent as we clattered along beside snow-blanketed fields. We pulled into the station in the small market town of Malton, which Mam said was called Derventia in Roman times.

The train to York was packed full of soldiers and airmen. Mam had somehow obtained permission for us to leave the train at Haxby station, which was normally closed to passengers but, since it had to stop there to deliver certain items, they could see no problem in us getting off. Several soldiers ('sojers' to me) got into our carriage. Their shiny black boots clattered on the floor as they carried in their rifles and bulging kit bags. Removing their forage caps, known as cheesecutters, they shoved them through the shoulder tab of their battledress blouses. As they lifted their bags and webbing packs onto the overhead netting of the luggage rack, the naps of their uniforms, which were wet with snow, started to curl up. The soldiers lit up their Woodbines and after a while the carriage reeked of smoke, so one of them opened the window a crack to let it out. Animal heat rose from the dampness of their uniforms as they slowly dried out. As we continued our journey, still following the course of the river, two of the soldiers, their coarse khaki uniforms feeling rough to the touch, made a bit of a fuss of me and gave me a boiled sweet to suck.

The train (and the soldiers) steamed on as we crossed and re-crossed the snaking Derwent, passing through the oddly named Huttons Ambo station and skirting the bare woodlands and the snow-clad parkland of the vast Castle Howard estate. Without stopping we passed through the pretty little stone station within a loop of the river that had solid and chunky chimneys. As we passed we caught a glimpse of the domed colonnaded family mausoleum that stood on the top of a snow-covered hill in the distance.

The piercing train whistle sounded as we continued our journey with the swaying of the carriages making us lurch from side to side as we clattered over the points. The smell of the men's warm, damp khaki uniforms pervaded the carriage as we passed through other tiny stations with quaint names such as Crambe and Flaxton. Every mile was taking me away from all that I loved and I resented it but, by then, the snow had stopped and the sky had begun to clear. We stopped at a place called Strensall where the soldiers put on their forage caps, heaved their bulging kitbags on to their shoulders and waved goodbye to us as they got down from the train.

We crossed the River Foss on a narrow railway bridge that had a wide iron pipe running alongside it, and after a further two miles or so we drew in at the small, neat station on the eastern side of Haxby. Mam put on my mitts and pulled my woollen balaclava helmet over my head before crossing the long, hand-knitted woollen scarf over my chest and tucking it under my armpits. She pulled my coat collar up round my ears and we stepped down onto the frost-rimed slabs of the platform.

A smiling, thickset, middle-aged man wearing a baggy, flat cloth cap and a thick brown overcoat came forward to meet us. I noticed that he had a pronounced limp and he introduced himself as Harold Mann, explaining that he was a close friend of my new foster parent. 'Ah'm sorry,' he said, 'but Mr Harris couldn't come as 'e's 'ad ter work on t'farm. 'E asked me to come and tek yer t' t'ouse.'

Mam thanked him for coming and he took hold of my small, scuffed and scratched cardboard case and we followed him along the white-edged platform. He led us through a white-paled wicket gate and over the shining metal of the twin railway lines. The low, sallow afternoon sun was making no impression on the rime of frost that twinkled like stars on the heavy wooden sleepers. As elsewhere, the station name boards had been removed, so as to make it more difficult (in theory) for the enemy (should they arrive) to establish their whereabouts. A wooden rest shelter stood on the up platform and nearby there was a row of white painted wooden palings and a small ticket office.

An old station house with an elegant Georgian entrance porch stood by the gates of the crossing. The countless steam trains that had passed close by for nearly a hundred years had turned its old stones black, and behind it there was a long-established and well-frequented coal yard. Beyond that was an elevated metal water tank that had a wide tubular arm with a canvas sleeve that could be swung out to refill the steam engine boilers. The wide, white-painted, five-barred gates were still shut and Mr Mann's pony and trap stood at the other side, with his horse, Monty, having a nap with one rear hoof, slightly bent at the hock, resting on the other. Mr Mann lifted my case up through the little door at the rear of the small open carriage and helped us up the iron step. We sat on its shiny, wooden-slatted seats that ran parallel with the panelled sides.

We sat in the little carriage wrapped in thick woollen blankets. The shaggy-coated pony trotted along very gingerly as the road was treacherous with a thin, glass-like layer of ice above compressed, frozen snow. Monty flared his nostrils and snorted from time to time and his warm exhalations hung like clouds of steam on the cold winter air. The pony's long, shaggy mane was blown about by the icy, cutting wind as Harold turned right onto Usher Lane immediately after passing a very large house on the corner. We stopped at the gate of a semi-detached house that had a small front garden behind a low privet hedge and, like its neighbours, it had a thin layer of frozen snow on top. Below its square-bayed windows was a small, snow-covered rockery, and on the wall to the right of the front door was a wooden plaque that read 'Lenmuir'.

Mrs Harris came out with a thick coat round her shoulders and carefully picked her way along the ice-covered path beside the house. Harold handed us over without much ado. As she led us slipping and sliding along the path past the coalhouse door, Mrs Harris instructed us that her evacuees were never allowed to use the front door. We went through a wooden gate between the corner of the house and the shed and, turning left, went up three steps and in through the kitchen door. Mrs Harris seemed to carry her own chill into the house with her along with a blast of icy, wintry air. Inside, on the left, a door led into a large walk-in larder and a second door opened into the bathroom. Due to the long journey and the effects of the cold, the pressure on my bladder was unbearable and I was 'dicky-dancing' as I desperately needed 'to go'. I couldn't wait and I dashed into the bathroom to go to the lavvy, which was tucked away in an alcove behind the larder. Above it a chain with a wooden handle hung down from a cast-iron cistern and opposite there was a white-enamelled, claw-foot bathtub with two shiny brass taps, which stood beneath the sloping ceiling below the stairs.

From the bathroom I could hear muffled talking and on going back into the kitchen, Mrs Harris seemed remote, forbidding and glacial in the cold wan light of that chilly winter afternoon. She had a pallid complexion and a blotchy face that reminded me of the poisonous foxglove bells in the woods at Grove House. She was wearing a faded, washed-out pinny over her ample bosom. Her face and arms were freckled like a bird's egg as she peered down at me through her heavy horn-rimmed glasses and when she shook my hand her limp, flabby fingers, which looked like pork sausages, felt cold and clammy. There was no smile and not a glimmer of warmth in her greeting.

To the right of the back door there was a cast-iron gas cooker and next to it a square, vitreous china sink, and a wooden draining board stood below the kitchen window. In the centre of the room was a table covered with a cream-and-blue-checked oilcloth. When the stiff formalities and the minor pleasantries were over, she made tea in a large brown pot placing a knitted tea cosy over it. The tea was poured into half-pint mugs and she invited us to help ourselves to the broken biscuits that lay on a chipped and cracked plate. The square table was slightly wobbly and a piece of cardboard had been stuffed under one of its legs to balance it. The oilcloth was covered in a network of tiny fissures and fine cracks that matched the mugs and the wooden forms that stood along three of its sides.

Mrs Harris seemed old to me and I heard Mam say in a tremulous voice, as she handed over my green ration book and National Registration Identity Card, 'I trust that you'll take good care of him.' To me, Mrs Harris's congeniality lacked conviction and she seemed formidable and icily polite as she studied the items in her podgy, nicotine-stained fingers. Mrs Harris then told Mam, 'He will sleep in the back bedroom with Donald and Jimmy. Don't worry about him Mrs Wright, he'll get the same treatment as the others.' This could have meant anything.

She then led us up the stairs by way of the front room, which was kept as a 'best room' only to be used for special occasions. It had a wooden picture rail high up on its faded, print-papered walls from which a couple of gloomy-looking pictures hung on long cords. There was a settee and two armchairs beside a small, tiled fireplace, and on the chimneybreast a round mirror with bevelled edges hung on a long chain. In the rectangle formed by the bay window was a sturdy wooden table covered with a velvety, maroon cloth with tasselled edges. In the centre of the room lay a threadbare rug with a margin of brown, bare floorboards around it.

Wooden stairs led up from the small entrance hall to a landing covered by a timeworn runner held in place by tarnished brass rods. To the left an open door led into the front bedroom. To the right was the door of the tiny box room, and straight ahead a door led into the back bedroom that contained a bed, a chair and a plain wooden wardrobe. The floor, which was covered with lino, had just one small clippy rug by the bedside, and a glass-shaded electric light bulb hung on a length of brown flex. A thin, decorated, paper frieze ran round the top of the distempered and stippled walls. Mrs Harris started to unpack my case, saying coldly, 'this is where you will sleep.'

In what seemed like no time at all there was yet another sad and tearful parting. Mam hugged me to her as if she would never let go and it hurt to see the pain and anguish in her eyes as she smoothed down my hair with a bit of spit, as it tended to stick up at the crown. She wiped the tears from my cheeks with her hankie and gave me a kiss, softly whispering, 'I must go now. Be a good boy. Jimmy will look after you and I will see you again very soon. Bye-bye sweetheart.' At that she was gone. She had to hurry to catch the bus into York and once there she would have to get the train to Darlington and hope that she did not miss her connecting train to Middlesbrough. Train journeys were slow and tedious at that time with many unscheduled stops and delays. She loved reading but the use of faint blue lights now made this almost impossible.

No sooner had she gone than Mrs Harris's false good cheer disappeared and she became brusque in her manner. She said, 'I will not tolerate any rudeness or cheek. I expect you to be quiet at mealtimes and to speak only when spoken to. Children should be seen and not heard and there is to be no swearing, shouting or running in the house. You must abide by all the dos and don'ts listed on the door of the cabinet in the kitchen or there'll be trouble.'

My feeling of well-being dissipated as quickly as the smoke that drifted up from Mrs Harris's seemingly ever-present cigarette. Not long afterwards, Jimmy, Donald, Thelma and Dot came in from school and I was introduced to them. I barely recognised Jimmy, who I had not seen for eighteen months, as he had grown a lot and was now a good-looking young lad. He had soft, light-brown hair that was combed back and parted on the left with a soft, wavy quiff topping his high forehead. Eighteen months is a long time at that age. Promising that he would look after me, he took me up to our bedroom to show me his toys and comics to take my mind off Mam's departure. I cried for a long time as we sat on the bed huddled together like a couple of street urchins. I felt lost and frightened in this strange, unfriendly and terrifyingly new place.

I was slow to settle in as I was very shy and I always felt ill at ease with the obsequious Donald, whom everyone called Ducky. He had clammy hands and shifty, darting eyes that always seemed to be watching me. Dot was a thin, droopy girl with short dark hair and a fringe cut just above her eyes. She seemed a bit dopey and slow-witted. I liked the congenial, lively and no-nonsense attitude of Thelma straight away and we got on well from the start. She was a good-looking, bright sort of girl with a small heart-shaped face and intelligent brown eyes.

When Mr Harris came home from work, I took to him immediately. He was a smallish man with muscular arms that had a thin covering of fine fair hairs. A smiling, ruddy-faced, down-to-earth man who smelled of soil and sweat. He said, ''Ow do, lad. Welcome to our 'umble abode. Mek yersel at 'ome and don't be frightened ter ask for anything.'

Wives always gave the working men the largest portions in those days and they were all hungry, tucking in to a meal of rabbit stew and dumplings with thick slices of crusty bread. I picked and fiddled with my food as I didn't like the tiny bones in it and my shyness and the strangeness of my surroundings had taken the edge off my normally healthy appetite. There was only room for the two adults and the two big girls on the home-made, wooden side benches, so Ducky, Jimmy and I sat, squashed together, on the bench at the front of the table. Mrs Harris was not given to kind words and she always seemed to wear an expression of displeasure and was very strict. She made it crystal clear that the house, and particularly our bedrooms, were to be kept neat and tidy at all times, saying, 'I'm not here to run after you lot or to pick up your discarded clothes,' before adding, 'and Jimmy you had better keep John right or you'll have me to answer to.'

'Yes, Mrs Harris,' he meekly replied.

To me she said, 'Our bedroom, the parlour and the pantry are strictly out of bounds.'

Her kitchen sink was stained brown and the gas oven was coated in burnt-on grease and it was obvious from the start that it was going to be a case of do as I say and not as I do. That night it took me a long time to get to sleep as I lay between the two bigger lads, snuggling up to Jimmy's warm back, but eventually I must have dozed off.

I was a resilient and amenable lad and I had no choice but to accept the new regime and get on with it. There was no laughter in the strict and bad-tempered Mrs Harris, who always seemed to look on us with unforgiving eyes, and her cold stare could take the warmth out of the sunniest day. She said and did many unkind and unpleasant things, which I felt deeply and thought very unfair. Her philosophy seemed to be: Give them a good hiding and they won't do it again. Such treat-ment came as a shock to me so soon after my cocooned life in the nursery school where I had been accustomed to love and tenderness. Mr Harris, although dominated and hen-pecked by his wife, was always kind, affable and gentle with us and, when she was not around, he let us get away with many minor childish mischiefs. He had smiling eyes that crinkled at the corners and he would often secretly slip us a sweet or two from behind the now depleted sheets of his *Daily Express* newspa-per when she wasn't looking.

The next day our Jimmy, who had picked up the local dialect and mannerisms of speech, said, 'I'll show yer t'way t' t'shops.' He took me into the village centre to show me Torvill's newspaper shop where comics could be bought, and it was just over the road from the school that I would be starting at on Monday. I became even more interested when he told me where mouth-watering gobstoppers, aniseed balls, penny chews, lemon barley and stretchy jelly babies could be had. He was referring to Bryant's little shop with its sweet, sugary-smelling interior and it was to become a regular port of call for us. I found that Haxby was very old with a quaint mixture of farms, ponds, greens, stone walls and wrinkled, red roofs.

Mr Harris had said that, ''Axby's typical of many o' t'auld North Yorkshire villages bein' originally just one long street.' Many of the locals, including Mr Harris, were happy to till the land and raise animals as their ancestors had done for years without number, but it was poorly paid work. The main road through the village followed the boundaries of the ancient fields. Life here had changed very slowly, and very little over the last few decades, and cows still ambled down Usher Lane at milking times.

Front Street with its wide grassy verges was the main thoroughfare. Jimmy informed me that, 'those old houses and cottages by The Green are two or three hundred years old and are still lived in.' The *Red Lion* on the north side and the *Tiger Inn* on the south had been public houses for over a hundred years. Behind Front Street there were back lanes, also lined with older houses and businesses. At the western end was Wyre pond; the boundary of Haxby where ducks skittered and floundered about on the thick layer of ice that covered its surface. There was a short open area before it became Wigginton Front Street.

Jimmy, who was one year older than me, held tightly on to my hand as he took me down York Road to call on my young uncle, Harry, who was living with two ladies called Miss Law and Miss Barker. I got a bit of a shock on going through the front door, for looming over us was the head of a large, shaggy Highland cow. It had great long horns that curved outwards and upwards and it had been stuffed and mounted on the wall of the hallway some years back. Apparently it had once belonged to Miss Barker's family, who had been farmers for many years. Miss Barker said, 'It won many prizes at agricultural shows, such as The Haxby Show, which was a very popular annual event before the war.'

I was very surprised by the poshness, the space and the superior – even though faded and dull – quality of everything. Compared to our humble and basic, but relatively new billet it was a palace. At Usher

Lane there was barely room to swing a cat, even if we'd had one. Harry introduced me to the Misses Law and Barker and they could not have made me feel more welcome and at ease. The warmth of their reception was in sharp contrast to the one I received at the hands of Mrs Harris and I found them very nice and friendly in their genteel old-fashioned way and came to like them very much. A pleasant, outgoing couple, lively of mind and well spoken, they delighted everyone with whom they came in contact. They were noted for their old-world hospitality and good manners and they obviously loved Harry a great deal, fussing and doting on him (much to his embarrassment).

Miss Elsie Law was a forty-six-year-old spinster of average height who was rather thin and wiry and of a slightly nervous disposition. She wrung her hands a lot and there was always a faint scent of Pond's moisturising cream, soap and smelling salts about her. She had an almost pathological fear of germs and there was not a speck of dust to be seen due to her obsessive dusting and polishing. She was of a more reserved and nervous nature than Miss Barker, who was a jolly fifty-two-year-old easy-going woman, on the small side with a matronly figure. She enjoyed life and exuded kindness and goodwill, and when she laughed, which was often, her whole body wobbled and shook. I never heard Miss Law laugh out loud, she only smiled sweetly from time to time. They were cousins and had been very close and loving friends for many years.

Miss Elizabeth Ann Barker was born at her father's farm. Her ancestors had lived and farmed there for 150 years or more. In 1923 when her mother died, her father worked on at Westfield Farm for a couple of years before retiring and buying the fine town house on York Road. His sepia-tinted photograph hung in an ornate, gilded frame above the mantelpiece in the parlour. He left the farm to his son, Arthur, and came to live at Haxby with his daughter. He promised to leave her most of his money on condition that she looked after him and didn't marry. Miss Barker's mother's maiden name was Law and she had a brother, whose daughter was born in 1895. Elsie had moved in with her cousin shortly after the death of her father.

They were a friendly and generous couple who had an air of gentility about them and had become accustomed to living the high life. The middle-aged ladies loved to entertain and be entertained and were wholesome company, and their friends and family were often invited to their garden parties. They had always dressed fashionably, but good clothes were becoming much more difficult to obtain and their pre-war wardrobe had to last much longer these days. After a day of shopping they looked forward to a cup of tea and a couple of mouth-watering, fresh cream cakes in the refined atmosphere of the restaurant of Betty's Café.

The large, imposing three-storey building had high, plate-glass windows, and square-shaped, white columns flanked its wide entrances – it had enjoyed a reputation as a high-class venue for many years. There was seating for up to 220 people and it was frequented by celebrities and the local rich and famous. It was a world of uniformed waitresses and white linen tablecloths; a place where fashionable people liked to meet for tea and a tête-à-tête. It seems that the place had recently become a magnet for servicemen based at the camps and airfields in the Vale of York. American, Canadian, Australian, New Zealand, South African, Free French, Czechoslovakian, Polish and British officers were now amongst its customers but it was out of bounds to 'other ranks'. Some left their photographs or other mementoes in what they called Betty's Bar or The Dive on the ground floor. Others scratched their signatures on the frame of the large mirror in the oak-panelled bar that the RAF crews nicknamed The Briefing Room. After the war it became a kind of memorial to the many young men who perished.

The middle-aged spinsters had been regular clients prior to and during the early months of the war and their self-indulgence had angered Mrs Harris, who often asked, 'Why should the well-to-do eat as much as they want? It always seems to be the common folk that have to tighten their belts and do without.' However, with her buxom bosom and generous behind, she didn't appear to be too undernourished.

Both women were shod in sensible, rubber-soled shoes. Heeled shoes had been the style for well-to-do ladies about town in the late 1930s, but in the early part of the war they had been asked to wear shoes with flat heels, and most of the ladies felt it their duty to do so. The aim was to save on wood, which was in short supply; even paper was now being made from straw. It had been recycled so often that it was now coarse in texture and of a yellowish colour.

They got in quite a flutter and blushed like peonies when a dashing Polish officer bowed, clicked his heels and kissed their hands. They thought that the Poles and the Czechs were so colourful and handsome. Some wore heavily braided uniforms with the tassels on their golden epaulettes dangling from the shoulders. The Poles, who were sometimes referred to as Polacks by the locals, had large floppy berets. Although embarrassed, the maidenly pair were quite flattered by the gallant behaviour of the flamboyant foreigners who all seemed to have extremely good manners and spoke politely in broken English. In recent weeks, the formerly well respected, licensed premises had started to lose something of its good name as too many young women were flocking there to consort with the free-spending servicemen.

People had started to suggest that nice girls should not be seen there, so they switched their allegiance to Terry's Restaurant and Café. Terry's was, of course, the city's other major chocolate-making firm and their brands were prominently displayed in the large bow windows. Later in the war part of their factory was taken over to produce aircraft propeller blades.

There always seemed to be a lad standing outside selling the *Yorkshire Evening Post* in all weathers and he would bawl out newsworthy items. In the refined and genteel atmosphere of the high-ceilinged establishment there was a low, genial murmur of refined voices as waitresses in black dresses and frilly white aprons passed in and out taking orders, and quiet, soothing music added to the relaxed ambience. Despite the clinking of teacups and cutlery and the clatter of food trays the paper lad's tortured, elongated vowels still managed to reach their ears. Miss Law wondered whether they were trained to do this or did it come naturally?

8

And So to School

It was cold and frosty with a leaden sky as Mrs Harris walked me under the large, ornate clock to the village school that Monday morning to be enrolled as a new and very apprehensive young pupil. Fortunately I was placed in the tender care of the gentle-natured Miss Francis in the 'baby' class at St Mary's hall. Not much older than Kitty, she was slim and of medium height with short, wavy, mid-brown hair. Wearing a Tweed two-piece, she tended to push her head forward as she clumped along on flat, sensible shoes. Of a kind and pleasant disposition, she usually wore a smile and she believed that you could accomplish more by kindness than you could ever achieve by force. She was not as bossy and strict as the slightly aloof and formidable Miss Curry, whose hair was tied back severely and held in place by Kirby grips. Miss Francis's friendly nature, calmness and gentle manner had a great deal to do with my settling in fairly quickly in the infant group.

Even so, initially, it was not a happy time for me. In my unsettled state, I felt rather lost and out of sorts as I gazed at the exposed rafters, purlins and tie beams of the rooftree above me. The schoolroom seemed dark and cheerless and the small windows only let in so much cold winter light. The atmosphere seemed strange and depressing and this was reinforced when I looked out of the window at the graveyard. I had a morbid mental experience in which I imagined that I could see the skeletons of the village forefathers lying cold and still beneath the snow-covered sods. Even the lichen-splotched headstones, which leaned at all angles, looked mottled and diseased. My imagination ran riot and I felt shivers up the back of my neck and I buried my face in my arms. Even though I was among so many children, I felt lonely, sad and apprehensive. To make matters worse it was said that some of the local parents had told their children not to mix with the dirty 'vaccies', as they called us. They were inclined to blame us when things went missing or if their kids got into arguments or fights.

Following so soon after the coddled and insular life of the nursery school I found this new way of life hard to accept and my heart ached for Mam, Kitty and my friends at Grove House. It had been an enchanted place to me and I longed to be back there being hugged and cosseted and told that I was loved. I resented being so cruelly torn away from the things that were familiar to me, and felt angry at having my loving and secure world so abruptly taken away for a second time. It seems that we do not appreciate what we have in life until it dawns on us that we may not encounter it again. I kept my head down hoping to go unnoticed, indulging in daydreaming the hours away 'wool-gathering' and clock-watching.

It was slightly reassuring to know that I would be with Jimmy again at playtime, as he was working away in Miss Curry's group behind a curtain that separated his group from mine. Time seemed to pass slowly and I tried to hide my sadness, shedding my bitter tears once I was alone. We had been told from our earliest days that big boys don't cry and I tried hard to suppress my tears and felt ashamed when they came unbidden. The only time that I was able to be by myself was when I visited the school toilet or in the Harrises' bathroom. There was no privacy to be had anywhere else. Gradually I made the necessary adjustments to overcome this new and daunting phase of my life.

The teacher on duty started the school day by blowing a long blast on her whistle. The powers-that-be had stated that a rattle was to be used only if toxic gas was present in the vicinity. On hearing the whistle we stood perfectly still waiting for the command, 'Get in lines!' A second whistle was the signal for us to march into the building where we hung our hats and coats on the rows of low wooden pegs in the cloakroom. Our teacher called out the names in the register and marked the column with a tick or a cross every morning and afternoon. We were called up to her desk each morning to be given a spoonful of cod liver oil, quickly followed by a spoonful of concentrated orange juice to mask the vile taste. This was followed by a spoonful of gooey, sweet-tasting malt, which I loved. The same spoon was used for all three and it was not washed between one child's turn and the next. Some of

the local children and many of the evacuees were entitled to free dinners depending on their family's ability to pay. We, always being hungry,
envied them and wished that we could stay, but that would have meant
Mrs Harris paying for the meals out of her evacuee allowances and it
was much cheaper for her as things stood.

We were then put in pairs and marched to the main school 'hall'. This
was actually two classrooms made into one by pushing back the fold-
ing glass and wood partitions, which had hinged, military-style, brass
handles that folded down to lay flat within a circular recess. In these
morning assemblies we had to endure the boredom of communal
hymn singing, starting with a hymn such as *He who would Valiant be* or
Jerusalem, led by the vicar, the Reverend K. Donald, whom I recollect
as being a kind, gentle and understanding man who seemed old to us
but was probably middle-aged. It was customary when prayers were
being said to stand with our eyes closed and our hands held with the
ends of our fingers pointing upwards and touching the chin. From his
high place on the platform the vicar looked down on the heads of our
now quiet and subdued group. He and the head seemed very posh to us
and we held them in awe, as they were figures of authority far removed
from our way of life. They inhabited a different world to us and, unlike
the kids of today, we would never have dreamed of approaching them
to ask anything.

The headmaster reiterated the fact that God had placed us where
we were in the social order and that to try to change this preordained
scheme of things would be sinful in His eyes. We were instructed that
we must order ourselves lowly and reverently to our betters at all times,
and had to listen to an arid lecture on morals and decent standards of
behaviour that, literally, went over our heads. Once we were in a quiet
and humble frame of mind the first lesson – Scripture – commenced,
during which stories and lessons from the Bible were read.

At the morning break the children collected a straw and a small,
wide-necked, glass bottle of milk, which held a third of a pint, from the
milk monitor. On pushing in the cardboard seal with our thumb, we
sometimes soaked ourselves with a fair portion of the contents, before
drinking the remainder. For many of the scruffy evacuees, the free milk
and dinners were about the only things that interested them in the
elementary education system. Unless they were exempt, the children
had to pay a ha'penny for the milk. We were told that it strengthened
our bones, thus reducing the risk of rickets, and we had seen too many

skinny, bow-legged children hobbling around in callipers in the streets of Middlesbrough before the war. If it was dry we were allowed to play outside, but we did not get out much during that first month because it was very cold, with days of snow and ice interspersed by slightly milder wet ones.

The alphabet was chalked on the blackboard and facts were relentlessly hammered into us by means of soul-destroying, rhythmic repetition that we chanted day after day until it was assumed that we knew them by heart. We learned parrot fashion. Again and yet again we rhythmically chanted saws like: 'Twelve inches in a foot', 'Sixteen ounces make one pound', 'Fourteen pounds make one stone', etcetera, *ad infinitum*, and the multiplication tables were taught by this same time-honoured use of rote. We repeatedly chanted our 'times tables' ending up, hopefully, still together with 'and twelve twelves are one hundred and forty-four'. The four fundamentals of sums were taught by using a range of coloured counters for adding, taking away and simple division.

The younger children were read to; the older ones had to take their turn at standing up to read passages out loud, and the-powers-that-be seemed to expect children to progress at the same rate. We now know that this is not the case. Miss Francis tried to enrich our vocabulary and use of words by means of group discussions but she was not able to give us as much individual attention as she would have liked, as there were far too many in the group.

I enjoyed Art, which involved drawing, painting and making things from all kinds of materials; Miss Francis allowed us a certain amount of free play and gave us pictures to copy. Sheets of newspaper, thick with paint as they had been used over and over again, were spread out for us to work on and most seemed to enjoy making a colourful mess with paints and crayons. I discovered, to my surprise, that I was better at pencil drawing than most of the other children, but I do not recall my latent talent ever being encouraged or exploited. In those early war years our work often revealed our inner fears and anxieties, and most of our drawings and paintings at this time took the form of lurid war scenes portraying soldiers fighting or ships being sunk by enemy U-boats. We often drew pictures of German aeroplanes, with black crosses on them, firing at people adrift in the sea. Following reports of raids on York, our pictures showed bombed houses with ambulancemen putting dead or injured people onto stretchers. It seems that we were regurgitating things we had seen in the papers or heard on the wireless.

Physical Training, known as PT, was of the 'arms stretch, knees bend' variety; Harry, Jimmy and I called it Physical Jerks. We were stood in lines in our white vests and baggy, navy-blue football shorts that were held up by a length of elastic in the waistband (if you were lucky like Harry), whose group had PT outside in the schoolyard where they shivered in the cold. Our PT lessons were carried out in St Mary's hall with the benches and desks pushed back to the walls or on the field out the back when the weather was fine. We had to run, jump and stretch to the commands, 'One-two, one-two' etc. The girls wore white blouses, and baggy, navy-blue school knickers with elasticated legs, that often had a small pocket on the front in which they kept their hankie and other mysterious objects. Both sexes wore plimsolls, known as 'plimmies' locally, which were usually carried to and from school in a cloth bag with a drawstring, but to us Middlesbrough lads they were always known as sandshoes. The girls sometimes had dance lessons accompanied by a teacher playing the piano and the older boys played football on the sports field behind South Lane.

I was paralysingly shy and extremely self-conscious among what seemed confident children, and if I became the object of attention for any reason, I tended to turn scarlet with embarrassment. If you wanted a pencil or needed to go to the toilet you had to raise your hand, and I had seen others doing it, but I had an irrational dread of being noticed. I tried to make myself small and kept my head down, putting my arm round my work so as to keep it hidden in the hope of going unnoticed. I hated going to the old brick toilet block in the playground, which reeked of urine and Jeyes fluid, but I would 'pay a call' just before going in to school and then try to last out until playtime. I was often bursting to go but would never ask to leave the classroom if I could help it. I could not get the slits in the thick, finger-like strips on the end my braces onto the buttons at the back of my trousers and, to my intense mortification and acute embarrassment, the teachers had to help me. I developed a strong aversion to trouser buttons, which exists to this day. People tried to hide their phobias in those days, unlike today, and I still dislike the look and feel of buttons. The introduction of trouser belts and zips was a godsend to me.

We 'vaccies' were often looked on as non-persons and were blamed for anything that went wrong and, in the 'big' school, there were sometimes fights in the playground between vaccies and the locals. It is easy to forget the mental pain that we suffered as children. Life, at that time, seemed fragmented and unreal as I tried to find my way in a strange and daunting environment. The longing to be accepted by our peers and to be a member of the pack can be very powerful and we choose to forget the devious, shifty and furtive methods we used to achieve this. I tried at all costs to avoid the wrath and the withering scorn of the adults in power over me. Children in those days did not have half of the confidence and assurance of the modern variety. I was a dreamer, like Mam, and was too timid to ask for things to be repeated when I did not understand them. I had a fear of appearing silly in front of my peers and, consequently, I did not learn the basics of most subjects and therefore failed to make much progress. In those days children were expected to be, as Mrs Harris repeatedly pointed out, seen and not heard. Speech was silver, silence was said to be golden; so who was I to challenge these tried and tested, time-honoured laws?

A lad in Jimmy's group that I got on well with was called Bernard Fisher, and when we played football in the field on the other side of North Lane, Jimmy and I always wanted to be in the same team as him. He was a very good player and his team always won. He was one of a large family living next door but one to us and was the eldest son of Mrs Mabel Fisher (née Brooke), a chubby, motherly and loving sort of woman who usually wore her dark straight hair cut quite short. Bernard was destined to become the Hull City and – at a later date – Bradford City goalkeeper. His brother, David, was four years old at that time and he had a cute little two-year-old sister called Maud.

All of the Fisher children were born at home – delivered by Nurse Lealman – as was the normal practice in those days. Being the district nurse-cum-midwife, she was a regular visitor at the houses over the years. Although a bit bossy at times, she was well liked in the village. Maud became a pretty, wavy-haired, rounded little girl; 'a right little moppet,' as the local folk said. I would often see her running about in her little cotton frock with white ankle socks and sandals as she played in their front garden. We were repeatedly told by Mrs Harris not to mix with the other children and *never, ever* to bring them to her house.

Maud's grandfather was living with his daughter and her family on Usher Lane. He had served his apprenticeship as a gardener and I remember him as a thin, serious and gaunt-faced man who always wore a black trilby hat with a muffler, tied tightly at the neck and tucked into his collarless shirt. We often saw him going about on his old bike

KILLED BY NAIL IN SHOE Sept Oct. 1932

Tragic Death of Middlesbrough Girl

The sudden death yesterday of an 11-year-old girl, Florence, the daughter of Archibald Bradford, of 15, Booth-street, Middlesbrough, following a slight injury to the foot, caused by a protruding nail in the shoe, formed the subject of an inquest held by the Middlesbrough Coroner (Mr O. H. Cochrane) to-day.

Dr. Power said that he examined the child on Monday when there were signs of toxæmia. On Tuesday his attention was drawn to a septic bleb in her left foot. The cause of death was toxæmia, set up from the wound.

According to the father, the wound caused by the nail had apparently healed up when deceased complained of pains in her leg.

A verdict in accordance with the medical evidence was recorded.

1. 1932 *Evening Gazette* cutting reporting the death of the author's Aunt Florence (aged 11). (*All images author's collection*)

2. Mother holding George and Aunt Renee (15) behind the author, Middlesbrough, 1939.

3. Mother (aged 18) in 1932.

4. Dad as a young man (aged 24) serving in the army.

5. Cousin Jimmy and the author in 1937.

6. Great-grandfather Henry
Knights, c. 1920.

7. Archie Bradford and Albert Crabtree (standing), Harry Bradford and Jimmy Nolan (sitting), Haxby, 1940.

8. Dad (second from right) as a cook in the army, *c.* 1940.

9. Sutherland Lodge in the 1940s. The bothy is to the right of the house.

10. Sutherland Lodge in April 2003.

11. Sutherland Lodge, Christmas 1939. Author (second from left, second row); George is being held up by Rosemary Waters; Kitty (third from right, back row); Mary (kneeling); Eric (second on left).

12. Steam train coming into Levisham Station in 2002.

13. Memorial Hall (previously Haxby School) sign.

14. Haxby Church in 2002.

15. Levisham crossing from Grove House in 2003.

16. Levisham station (postcard).

17. The Artley children by the platform hut in 1940.

18. Grove House, October 1940. George is on the far left; author is third from right, front row.

19. Grove House.

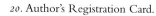

NATIONAL REGISTRATION

| | 8 | 1 | 4 |

WRIGHT
John J.

1. This Identity Card must be carefully preserved. You may need it under conditions of national emergency for important purposes. You must not lose it or allow it to be stolen. If, nevertheless, it is stolen or completely lost, you must report the fact in person at any local National Registration Office.

2. You may have to show your Identity Card to persons who are authorised by law to ask you to produce it.

3. You must not allow your Identity Card to pass into the hands of unauthorised persons or strangers. Every grown up person should be responsible for the keeping of his or her Identity Card. The Identity Card of a child should be kept by the parent or guardian or person in charge of the child for the time being.

4. Anyone finding this Card must hand it in at a Police Station or National Registration Office.

Age 5.

Born 5 April 1935.

51–3120 1

NATIONAL REGISTRATION

| | 8 | 1 | 4 |

WRIGHT
John J.

**DO NOTHING WITH THIS PART
UNTIL YOU ARE TOLD**

Full Postal Address of Above Person :—

Sutherland Lodge,

Pickering,

Yorks,

(Signed) Florence A. Thorne

Date 21st May 1940

20. Author's Registration Card.

21. Photograph of Jimmy with his mother (in ATS uniform) in 1943.

TELEPHONE Nº 3281.

County Borough of Middlesbrough

ERIMUS

R. Sutcliffe, F.S.A.A.
Borough Treasurer

PLEASE QUOTE

WRH/MTP

MUNICIPAL BUILDINGS,

MIDDLESBROUGH

10th July 1942.

Dear Sir or Madam,

      I am informed by the Borough Engineer that the house recently occupied by you, No. 27 King George Street, Middlesbrough, has now been repaired, and that the premises will be ready for occupation on the   13th July 1942.

      You should communicate with your own landlord and also contact the Billeting Officer at No.36, Dunning Street, in order that the necessary arrangements may be made for any furniture which has been removed from the house to be returned thereto.

                  Yours faithfully,

                  Borough Treasurer and
                  Chief Billeting Officer.

Mr Bradford,
    c/o 382 Linthorpe Road,
      MIDDLESBROUGH.

22. Letter stating that Gran's bombed house is now repaired, July 1942.

WAR ORGANISATION

OF THE

BRITISH RED CROSS SOCIETY and ORDER OF ST. JOHN OF JERUSALEM

President:
HER MAJESTY THE QUEEN.

Grand Prior:
H.R.H. THE DUKE OF GLOUCESTER, K.G.

R.L.10.

WOUNDED, MISSING AND RELATIVES DEPARTMENT

Chairman:
THE DOWAGER LADY AMPTHILL, C.I., G.B.E.

TELEPHONE No.:
SLOANE 9696
TELEGRAPHIC ADDRESS:
"WOMIREL, KNIGHTS, LONDON"

Re *Cpl. J. Bradford. 4390218. Queen's* LONDON. S.W.1

7 BELGRAVE SQUARE

1 - 9 - 42

Dear *Mrs Bradford –*

We have received your letter of *13 - 8 - 42* in which you tell us that you have information that your *son* name has been broadcast as a prisoner of war. We have been in communication with the B.B.C. and have verified that the news was given out from *Breslau* on *22 - 6 - 42.*

As broadcasts from foreign stations are not always entirely reliable we fear that this news cannot be taken as official, but in this case as the particulars given were correct we think you have every reason to hope that it is true.

We are very glad that you have had this good news and sincerely hope that you will soon receive an official notification confirming that your *son* is a prisoner of war.

P.S. *address broadcast as*

c/o Mrs A. Knight.
15 Fawcess Road
Doncaster - Redcar - Yorks

Yours sincerely,

Margaret Ampthill
Chairman.
LVB

23. Letter from the Red Cross stating the facts of Uncle John being a prisoner of war.

24. Uncle John (second from right, front row) as a POW in Stalag 344 in 1944.

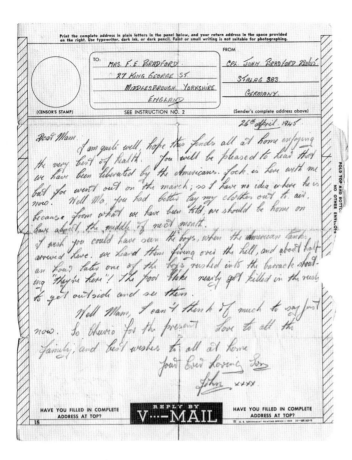

TO:
MRS. F. E. BRADFORD.
27 KING GEORGE ST
MIDDLESBROUGH YORKSHIRE
ENGLAND

FROM
CPL. JOHN BRADFORD 7603675
STALAG 383
GERMANY.

(CENSOR'S STAMP)   SEE INSTRUCTION NO. 2   (Sender's complete address above)

FOLD TOP AND BOTTOM
NO OTHER ENVELOPE

26th April 1945.

Dear Mam.
I am quite well, hope this finds all at home enjoying the very best of health. You will be pleased to hear that we have been liberated by the Americans. Jock is here with me but Joe went out on the march; so I have no idea where he is now. Well Ma, you had better lay my clothes out to air, because from what we have been told, we should be home on leave about the middle of next month.
I wish you could have seen the boys, when the American tanks arrived here. We heard them firing over the hill, and about half an hour later one of the boys rushed into the barrack shouting "they're here"! The poor bloke nearly got killed in the rush to get outside and see them.
Well Mam, I can't think of much to say just now. So cheerio for the present. Love to all the family, and best wishes to all at home
Your Ever Loving Son
John xxxx.

HAVE YOU FILLED IN COMPLETE ADDRESS AT TOP?
18

REPLY BY
V····MAIL

HAVE YOU FILLED IN COMPLETE ADDRESS AT TOP?

25. Letter from Germany telling of Uncle John's liberation from the POW camp.

26. The Reynolds family and author (on right), King George Street, Middlesbrough in 1945.

GOVERNMENT HOUSE CANBERRA

The appeal made in my name has produced over Fifty Million Pounds thus enabling the War Organisation of the Red Cross and St. John to carry out its task of alleviating the sufferings of our sick, wounded and prisoners of war to the fullest possible extent.

It gives me great pleasure to record my grateful thanks to you for your help through the Red Cross Penny-a-Week Fund in bringing about this magnificent result.

Henry

PRESIDENT
RED CROSS & ST. JOHN FUND

June 1945

Mrs. Bradford.

27. Certificate awarded to Gran.

28. The author's parents' grave,
Acklam Cemetery, Middlesbrough.

29. Certificate awarded to those
people who took in evacuees.

30. George, Mam and author, Grove House, 1940.

31. Author sitting next to Mam, Grove House, 1940.

32. Mother and author (third and second from right), Grove House, 1940.

carrying a scythe and sickle. In his later years he worked as a lengthman for the council maintaining a set area of the local roads. Maud's grandad slept in the box room, and she had initially slept in a drawer as a baby.

Talking of sleep, we infants still had a half-hour catnap in the early afternoon but we did not lie down as we had at the nursery school; we rested our heads on our forearms on the deeply etched lids of our old wooden desks. It was often difficult to sleep, especially when the great circular saw was whining and screeching, as it sliced through the great balks of timber at the carpentry business along the lane. On quiet days sound travelled a long way. The teachers were ordered to carry out kit inspections on the evacuees at least once a week, and if clothes needed repairing or replacing their parents were contacted. Mrs Harris was forever sending letters to Middlesbrough asking for more clothes for us, but for some reason we didn't always get them, even though Mam and Aunt Hilda swore that they had sent them.

A local ARP unit had been set up and they came to our school to give demonstrations; and they put up aircraft wall charts showing the silhouettes of British and German aircraft. They told us where we could and could not go and what to do if an air raid took place. They showed Jimmy's group how to use sand, stirrup pumps and buckets of water to put out small incendiary fires, explaining how to deal safely with the strange-looking butterfly bombs which had a metal casing that split open on impact to look like wings. We carried out regular air-raid drills when – on the teacher's command – we practised getting down quickly to sit cross-legged underneath our desks.

We practised putting on our heavy gas masks. On duty the wardens wore wide-brimmed tin helmets with a white W painted on them and a navy-blue, one-piece, denim boiler suit with a badge on the breast. They put up a poster that stated: 'Hitler will send no warning – so always carry your gas mask.' The rubber mask had a large, lozenge-shaped, celluloid eyepiece, and at the front was a canister that had small circular perforations, which filtered out any gas but allowed air through. The chin was placed inside and the mask was pulled over the top of the head by placing the thumbs under the three white canvas straps attached to the rubber by metal buckles at the back. They could be adjusted to give a close fit and the mask was removed by pulling the straps forward over the head from the back.

The fitting instructions were printed on the underside of the lid of the box, ending in a warning printed in bold capital letters and underlined, which stated: 'Do NOT TAKE RESPIRATOR OFF BY PULLING THE CONTAINER UPWARDS OVER THE FACE'. Initially, I experienced an awful choking sensation when the mask was on and I would start to sweat, which caused the eyepiece to steam up, at which point I began to cry and panic before quickly ripping the mask off. Later, Miss Francis was given a supply of green demisting capsules to rub on to the visor, and when these ran out we used soap to keep it clear. In time I got used to wearing it, as did thousands of other children. To test that the mask was properly fitted an ARP man placed the palm of his hand over the front of the cylinder for a few seconds, and if you struggled to breathe it was correctly fitted. The rubber sides of the mask would sometimes make a rude fluttering noise as we breathed out, like the present-day whoopee cushion, and we laughed until our sides hurt. Embossed on the lid of the box was the word TOP which enabled people to find the lid in the dark.

In my class group there was a shy little girl called Eva Pulleyn who was usually better dressed than the rest and lived in a big house. Behind it there were a number of old brick outbuildings surrounding a long courtyard. Eva came from a large family and her father was a bricklayer and a brickmaker by trade. He used the ground floor of the granary as workshops and her elder brother, Bill, kept a vintage Lanchester car in the stables. The old car dated from before the Great War. Building materials, such as cement, bricks, timber, sand, flagstones and the like, were piled up around the yard or were stored in the outbuildings.

On the eastern side of the yard there was a huge two-storeyed barn half full of rectangular straw bales where Eva kept a lamb. With its winches, wooden steps and trapdoors, it was a paradise to Jimmy and me when we played there. We would leap about on the straw and jump down from the loft into the area where her three squealing pigs were kept. Next to it was another brick building in which there was a washhouse and copper. On a shelf in one of the outhouses, above the iron mangle and the fluted, aluminium poss tub, there were bags of Sharp's meal, which was mixed with the potatoes that were too small to sell and boiled-up for pig feed. Rhode Island Reds and scarlet-combed Wyandottes busily clucked, scratched and pecked at the grain scattered on the concrete of the yard, and the family kept battery hens in the old brick granary above the stables. Nearby were tins of Jeyes Fluid, which was used to sterilise the hencoops that always had a slightly sour smell. On other shelves there were packets of Colman's starch with red and black labels; packets of Sunlight soap; red-and-white boxes of Reckitt's Blue Dolly Bags; white cardboard boxes of Borax; Lux Soap Flakes and other washing products.

At the far end of the yard there was an old wooden shed with open areas of grassland at each side. On the roof of the granary was a white-painted dovecote but all we ever saw going in and out of it were pigeons, and Eva had to explain that, 'Pigeons with their pink chests and bronze backs are known as turtledoves and their fledglings are called squabs.'

When the weather was dry we were allowed to play in the field behind the school at break times and sometimes lessons were held in it. There was no playground at St Mary's hall and the church graveyard was out of bounds to us. If it was too wet and muddy we had permission to go in Mr Pulleyn's courtyard on the understanding that we did not move or damage anything. We made dens in the prickly straw bales stacked in the barn, getting our arms and legs scratched and sore in the process, and we scrambled up the wooden ladder to the loft as nimbly as spiders. Wide-eyed with wonder we gathered round to watch the men as they worked on the black, open-topped vintage car that had large, shiny brass lights, thin white-walled tyres and wire-spoked wheels. They cranked the old engine with the starting handle until it puttered into life, but the long metal handle had been known to suddenly whip back. It could break a thumb or crack the wrist if it was not held properly and released at the moment the engine fired. We giggled excitedly when we were allowed to sit on the shiny leather back seat that was forward of the back axle so that the passengers were not bounced about too much. The highly polished, wooden dashboard gleamed in the weak winter sunshine as I sat on the box set into the wide running board and the car was driven around the yard. We took turns at squeezing the rubber bulb that made a deep honking 'parp' come from the shiny brass horn.

The Pulleyns were a respected and long-established family in the village and Eva was the youngest. Their family tree had many branches and its roots had been firmly set in the local soil for generations and members of her family had built many of the houses in the village. Some, like her sixty-year-old uncle, Robert James Pulleyn, were to play an important part in the civic affairs of the area, becoming Lord Mayor of York from 1939 to 1940. The founder of a successful firm of building contractors, he owned the Grand Picture House on Gillygate and was still an eminent member and alderman of York City Council.

Mr Wray, whose flat cart was known locally as a rulley, delivered our coal, which was neatly stacked in hundredweight hessian sacks next to a pair of heavy metal scales. Humping the sacks on his leather-clad shoulders, he emptied them into the coalbunker. The bottom of the coalhouse door must have scraped across the path for a long time, as it had left an arc-shaped mark on the flagstones.

Leaflets and items appeared in the newspapers under the title 'Food Facts' giving advice on how to make cheap and tasty meals and how to cope with the food shortages. The aim was to help people make the best of what was available, and one of the recipes, using vegetables, no meat and a little fat, was for Woolton pie. Although some were helpful, many of the food leaflets became known as bumf (i.e. bum fodder) and ended up hung on a loop of string in the village lavs. Mrs Harris listened regularly to the five-minute wireless programme called *The Kitchen Front* that was broadcast at 8.15 a.m. from Tuesday to Friday, while Dot would stand at the sink washing the breakfast dishes; when she was finished we set off for school.

During the half-term holiday Mam, Aunt Hilda and Uncle John paid a short visit. Jimmy and I enjoyed being seen with our Uncle John as he was now sporting sergeant's stripes on his army uniform that had knife-edged creases. Being in the forces gave a man standing and Gran felt proud to sew the stripes on for him. He was on embarkation leave again and his battalion had been in training near Dorchester and in the Cheddar Gorge area. On seeing the long list of dos and don'ts pinned up on the Harrises' kitchen cabinet he said, 'It's worse than being in a prisoner of war camp.' The belts and cane that usually hung there had disappeared and his words were to prove to be prophetic. He told us that during the recent snowstorms, 'Our platoon got cut off at the notorious Porlock Hill and we had to dig our way out to get back to camp.'

Each time Mam had to go it became more and more heart-rending for both of us, and just before leaving, she held me close and cuddled me into the warmth of her well-rounded bosom. Tears welled up in her eyes and in my mind's eye I can still see the red double-decker bus, with its advertisement for Tower Ales distorted by my tears, as it left for York. That night, and every night, I knelt by the side of the bed and prayed to God asking him to keep Mammy and Daddy safe until the war was over so that I could go home with them again.

Pointing out where Libya was on the large world map, Miss Curry told the assembled school that, 'British and Australian troops under the command of General Wavell have carried out a surprise attack capturing the port of Tobruk and, during the advance, over 25,000 Italians have been taken prisoner. This great success has helped us to secure the eastern Mediterranean.' Being so young and with the fighting so far away we felt safe here and the facts did not really register. We thought that it was all very exciting and Miss Curry kept us up to date on the fluctuating progress of the war. It was one of very few successes up to that time and, as such, the news was gladly received by the people of Haxby.

9

Village Life and People

That February there were several keen frosts with deep snow lying on the fields and, on the Monday of our half-term holiday, a bone-invading chill crept under the back door and slid across the floor before climbing up our backs. Being washday, condensation misted the windowpanes, distorting the view of the back garden as it streamed down wetting and lifting the edges of the criss-crossed anti-blast tape. The kitchen was the centre of most of the household activity and articles of damp laundry hung everywhere, blocking off any warmth from the fire and adding moisture to the choking fug already caused by Mrs Harris's constant cigarette smoking. She coughed and wheezed as the blue smoke curled up towards the brown tobacco-stained ceiling. The heavy dankness, which hung like a sullen cloud, made us feel listless and lethargic.

Rousing ourselves with an effort, Thelma, Dot, Jimmy, Ducky and I put on our warmest clothes and got the wooden sledge from the garden shed. Mr Harris, who was at work on the farm, had made it in his spare time. We were glad to get out to breathe the clear, sharp, frosty air, which lifted us out of our stupor. Blinking like emerging moles, we came out into the weak sunshine that shone from a cloudless, pale-blue sky and, being low on the horizon at that time of year, it cast long shadows. As we crossed Usher Lane with great care, the icy wind blew the cobwebs from our minds. The surface of the road glittered and sparkled like diamonds as the sun glinted off it and every roof and hedge was white with hoarfrost.

We made our way beside thorn hedges to the frozen Windmill pond that lay at the far side of a snow-covered turnip field, and there was a hard glistening layer of ice on top of the deep snowdrifts. Beside the pond, which we were told was bottomless, stood an old, rusting irrigation pump with its twisted metal vanes creaking and groaning as they turned slowly in the bitterly cold north-east wind. The surface of the pond was frozen solid and we skittered about on it in our hobnailed boots, landing on our backsides more often than we stayed on our feet. For a while we took turns on the sledge, two at a time, while the others held the rope and pulled it along. We whizzed up and down trying not to crash into the crowds of villagers on the ice; most of whom were floundering about and falling down just like us.

We decided that we would slide the sledge down a bank of frozen earth that sloped steeply down towards the ice-covered pond. Jimmy, who was a bit of a daredevil, volunteered to go first but, when the sledge hit the thin ice at the edge, it creaked and then there was a deep, ominous growl as it split open into several clear, green-edged shards. Jimmy and the sledge shot straight through into the icy water, but luckily he did not go completely under the ice and was able to hang on to the floating sledge. A group of grown-ups, on seeing what had happened, quickly dragged him out of the bitterly cold water. He was shocked, shivering and soaking wet but we soon got him back to the house where he was put into dry clothes and warmed through by the fire.

We thought that he would get a really good hiding from Mrs Harris, but she, surprisingly, felt sorry for him. It seems that she had a bit of a soft spot for him, and the canes and belts remained untouched on that occasion. She was, apparently, just greatly relieved that he was all right and none the worse for his icy ducking, and decided that it was best to say nothing and let it pass. Shortly afterwards she turned on me, saying, 'Just look at the muck on your bum.'

I foolishly replied, 'I can't see my bum from here.' At which she clouted me round the ear, saying, 'And that's enough cheek from you!' Stars danced before my eyes and my ear rang.

Several people had accidents on the icy roads and Harold Mann was often late in delivering the milk as his shaggy pony, Monty, had difficulty keeping its footing on the hard-packed, frozen snow. Snow fell from the milky sky on ten consecutive days, piling up in deep drifts by the hedgerows. Mrs Harris and the other women still had their milk ladled into jugs, as glass bottles were hard to come by, and it was not until the end of March that winter loosened its icy grip, with the snow finally thawing leaving heaps of dirty slush at the roadsides.

By this time cooked dinners had become available to the pupils of both schools, which was a real boon to parents that worked. The meals were served from the counters, hotplates and gas ovens newly installed in the corner of St Mary's hall, and the ovens helped to keep the place warm on cold days. The meals were brought by van from the cookhouse at Strensall army camp. The overcrowding meant that the dinners had to be served in two separate sessions and we were pleased to learn that we would have to finish our morning lessons a little earlier to allow time for the hall to be prepared.

The milk was delivered in aluminium crates with the one-third-of-a-pint bottles stood in wire compartments. They were stacked outside in the playground at the back of the main school, and when playtime arrived we often found that they were partly frozen, with plugs of solid cream standing about an inch above their necks. We sucked on them as if they were creamy iced lollies. During the long spell of snow and icy weather the crates were brought into the classroom a little earlier and placed near a green cast-iron radiator to thaw out. The bottles had thick, waxed paper seals that had an indented portion that you pushed in with your thumb. At playtime Harry, Ducky and their pals made slides on the icy playground and had great fun adding a few more bruises to the collection that they had already acquired.

Earlier in the year, the army had set up a searchlight in a field on the western side of Moor Lane opposite the Home Guard blockhouse. We went up there to help fill the sandbags and, when we were given a penny for our troubles, we were thrilled to bits but we soon tired of it. It was too much like hard work and there were easier ways of earning a penny to spend on sweets. Harold Mann often gave us a penny for helping him on his milk round.

Sometimes we heard distant explosions from up Moor Lane way, where the Home Guard were practising lobbing live hand grenades into Beresford's pond. At first they had no Mills bombs, so they used potatoes or large stones instead and, on finding out, Mrs Harris retorted, 'It's a waste of good potatoes if you ask me!' Their ammunition was stored in corrugated-tin huts on the grass verges alongside Cross Moor Lane, and these were guarded and kept well padlocked at all times. We would have liked to watch the action but they had closed off the road with Home Guard men manning the roadblocks.

At the end of March, we learned that Uncle John was home on yet another embarkation leave. He had been vaccinated again and issued with a khaki drill uniform (KD), so it looked certain that he was going to see active service; but this time in a hot, desert region. There were rumours that they were to join the Middle East Force (MEF) in Egypt. All their equipment and stores were packed and they were ready for the off.

In January the amount of meat allowed to each adult per week had been reduced, and it was then reduced further to only one and tuppence worth (nearly 6p). In February the off-putting, muddy-looking wholemeal bread – the so-called National loaf – was introduced. It was a heavy blow when jam, syrup, marmalade and treacle were put on ration in March; collectively a total of 8 ounces (227g) per person per week being allowed. Rationing was at its lowest level so far and it was even officially forbidden to feed crumbs to the birds. From that time onwards Mrs Harris would only let us have margarine or jam on our bread – never the two together! The margarine was thinly scraped on and off again and we seldom tasted jam or syrup. We lived mostly on bread, lumpy potato, heavy suet dumplings or we had rabbit meat made into stews or pies as it was not rationed and was readily available. We were growing kids and were always ravenous so we ate whatever was put in front of us or we stayed hungry. After every meal our plates were always shiny and clean, as we soaked everything up with bread or even licked the plate when Mrs Harris had her back turned.

Nature Study at school now took the form of walks beside the piebald ploughed fields armed with bags, nets and a wide variety of containers. We skipped along in pairs, with the girls hand-in-hand with their best friends, and we added our spoils to the cluttered-up nature table. Drawing things, which I enjoyed, helped me to remember details of shape, number of legs, parts of an insect's body and suchlike, and I was to find this approach invaluable later in life. In March, when the weather turned slightly milder, we collected frogspawn and watched the tadpoles hatch out to hang on the stems of the pondweed in their fish tank. The tiny frogs lost their tails and were then obliged to leave the water, feeding on aphids by shooting out their very long, sticky tongues, which happened so quickly that it could not be seen by the naked eye. They had, by that stage, to breathe through their newly formed internal lungs. At this point we trooped along to Widd's pond and released them back into the water, which had become churned up and made murky by the dabbling, beady-eyed ducks and the shy and furtive moorhens.

Some of the older boys at the main school were kept busy digging, planting and weeding on the school allotments. This backbreaking activity had assumed much greater significance as many vegetables were now in very short supply. A certain group of older boys, who the headmaster classed as thickheads or numbskulls, had to take care of his garden and woe betide them if he saw any of them messing about. He used to give them a crack on the back of the neck with the end of his RAF swagger stick. He thought that these lads would be more gain-fully employed out of the classroom where a close eye could be kept on them. They were quite happy to be outside away from the soul-destroying syllabus, averring, 'School's a bloody waste o' time any'ow. It stops us gettin' on wi' t'real work on t'farm. Yer can't learn farm jobs from books!'

Mrs Harris always seemed to send us on errands just as we were planning to go out to play and, when I came back empty-handed, Mrs Harris shouted in my face, 'Are you completely empty-headed or what?' Due to daydreaming I often forgot what I had been sent for, and after getting a clip round the lug I had to go back with a written order.

Chalked drawings had started to appear on walls and doors in the village showing the top half of a face of a bald-headed character, with a question mark growing from the top like a single hair. He had big round eyes, a long, blobby nose and the fingers of both hands show-ing over the top of a brick wall. Remarks like, 'Wot no jam!' (or any other commodity) were written beneath it. This little character, known as 'Chad', became a symbol for the increasing wartime shortages.

Poor Dot was made to clear out the fire-grate every morning and reset the fire for the day. She would put loose paper on the grate, place screwed-up newspaper and small sticks above it, before adding a few lumps of coal and lighting it. When the fire took hold she would prop the shovel up and cover it with an opened-out sheet of newspaper to make it draw. Sometimes the sulky fire went out and at other times the newspaper caught fire sending bits of black, charred paper floating everywhere; either way, Dot, who just stood there looking blank, got an earful and a clip round the ear from the irascible Mrs Harris. She was told to put yesterday's ashes on the flower borders and to spread the cinders on the garden path, as Mr Harris said they kept the weeds down and helped kill slugs and snails.

Mr and Mrs Winterburn, a childless couple, were our next-door neighbours and had a succession of airmen billeted with them. On

Saturday mornings Jimmy's chore was to stand in the queue for bread; it was the custom that only regular customers could have it put aside for them. It seemed that every time Jimmy left the house Mrs Winterburn would stop him and ask him to fetch her bread. He willingly obliged but, after a time, he got fed up with it as he suspected that she must be hiding behind her net curtain waiting to waylay him and she had never given him a penny for saving her the time and effort of going for it herself. So, one Saturday, when he had been waylaid for the ump-teenth time, he went to the bakery for our bread and told Mr Rowland that Mrs Winterburn was not happy with the bread and that she did not want any more from him. When the angry Mrs Winterburn told Mrs Harris of this, she was furious and made her husband punish him. Reluctant to do so, but not daring to oppose her, he took Jimmy up to the bedroom where he administered half a dozen whacks with his thick leather belt. One landed on his backside, but five of them 'acci-dentally' landed on the bed, and he told Jimmy to cry out at each stroke so that Mrs Harris would be none the wiser.

The lend-lease system with the USA was agreed, as the country was on the verge of bankruptcy, and a relieved Winston Churchill made one of his more eloquent and stirring speeches in which he said: 'Give us the tools and we will finish the job.' The loan was needed to provide these tools as well as food and weapons. Rowntrees was one of the fac-tories involved. Single women aged twenty to twenty-one years of age had recently been 'called up' by Ernest Bevin, the Minister for Labour, so that more men could be released for active service. Thousands of women chose to go into the works and factories but married women with young children were still exempt. Men aged over forty-one years of age, who were exempt from military service, were also involved and they were paid a basic wage of £3.0.6. (£3.02p) a week, while the women received only £1.18.0. (£1.90p) for doing the same work.

The outside of the huge chocolate factory was camouflaged in green and brown, and the windows were blacked out making the atmosphere inside claustrophobic and the lights were kept on all day. The Rowntree family held anti-war convictions like all Quakers, but this did not prevent them from forming a new company under the innocuous-sounding name of *County Industries Limited*. Under the umbrella of this company the upper floors of the building, which had formerly produced Rowntrees Fruit Gums, were being used to pack and arm 37mm shells, with only a small part of the factory now making chocolate. The fuses were inserted into the nose of the shells on the top floor behind a protective screen. It was a highly dangerous occupation, but the workers were prepared to do it if they felt they were making a significant contribution to the war effort, and the factory was in full production twenty-four hours a day, six days a week.

They worked twelve-hour day shifts for two weeks, then night shifts for the next two, and as a precaution they were obliged to rub a clear, red, jelly-like barrier cream called Rosalex onto their hands to reduce the risk of dermatitis, as some had developed red and itchy skin rashes in the early days. They were entertained, during the long boring work hours, by means of a Tannoy system that blared out popular music and songs recorded by the stars and the big bands of the day. The BBC broadcast *Music While You Work* twice a day, especially for war workers, and a new variety show called *Workers' Playtime* was relayed at lunchtimes. Big names of the day, like Vera Lynn and Flanagan and Allen, broadcast *from a factory somewhere in England* – the place never being named for security reasons. These broadcasts were received in households all over the country and were very popular. Mrs Harris always had her wireless on.

The factory had installed a huge reservoir of water on the roof, the contents of which could be released to dowse any fires that broke out. Royal Observer Corps members on the roof worked shifts round-the-clock, straining their eyes searching for the tiny specks in the sky. It was not easy to identify enemy planes when there was cloud cover and so they kept in contact with a linked network of military tracking stations; these relayed messages informing them of the whereabouts and numbers of enemy aircraft sighted while a small army of girls worked below. They were still producing the famous Rowntrees milk chocolate bars, fruit gums and pastilles, and the air was full of the sickly sweet smell of cocoa and chocolate. A great deal of the dark chocolate was used in aircrew rations and it was an important component of their escape kits, along with maps, a compass, a razor and a rubber water bottle, only to be used if they crashed or had to bail out in enemy territory.

At least once a week our Jimmy took me to Bryant's shop to buy sweets with our bit of pocket money. We liked the black liquorice bootlaces and the round, penny-sized Pontefract cakes the best and, for some reason, we always called them Pomfret cakes. Bryant's shop no longer housed the post office, which had been taken over by Mr Eric Rowland and his family and set up in what had been the bakery. Where the post office counter had been there was now a wooden framework with rows of biscuit boxes fitted into it. Broken biscuits could be bought quite cheaply.

The large and fast four-engined Halifax bomber had only recently been brought in to service and we heard on the grapevine that a squadron of them had arrived at Linton-on-Ouse airfield. We often saw them over the village and new aircraft were being delivered every few days. The exhaust flames from the cowlings of their Hercules engines could be clearly seen at dusk, and their vibration rattled the ornaments and plates on our shelves. It seems that they were to replace the relatively slow and obsolete Whitleys that were by then nobody's friend. In the early months of the year the newspapers reported that Halifaxes of Bomber Command were attacking targets on the French coast.

The air-raid warnings had increased in recent weeks and one night in early March the mournful wail of the siren sounded yet again. Just after 9.30 p.m. we were rushed downstairs to lie under the front room table, which had been pushed against the wall as directed. The girls were with Mrs Harris in the cupboard under the stairs but the long sustained note of the all-clear was not sounded until quarter to four in the morning. We trooped wearily back to bed, but at least we didn't have to start school until ten o'clock that morning. In the darkness of those winter mornings we sometimes saw the returning bombers briefly lit up by the beam of the local searchlight, which was flicked on and off to show that the aircraft had been recognised. Our sleep was often disturbed and we turned up at school dull from the lack of it.

On my sixth birthday Mam, with her gentle ways and winsome smile, paid us a short visit, and whenever she appeared it felt as though the sun had just emerged from the clouds. Before she left she gave us a few coppers to buy sweets and a comic, and Jimmy still had a bit of the money that his mother had given him on his seventh birthday two weeks back. We thought we might try another visit to Torville's little shop, as Bryant's was always busy and crowded. It was set back behind the wide grass verge that bordered the south side of the main road and the front door was a bit difficult to open, as its wooden frame tended to swell after a spell of wet weather. On this occasion, Jimmy gave it a hefty shove with his shoulder and it burst open, and we startled the customers as we staggered in amongst them accompanied by the loud clanging of the bell above the door.

The wooden counter was almost hidden beneath newspapers, magazines and comics. It was owned and run by a small, busty spinster called Miss Susanna Torville who was going grey, even though she was probably only in her fifties. She seemed like a real old biddy to us and her parents had bought the shop before the turn of the century and it had not changed much in all that time. Miss Torville weighed our sweets in the large, gleaming brass pan of the Avery scales with extreme care, even to the point of taking off three small sweets and replacing them with two slightly heavier ones to make sure that the weight was absolutely spot on and not a fraction of an ounce over. There was a step towards the rear of the old shop, which led to her private living quarters, and in the gloom of the interior customers, including us, had a habit of stumbling down it. After that we went to Bryant's for our sweets as they were not so fussy if the sweets weighed a little more than our few coppers justified, and they always put them into a conical-shaped paper bag twisted at the top to close it.

Comics were very popular with children in those days before there were any television sets, but many of them, such as *Tiger Tim's Weekly*, had been forced to close down due to paper shortages. The *Beano*, which cost tuppence (less than 1p), had previously had twenty-eight coloured pages, but now it was smaller and only had eight with coloured print only used on the cover pages. The comics were now full of war themes, with spy stories and tales of unexploded bombs, and every day, while we waited for our tea in the kitchen, Thelma would read to me out loud the rhyming couplets under the Rupert Bear cartoon strip in the paper. I really looked forward to this as I loved the adventures of the little bear in the red, high-necked jumper, yellow scarf and large-checked trousers.

In April it was said that Mr Harris's hero, Leonard Cheshire, had completed his tour of thirty operations when he flew out on his first bombing expedition in one of the new Halifax bombers; he was assigned to attack the Baltic port of Kiel with its dockyard facilities and U-boat pens. The Germans had destroyed Yugoslavia's army in just one week and had driven the Allies out of Greece with another Dunkirk-type retreat to the beaches. This was terrible news for the people at home, with Crete and Malta now the only British outposts in the Mediterranean Sea.

On 13 April 1941, Easter Sunday, we were bathed and put in our Sunday best, and I remember wincing as Mrs Harris roughly combed the cotters out of my hair. We were then taken to matins at St Mary's church. At the end of Holy Week, as the large, brown, sticky buds on the horse chestnut tree by the gate were starting to open, it was nice to see the greenery and the spring flowers after the long, snow-covered winter. The daffodils, growing in profusion on the green and between the graves, were dancing and rocking in the gentle breeze as our group of seven went in through the arched doorway of the old stone porch. As we walked behind the high-backed wooden pews, Mr Harris, looking very smart in his highly polished Sunday shoes and dark pinstriped suit, removed his black trilby hat, but the women kept their hats on. A musty smell mingled with the pungent, earthy odours emanating from the villagers packed in serried ranks on the shiny pews. 'Was it the smell of God?' we wondered, as the slanting rays of the sun shone through the lancet windows illuminating the dancing dust motes. It took some time for our eyes to adjust to the dim interior, where stained-glass windows depicted saints with links to the North Country such as Bede, Hilda, Oswald and Cuthbert; each one crowned by delicately carved, cinquefoil, stone tracery.

My Uncle Harry – now thirteen years of age – was prinked out in his Sunday best, wearing a smart, short-trousered suit with a white shirt and tie. The Misses Law and Barker, resplendent in white gloves, smart hats and fashionable coats with expensive brooches on the lapels, were a picture of sartorial elegance as they listened intently to the resonant voice of the Reverend Donald. When we stood up we were always slightly behind everybody else, opening and closing our mouths pretending to sing hymn number 143 that begins 'Christ the Lord is risen today, Hallelujah!' Our voices were drowned out by the loud, heartily singing congregation and the choir, who stood behind the intricately carved reredos screen looking clean and smart in their long cassocks and freshly starched white surplices.

The deep, bass voices of the farmers and the farmhands, with their weather-beaten faces and big red hands, rang out as they sang uninhibitedly, with great joy and thanks to the Lord, as their ancestors had always done. Their intense masculinity and simple primitive faith was plain for all to see as they enthusiastically belted out: 'Sing to the Lord with cheerful voice.'

The brass cross on the altar shone with the effulgence of burning gold, and the brilliant white of the altar cloth matched the pure white of the vicar's chasuble. He had worn a purple one in Lent. There were

arrangements of beautiful spring flowers decking the choir stalls and
the ends of the pews, and the freshly picked primroses and daffodils
stood out in the dim light, brightening the more sombre and shad-
owy areas of the old church. Several of the pews emptied as the vicar
began the ritual of Holy Communion and the villagers returned to
their places one by one having knelt at the altar rail to take the sacra-
ment. Some still had the consecrated wafer melting in their mouths
and a few had a look of smug satisfaction feeling that they might just
have opened the door to heaven a chink wider. Our tall, bald-headed
headmaster, Mr Fox, sat there playing the organ, pulling out the stops
and pumping the pedals enthusiastically as the music boomed out from
the organ pipes and echoed back from the high roof space. The organ
was tucked away to the left of the altar and behind it a young lad sat
fervently pumping the bellows.

The vicar then read the sermon from the wooden lectern above the
intricate stone carvings of the old pulpit. In honour of Easter he was
wearing a more splendid alb, amice and chasuble than usual, with his
chasuble symbolic of Christ's seamless coat. During his sermons hellfire often seemed to crop up as, in his clear, deep-timbred voice, he
proclaimed the Easter message and read the collects appropriate to the
day; but the words were almost meaningless to us and most of them –
figuratively and literally – passed over our young heads.

Before long we grew bored and started to fidget, gazing up at the
pine hammer beams and the Douglas fir roof panels that were difficult to make out in the deep shadows. Below the hammer beams, long
chains supported the large, wrought-iron hoops of the chandeliers, and
Mr Harris whispered to us, 'They once 'ad candles in 'em thar knows.'
They looked like wagon wheel rims to me and I moved sideways so
as not to be directly under one in case it came crashing down on my
head. We started whispering to each other until we were shushed by
the cantankerous Mrs Harris. She had given each of us a shiny penny
coin to place on the collection plate that was being passed round. In
our boredom we squinted at the words 'D: G: OMN: REX F: D: IND:
IMP' that were embossed round the head of King George VI without
understanding what any of it meant.

Our foster parents were not especially religious although they
believed that we had been put on this earth for a purpose, and if there
was a purpose in life this presupposed that there must be a God. They
believed that Jesus Christ's lessons taught us how we should behave

towards each other, although Mrs Harris did not seem to adhere to them herself. She had the good book in her hand but apparently not in her head and could be, as we were to learn, nasty and mean spirited. She seemed to think that going to church was a kind of insurance, just in case there was an afterlife. She might have been better occupied pondering on the wrath of God rather than on His loving and caring aspects alone.

We were unthinking believers in religion but Mam believed in the Bible in a more profound way and really felt the horror of Christ's crucifixion. She used to say, 'If God is with you nothing on earth can harm you.' And she thought that Christ's love gave us the strength and patience to tolerate the bad things in life. Religious life had long been all-pervasive to her and she suffered the sadness, the joy and the ecstasy of the various Holy days. At Easter sorrow and joy were closely inter-mingled, just as they were in her, but there was also a feeling of hope abroad in the spring air. Of a gentle nature, she was a pacifist at heart, but she truly believed that without religion mankind could quickly degenerate into savagery; and she believed that that is what had hap-pened in Germany. Her God was a merciful God and she just *knew* that there was a life after death. To her life was only a temporary state, after which all would be reunited with their departed loved ones. She was pleased that we were gong to church services and the Sunday school classes in St Mary's hall where Miss Curry conducted the singing.

The following Tuesday night we went to bed at the usual time only to be woken in the early hours by the plaintive wailing of the air-raid siren. Scurrying downstairs we heard the unsynchronised drone of German aircraft engines and then there were two muffled booms from across the fields to the north-west. Soon afterwards the continuous tone of the all-clear sounded and we went back to our bedroom, but on peeping round the curtain we could see the flames of several fires burning in the distance. There was a red glow in the sky over towards the Plainville area and the next day we learned that a Heinkel 111 had developed engine trouble. The starboard engine had burst into flames, and some said it had been shot down by one of the Bofors guns defend-ing Linton-on-Ouse airfield. The pilot had jettisoned his 1,000kg bomb and the five-man crew managed to bale out, with eyewitnesses stating that, 'The great plane somersaulted and looped through the night sky like a giant Catherine wheel with its engines revving out of control.' It crashed in a field about two miles from Haxby.

Several kids failed to turn up at school when we started at ten o'clock the following morning and one of these was the mischievous ten-year-old Derek Robinson, who had gone to the crash site to collect shrapnel. Shrapnel was greatly treasured and highly swoppable in school. 'A right cheeky little devil,' Mrs Harris called him. Unfortunately for him, our village policeman, PC Bill Manging, who lived with his wife in the bungalow next door but one to Harry, also arrived at the crash site that morning. With his black cape flapping in the wind he chased Derek across the fields holding on to his steel helmet, but the fleet-of-foot little lad was too fast for him this time. However, PC Manging knew where he lived, and, on catching up with him later, tore a strip off him. By that time Derek's precious 'treasures' were safely stashed away to be proudly displayed to the kids in the schoolyard later.

The engine left a deep crater in the soft earth and the wreckage was scattered over a wide area. Soldiers had rounded up the crew and put the men under arrest. It was definitely the highlight of the week and it was amazing how quickly the news had spread. Later that day, Harry said, 'We rushed to the main gate and sat on the low wall, getting there just in time to see a party of soldiers and the local Home Guard escorting a German airman past the school. They had their bayoneted rifles cocked and looked ready to use them. The German had on a wool-lined, one-piece flying overall with zips on the pockets and wore a leather belt with brass buckles, a close-fitting leather helmet and fur-lined flying boots.' I was green with envy at missing out on such a major event and Jimmy and I drew and painted pictures of Luftwaffe pilots for weeks to come.

Soon afterwards, under the strictest of security, the crumpled, oil-streaked wreckage was taken away on a 'Queen Mary' trailer covered with a tarpaulin. It was taken to 60 MU at Shipton and we often saw the long, low vehicle parked opposite the school or by the level crossing gates. Many years later the crash site was excavated and bits of the engine, propellers and other parts were found, and a five-foot-long propeller blade was kept in a barn for many years.

On 4 May the clocks were put forward one hour giving us two hours of extra evening daylight, known as double summertime, as the clocks had not been put back the previous autumn. It meant that it was light well after bedtime and light again before we got up in the morning, and we took full advantage of this, playing in Widd's field until long after tea. The farmers and the farmhands, a robust, cheerful lot with shining red faces and large, rough hands, worked late in the fragrant summer fields behind the snorting, stamping horses, and there were no jarring mechanical noises.

We were always made to say Grace before meals, but it wasn't the swift hand of God that we feared. If any of us ate anything before Grace was said we got a clout from Mrs Harris. Breakfast usually consisted of porridge made from Quaker Oats mixed with milk and water. I tried hard to be good and polite at breakfast, as Mam had told us that, 'God is a silent listener and a guest at every meal.' But it was difficult to be good all day; especially when Jimmy kept pulling faces at me and trying to get me annoyed. It had been light for a good two hours as our little group walked to school on those early summer mornings.

The east coast was now easily accessible to the Luftwaffe and the evacuees from Hull were anxious about their parents' safety and couldn't wait for them to visit again. The evacuees from there told us that the town had suffered repeated bombing between March and May, with hundreds killed and thousands of houses damaged. At night the raging fires lit up the night sky and the orange glow could be seen from Haxby. When Mam visited us she told us that six bombs had been dropped on the Newport area and one had landed inside the steel casing of one of the gasholders not far from our house, setting it on fire and providing a spectacularly frightening display.

The Wigginton and Haxby Women's Institute (WI) were doing their bit for the war effort. Their needles busily clicked away as they knitted scarves, jerseys, woollen hats, balaclava helmets and socks, which were parcelled up and sent to local men serving in the forces. They also made garments for the local children and the RAF men billeted in the two villages. They made lots of jam and the local housewives snapped the jars up eagerly, with Mrs Harris making sure that she got her fair share, but we were still denied jam and margarine on our bread at the same time.

To help the worsening food situation, Mr Harris went out and caught rabbits using hand-whittled wooden pegs to which he attached wire snares (locally called 'sniggles'). His big square hands were callused and ingrained with soil and were those of a man accustomed to hard manual work. He knew all the rabbit runs near his allotment and in the local fields and he set snares in the deep grass under the hedgerows in the evenings. He would then go out early in the morning when the dew was still on the grass, picking a few mushrooms on the way. Once the rabbits were removed from the sniggles he spliced the skin of their hind legs and brought them home slung on a long stick taken from the hedgerow that he rested on his shoulder. The open fields, with their covering of fresh, lush grass, were alive with rabbits and field mice, and Mr Harris told us that he often heard the forlorn cry of a rabbit as he approached. Death was always waiting in the wings in the form of slinky stoats with black-tipped tails. Brown on top and white underneath, their kittens would eat anything, including insects.

We were often given rabbit stews and I came to like the taste of the white meat that was a bit stronger than chicken. We had also started to have bland-tasting, mass-produced vegetable rissoles that had only recently been introduced and could be bought at the Co-op store for eight pence (3p) per pound.

10

Stormy Waters

The Wiggy Rec, a wooden building on the main street at Wigginton, was shared with the RAF. Several lorries painted in dull blue were usually to be found parked in its grounds and Sergeant Ellery made it abundantly clear that he was the man in charge there. He was responsible for getting the large numbers of airmen billeted in the area – most of whom worked at the aircraft maintenance unit at Shipton – to and from their places of work every day. The large hut was also used by the RAF every Wednesday to show films. The latest, *Turned out Nice Again*, starred George Formby as a half-soaked but loveable, ukulele-playing, working-class chap who was always being put upon, and its title became one of Mr Harris's favourite sayings. Maybe Mr Harris identified with him. The musical 'Broadway Melody', featuring the suave Hollywood song and dance star Fred Astaire, was also shown around that time but I don't recall ever being taken there.

Regular Saturday night dances were held there as the RAF lads had formed a good dance band and many of the local ladies were to have fond memories of these dances in the years to come. Many of the RAF lads used to call in at Walker's fish and chip shop on Front Street, Haxby, for their suppers.

RAF Sergeant Ellery received regular news bulletins on the wireless that the RAF had installed and he passed these on to Miss Curry, who then informed us. The latest news concerned Rudolph Hess, Hitler's former deputy, who had flown across the North Sea and parachuted on to a farm near Glasgow. He was said to be mentally ill. By this time Greece was in German hands following a huge airborne invasion with heavy losses on both sides. Many Allied troops had been taken prisoner and the remainder were evacuated to Crete, which fell to yet another massive German airborne attack near the end of May. Another defeat was a bitter disappointment to the British public.

At that time Germany was at the height of its military power and was sweeping all before it. The prospects of victory for the Allies seemed remote. The continent of Europe was under Nazi oppression and they now occupied or controlled most of North Africa. We learned that German troops were massing on their eastern borders and on the 22nd Hitler, blinded by his own conceit, hurled his mechanised divisions at the vast Soviet Union, and his former allies were in retreat. This meant that he now had war on two fronts and the threat of an invasion on Britain all but disappeared. It was to be Hitler's greatest mistake.

Mrs Harris was in an even viler frame of mind than usual around that time, as a stray bomb had landed on the gas works in York which caused the gas pressure in the village to be low for a week, making it difficult for her to provide hot meals. Times became even harder when it was announced that clothes were to be rationed from 1 June. No special ration books for clothing were issued and the locals were obliged to use spare coupons from their food books for some considerable time. The ribs of Mrs Harris's corsets where made of whalebone, which was now hard to come by, but she only wore them when she went somewhere special and most of the time she looked like a sack of potatoes tied in the middle.

We enjoyed fifteen hours of sunshine on one day in June and long, hot sunny days thereafter as the summer seemed to go on forever. When coal was put on ration on 4 July, it was not really noticed until the weather changed for the worse later in the year. The sugar ration was doubled from eight ounces to one pound, for that month only, as large amounts of summer fruit were readily available. Mrs Harris's excess fruit was stored in her larder in sealed Kilner jars.

We were made to change into our old shabby clothes as soon as we came home from school and we each had a list of household chores and errands that had to be done before teatime. By now the long list of dos and don'ts had grown and God help us if we didn't abide by them. We had to clean and polish our school shoes over an old newspaper and the girls had to help Mrs Harris in getting the tea ready and had to do the washing up afterwards. After tea we were sent out to play until near bedtime, unless it was raining, when we were sent up into our bedrooms to play with our meagre toys and games. There were no books in the house, only newspapers and the odd magazine like *Picture Post*, *Illustrated* or *Woman's Own*, which cost tuppence (1p) and came out every Wednesday. Although I was unable to read I enjoyed looking at the pictures.

We often found small white booklets in the house called *Old Moore's Almanack*, which Mrs Harris bought at Torville's shop. There were prophecies in black print on the front cover and they had black and white hieroglyphics and cabalistic sketches on the inside pages. There were things like the phases of the moon, tide tables and rhyming verses predicting catastrophes and disasters yet to come. It all seemed a bit spooky to us but most people were superstitious in those days. Mrs Harris was *very* superstitious and she told us that we must never pass each other on the stairs, put our shoes on the table, or leave our knives and forks crossed on our plate. If we did so we would always have bad luck and she believed implicitly in the horoscopes printed in the *Daily Express* that cost one pence (0.4p) at that time. We practised our own magic rituals, one of which involved touching the top of our front gate and walking backwards up to the Fisher's gatepost. We then had to touch that before we could turn to face the right way, and I repeated this ritual every time I went out.

Living next door to us was a young childless couple called Len and Sarah Hayes. He was a rat catcher on the local railway and kept long, flat-backed ferrets with beady, pink eyes in cages at the bottom of his back garden. He had one of them peeping out from inside his shirt as he told us that the males were called 'hobs', and he didn't mind us watching as he fed them on mice and old chicken legs that were unfit for human consumption. As they ran about the slinky creatures had a strange habit of suddenly leaping up into the air.

Mr Maurice Nolan, who lived in the first house in the next pair but one to us, had a son and a daughter from an earlier marriage, and we overheard Mrs Harris say disapprovingly that he was now living tally with his new wife-to-be. She added that there had been a shotgun marriage, but we didn't understand what she meant and that year a new baby arrived at the house. She told us that it had been found in their rhubarb patch and, for a while after that, whenever Mr Harris took us to his allotment, we looked under the rhubarb leaves to see if one had been left there. We were nowhere near as worldly-wise, knowledge-able or confident as the youngsters of today. Mr Nolan was employed locally as a bookie's runner and one day, passing the couple on Usher Lane, we asked if we could see the baby, but when we looked into the pram a horrible 'pong' assailed our nostrils. From our back garden we could see a long row of Terry towelling nappies flapping and fluttering in the breeze.

When the summer holiday arrived we were sent out to play; but not until we had done our chores, eaten our breakfast and completed our errands. We all had to run messages but poor Dot always had more jobs to do than the rest of us. We were given orders not to come back until dinnertime, and God help us if we were late for that. Then we were let loose again until teatime; unless Mrs Harris heard on the village grapevine that one of the shops was selling some hard-to-get product, in which case, one of us had to go and stand in the queue to save a place for her. On Sundays and Wednesday afternoons we were safe as all the shops were shut. After tea we were sent out to play again until near dusk.

When we came back after playing out, our legs were usually scratched and sore from the hay, the brambles and the grass seed-heads (that we called arrows) which got stuck in our woollen socks; and these were usually concerntina'd round our ankles and looked like the blacksmith's bellows. In the heat of the afternoon, leg-weary after hours of incessant activity, we would flop down on the grass and give way to indolence. We would lie spread-eagled on our backs, half-hidden in the Yorkshire Fog in Widd's field. I enjoyed the feeling of somnolence as the heat was reflected upwards from the sun-warmed soil. Lying in a tangle of bodies, we used each other as pillows, and I would watch the fluffy, cotton-wool clouds floating serenely by across the azure of the wide summer skies and surrender to the moment. As the sun warmed my face the sunlight that filtered through my closed eyelids turned the insides pink. One moment I lay quiet and relaxed; the next my sleepy, languorous reverie would be brought to an abrupt end as Jimmy or one of the others jumped on me and knocked the stuffing out of me. The still, restful moment then turned into scrimmaging and horseplay that usually ended up in a 'roughhouse'.

On those glorious summer days we ran wild and free. We climbed trees and fell over sustaining bruises and cuts that bled, dried and formed scabs. Our knees and elbows were always yellow with iodine. We wandered round the local countryside, getting hotter and sweatier as the day wore on and we came to know every lane, snickleway (i.e. ancient tracks and rights of way), house, farm, barn and field in the area. Day after day the sun beat down, bleaching our hair and turning our faces, forearms and legs a ruddy bronze in colour. Occasionally the sky darkened and the air cooled and when heavy summer showers fell we sought shelter in a barn, taking the opportunity to make dens in the hay and secret passages between the straw bales until it faired up. The parched and dusty earth darkened as it soaked up the life-giving rain and we left the cool shady depths of the barn, blinking like coal miners emerging from the pit. Screwing up our eyes against the dazzling brightness, we enjoyed the warm kiss of the sun on our skin. After the chill of the rain we felt newly invigorated as sweet, freshly released scents emanated from the flowers, the wet leaves and the steaming grass. Sadly, the tassels of corn that had danced in the sun now lay forlornly on the earth following their heavy battering. The smell of the rain-wet soil rose up to mingle with the summer air and we drew its nectar-like freshness deep into our lungs and it was sheer bliss to be young and alive.

Mrs Harris lacked the gift of loving kindness and didn't seem bothered whether we got lost, injured or drowned as long as we kept well out of her sight. The open countryside was ours and free for the taking and we revelled in it, spending most of our time outdoors, returning to the house just to eat, sleep and do our chores. 'Seeing' German soldiers hiding behind every hedge and tree, we stealthily crept up on them and killed them. As we played in Widd's field amid scents of rye grass and foxtails, we would sometimes see real soldiers walking along the lane and, one day, we knew it wasn't right when one of them exposed himself and we edged further away from him. From the field we were able to see whether Mrs Harris had come out into the back garden to wave a tea towel above her head – her way of indicating that it was time to go in. While we waited there were always newts and things to be caught below the coruscating, breeze-ruffled surface of the shallow pond.

During that glorious late summer the days were long and hot and the nights were short and warm, and life was seldom dull. After expending so much energy in constant activity we slept soundly in our beds at night and I developed a deep and lasting love of nature. On 10 August the clocks were put back again by an hour bringing the double summertime to an end. The evening shadows lengthened, but it was still light until ten o'clock at night. Ecstatic days were followed by humdrum days when nothing much happened and Jimmy and I often argued and fell out, but the bond of blood and friendship was strong and we soon made up and became the best of pals again. We stood together if anyone threatened the other but, more often than not, it was Jimmy who protected me.

Mr Harris often read out items from the newspapers, which were getting thinner and thinner. Leonard Cheshire, the brave and widely admired bomber pilot, was often mentioned and he had become something of a hero to us. It was said that bomber crew survival rates were now averaging around three weeks and Leonard Cheshire was living on borrowed time. He had either been very lucky, was a brilliant pilot or both to survive this long. Mr Harris lionised him and to him he was the bravest pilot that ever lived. He was to become the most decorated pilot in the RAF.

When Mam visited again she told me that she had given up her job as a housemaid in the large house on Newport Road owned by Mrs Ethel Gaunt, who was later to become the Lady Mayoress of Middlesbrough. Mam couldn't bear to be parted from her 'baby boy' for long and she was now back at Grove House with our George working as an assistant cook to Mrs Ruonne. She said, 'It makes it much easier for me to visit you now and I missed you both terribly when I was in Middlesbrough. I now go to the little church in the valley with the Artleys every Sunday and they send their best regards.'

Dad was now attached to a Durham coast light anti-aircraft unit and could not get home very often, and Mam had temporarily rented our house to a female acquaintance called Mrs Miller who was of the Mormon persuasion. Mam had felt sorry for Mrs Miller when she found out her husband had beaten her and kicked her out, as her sister's bad experiences with her estranged husband were still fresh in her mind.

Mam could now catch the early train to York from Levisham Station right outside the door and then catch the double-decker bus to Haxby. She would write to Mrs Harris about once a month to tell her when she was coming, and when Jimmy and I found out what time the bus was due we would run excitedly down the road to meet it as it pulled in by the Co-op store. Mam, not being invited to stay for a meal, often took Jimmy and me to our Harry's billet on York Road. Here the homely Miss Barker and the friendly Miss Law made us feel very welcome and we sometimes played clock golf on their lawn. Afterwards we stayed for a nice tea with lots of cakes and sandwiches sat at the wooden table in the back garden, but I keenly sensed Mam's pain each time she had to leave.

When the new school year started at St Mary's hall that September it was as crowded as ever, but the warm and gentle Miss Francis was still my teacher. She had a quiet, clear voice, which she seldom raised, and she encouraged us to be more sensitive to each other's feelings in the hope of making us better children. Jimmy had moved up to the main school and, much to his delight, he was now in Miss Rutter's group in the high-ceilinged classroom adjoining the headmaster's house. She was his acting, unpaid deputy. Slim, voluptuous and athletic, with graceful wrists and ankles, she was sometimes to be seen hurdling over the low wall at the front of the school giving the sniggering lads a brief glimpse of white underwear. Jimmy had a bit of a crush on his pretty, dark-skinned teacher with her Italian looks.

She had an oval face, high cheekbones and dark, soft, luxuriantly wavy hair and Jimmy loved the way it swayed as she moved. Her eyebrows were dark and she had big brown eyes with long lashes and to Jimmy she was beautiful. Her vivacity and poise were her greatest assets and he thought she looked like a film star; she could do no wrong in his eyes. The lips of her well-shaped mouth were soft and full and often broke into a glorious smile. I often saw him following her around like a puppy dog being as helpful and polite as could be and making calf's eyes at her. When I exaggeratedly mocked him he gave me a swift punch in the ribs. Harry was now in the 'big boys' form presided over by Mr Fox.

In mid-September the Ministry of Food compelled the subsidised grocers to sell hard-to-get potatoes at one penny (0.4p) each, as they felt that people needed more complex carbohydrates in their diet to correct the imbalance caused by rationing and shortages. Even off-ration foods, like fish and sausages, were hard to get and Mr Harris said, 'It's a darn mystery what's in them sausages any'ow.' When they became available long queues formed. We were seldom given real potatoes except when Mr Harris brought a few from his allotment at certain times of the year. More often than not we were given tinned corned beef or Spam with a tasteless dollop of unappetising 'Pom' made from potato powder to which hot water had been addded. We now started our day with a splodge of hot porridge made with water, not milk. 'That'll put a lining on your bellies and keep you warm,' contended Mrs Harris.

Overall our diet was pretty bland and we were always hungry. We ran, walked and skipped wherever we went which kept us lean and fit. We seldom saw any fat kids. For our main midday meal we still had lots of rabbit stews with dandelion leaves, nettles and greasy suet dumplings floating in them. Mr Harris kept a plot at the bottom of the back garden on which he grew dandelions and nettles to supplement our intake of greens but Jimmy always called it rabbit food. Mrs Harris used the leaves for salads and as pot herbs believing they were good for us. This was reinforced by the avuncular Dr Charles Hill, MP, when he spoke of 'his friend the dandelion'. Known as The Radio Doctor he gave a five-minute talk on health every morning. We called dandelion flowers *pee-the-beds*; others were not quite so polite. We had to say Grace before and after every meal, which never altered from, 'For what we are about to receive, may the Lord make us truly thankful, Amen', and 'For what we have just received …'

Quite often we were given a plateful of heavy suet pudding with salt on it, which Mrs Harris had steamed in a muslin bag over a big pan of boiling water. It was about the size of a football and it filled us up but it lay like lead in our bellies. We ate what was put in front of us or we went hungry. One day, for a change, she made a Spotted Dick (suet pudding with raisins in it) and I remember getting a clout round the lug for saying something rude about it.

On our nature walks Miss Francis encouraged us to collect the rose-hips that bulged red and shiny on the briars, and she told us that they would be made into rose-hip syrup which was rich in vitamin C. In the past we had used their hairy, close-packed white seeds to put down each other's shirt collars and we called them itchy-backs. In our spare time we scoured the hedgerows until barely one was left on the bushes for the poor birds to feed on in the winter, and for our efforts we received four pence per pound. I think I made about tuppence profit, but Mrs Harris – to my dismay – made me put a penny of it into the collection plate at church that Sunday.

So the swallows departed for warmer climes and our days in the village passed uneventfully. We popped the white snowberries that clung to the spindly twigs in the hedgerows. The rosy-cheeked apples reached full ripeness and the sweet smell of cider filled the air beneath the trees as the fallers fermented. We ate many of those that were still in reasonable condition, but it was customary to leave the last apple on each tree for the fairies. Locals called the curved, brownish-green, sweet and succulent Conference pears, 'banana' pears. As their weight bent down the boughs in the orchards, it made it easier for us to do a bit of illicit scrumping. We did not see it as wrong when fresh fruit was so scarce and we were so hungry. When some of the kids were seen and recognised, they were reported to the school and, after they had received their just deserts from Mr Fox, they spit on their hands and held them under their oxsters (armpits) as that seemed to ease the stinging pain a little. Mr Harris said, 'We used ter rub a raw onion on our 'ands to deaden t'pain but they're 'ard to come by these days.'

The blackberries in the hedgerows grew fat, turning from red to juicy black and they stained our lips, tongues and fingers. As autumn moved on, the leaves of the horse chestnut and beech trees were tinged with brown making them engaging to the eye. We had watched the spiky, tri-lobed fruits of the horse chestnut trees slowly growing to full size all through the spring and summer. Conkers became the 'in thing' again, and as we took the mahogany-brown seeds from their cocoons they had a slight smell of iodine.

Using an old skewer from Mr Harris's cluttered shed, we bored a hole through them and suspended the best ones on thick string. We had dried them slowly in the airing cupboard and soaked them in vinegar to harden them, and Jimmy had a few from the previous year that were now dry and really hard. Thinking we were in with a chance, we set forth to conquer the rest but someone always seemed to produce a better one. After many hits and a few wins, the first fatal cracks began to appear in our would-be champions.

The seven-fingered leaflets on the horse chestnut trees were just starting to turn brown, but they became a sorry sight after the lads had bombarded them with large sticks in an attempt to knock down the spiky seedcases. The ground inside the graveyard gate was thickly littered with fallen twigs and leaves and some of the boys received 'six of the best' on their backsides from the headmaster. A number of irate women had complained that the heavy sticks the boys had thrown up just missed them when they were blown down by the strong winds.

Jimmy sometimes walked up to Mrs Evans's bungalow to see the various aeroplane models that Terry Waddington's dad had carved for him, but he would not be getting any more. While working at Linton-on-Ouse airfield, he had been asked to swing the propeller of a Tiger Moth biplane to start the engine. His foot slipped, and as he staggered forward the spinning propeller almost severed his right hand and he had to undergo major surgery and receive treatment for a long time.

At potato picking time, the farmers were starting to get extra help. We saw groups of prisoners of war, from the camp that had been set up at Strensall, working in the fields for the first time. The Italians wore dark-brown battle dresses with a large red circle sewn on the back, but the Germans had yellow, diamond-shaped patches on their grey uniforms. They were brought over every morning in army lorries and groups of four or five were dropped off guarded by a soldier armed with a loaded rifle and fixed bayonet; they were then returned in the evening. In July, thousands of them had been brought to Liverpool by ship and were put in barbed wire-encircled enclosures all over the country. The farmers were delighted with their new 'hands' and Miss Curry told us that they found the Germans to be the hardest workers. She had said to the whole school, 'Don't worry, they are not Nazis. Those have been taken out and put into other special, well-guarded camps.' Even so, we were very wary of them and never went near them, as we had heard too many horror stories about them.

Living four doors up from us was Mr Cliff Hartshorn and his wife, Mary. They had no children and he was a harness maker, cobbler and shoe repairer by trade. Partially deaf, he worked in the large wooden shed in his back garden mending shoes for a small fee, and he didn't seem to mind us standing there watching him. We would stand there for ages – especially if the day was wet – looking on and marvelling at his speed and dexterity. At last, after many long weeks, he got round to repairing our leather case ball, and we were eager to get the precious 'casie' back so we could play with it in Widd's field. I measured my success by how many kicks I got rather than how many goals I scored, which was usually nil. Widd's field was the centre of our little world when we were out of the house.

On Saturday mornings we would sometimes go to watch the village football team. The footballers used to change in the old Memorial Hall that reeked to high heaven of Elliman's and Algipan embrocations (sometimes called Fiery Jack), dubbin (to soften the leather), sweaty feet and cigarette smoke. The tops of the players' leather boots, tied round and round with long leather bootlaces, came above their ankles and had leather studs nailed on to the soles. When it rained the hundreds of round holes that they left all over the pitch filled up with water, as we watched from the doorway of one of the two breeze-block air-raid shelters at the end of the field. I never understood how the players managed to head and boot the large, heavy casie so far. When it was wet and muddy it became as heavy as lead, and whenever it came near us we could barely shift it.

There were sporadic bombing raids by enemy aircraft and we knew by the sound of the engines if they were German or British. On clear moonlit nights they seemed to follow the railway lines towards York, but no fatalities occurred and the local Home Guard got in some much-needed target practice. Working with the regular soldiers from Strensall Camp, they often had firing practice in the field across the road from our classroom, and we could hear the shouting of orders and the loud 'pom-pom' sounds of the Bofors light anti-aircraft gun. When the wailing air-raid siren woke us during the night we were not too dismayed, as it was usually a false alarm and it meant that we could go to school late the following morning. If the all-clear sounded after one o'clock in the morning we were allowed to start school at ten, and if it was after three we didn't go until after dinner. Even in our little village the war was never far away and Harry said, 'You should think yourselves lucky to be living here in safety and stop chuntering on about everything.' It was all right for him; he was living in luxury while we were always hungry and getting belted for next to nothing.

V for Victory signs began to appear on walls and doors, in windows, on the buses, in newspapers and magazines – in fact, everywhere. The determined and pugnacious Winston Churchill, affectionately known to the people as Winnie, gave his famous palm-forward, two-fingered V sign whenever he appeared in public. It was all carefully designed to raise the morale of the people and to keep up their fighting bulldog spirit, and, because of him, the British never doubted that we would win in the end. The dark chilly nights started to draw in with more dull and rainy days and, if we were 'good,' we were allowed to stay up late to listen to the wireless on Thursday evening at 8.30 p.m. We had to promise to be quiet or else we would be sent 'up the wooden hill to Bedfordshire'. The extremely popular fast-paced comedy show *I.T.M.A.* (It's That Man Again) was on for half an hour on the Forces Programme, having switched from the Home Service early in the war. The title had originally referred to Hitler but people thought it meant Tommy Handley. We picked up all the catchphrases – everyone in Haxby seemed to love the larger-than-life characters and their sayings. One of the much-loved characters was Fusspot, which was what Mrs Harris called me.

Sam Costa (as Flying Officer Kite) had a huge handlebar moustache and the airmen in the village said that it wasn't a proper moustache unless it could be seen from behind on the port and starboard sides. The character that sticks in my mind most was that mysterious and scary character called Funf, who was supposed to be a German spy. It was actually Jack Train speaking into an echoing empty tumbler and Mr Harris used to frighten us, if we were talking or making too much noise in the bedroom, by shouting up the stairs, 'Watch out, Funf's coming!' Whenever we heard that and slow, heavy footsteps on the stairs, we scurried into bed and hid our heads under the covers, too scared to utter another word.

The call-up age for men had been lowered to eighteen and a half years, and at the other end of the age scale men up to fifty years of age were now eligible for military service. There was a drive for salvage, including jam jars, paper, scrap metal and the like, and the people were told that it was to be recycled and used to make military vehicles, weapons and aeroplanes. The vast quantity of weapons and vehicles lost at Dunkirk had to be replaced and even old rags were pulped and used to make paper. Collection points were set up and we got a farthing for a jam jar and a ha'penny for a bottle, but they were not easy to come by.

The news, delivered in the comforting, authoritative, cultured tones of Alvar Liddell and Robert Dougall, announced that the *Wehrmacht* troops (the regular German army), in spite of the Russians' scorched earth policy, were at the gates of Moscow and thousands of Jews were being shot or sent to the camps as slave labourers. When the rains started the German vehicles got stuck in the mud and when the snows came they had to endure temperatures of −27°F (−15°C). Without winter clothing thousands of them froze to death. It was a war of attrition and the German offensive was grinding to a halt.

In North Africa the British and Commonwealth forces had been reinforced (including Uncle John) and the Western Desert Force was now known as the Eighth Army. Tobruk was relieved after a siege of thirty-three weeks and the top brass wrongly believed that they had won the war in North Africa and that one more push would give them Tripoli. In truth, it had been a close-run thing with confusion, lack of communication and outdated tactics.

On 7 December the US Pacific Fleet, laying at anchor in Pearl Harbor, Hawaii, was devastated in a surprise attack by over 400 Japanese warplanes that flew in at speed, sinking many ships and killing 3,000 servicemen. The USA and the British Commonwealth responded by declaring war on Japan, and Germany and Italy declared war on the USA. It was now a worldwide conflict.

From mid-December onwards snow fell at Haxby and the ground was covered in an unbroken white sheet. We brushed the snow from our clothes, which were becoming threadbare, patched and shabby by this time, and watched as it scattered on the icy wind. No lights were to be seen twinkling in people's front windows because of the blackout and after dark the village lay hushed and submerged in a deep stygian blackness that is hard to imagine these days. No light reflected upwards which made the stars appear exceptionally bright and far more numerous.

One night we had just got to sleep when a local air-raid warden, on seeing a chink of light at the bedroom window, knocked on Mrs Harris's door. The brave man, in his steel helmet and dark blue boiler-suit, told her in no uncertain terms to 'Put that bloody light out!' When she confronted him with a coat over her nightie and her hair tied up in rag curlers, she must have been a fearsome sight, with her doughy jowls wobbling as she told him what she thought of him. 'Why don't you go and join the army like a real man instead of harassing people,' she shouted. 'Don't come here bothering law-abiding folk.' She was not amused; in fact, she was fuming. 'Doesn't the man understand that it's a damn nuisance having to go outside in the cold to check that no light is showing!' We, and poor Mr Harris, suffered the brunt of her ire over the ensuing days.

As another Christmas approached we were kept busy at school drawing greetings cards and hanging decorations that we had made from strips of coloured card and paper. We enjoyed the school Nativity play, the carol singing and the school Christmas party, where we played games and made right pigs of ourselves.

Just before we broke up for the festive season we were gathered together, and a hush fell as Mr Fox entered the room as we felt constrained in his presence. The assembled children were told of great changes that were soon to take place and we were given a letter in a sealed envelope. As I hopped and skipped up Usher Lane the glittering, frozen snow that crackled under my feet sounded like cornflakes being trodden on. There was a spring in my step and by the time I reached 'Lenmuir' it was snowing heavily again, with the fat, swirling flakes bringing the promise of a white Christmas. It was my first at Haxby and, to my delight, that promise was kept.

The government tried to make things a little easier over the Christmas and New Year period by relaxing the strict rationing of certain foods. In December a 'points' system for foods that were scarce but not rationed was introduced to prevent food being bought up in huge quantities by the well-off. A set number of points per month were allocated but it still had to be paid for.

Ever-smiling Mam, whose love was boundless and unconditional, came to see me on Christmas Eve, and she blushed like a peony when Mr Harris gave her a kiss under the mistletoe hung over the kitchen door. She must have left a present for me with Mrs Harris when I wasn't looking. She was sorry to go but she had to be with George on Christmas Day. The next morning I ripped the brown wrapping paper from my present in great anticipation, not thinking about the difficulty Mam had probably experienced in getting it, and we had a nice Christmas dinner as Harold Mann had killed one of his chickens for us. As a special treat at teatime, Mr Harris roasted the chestnuts that he had collected earlier. Putting them on a shovel, we watched them jumping and splitting as he held it over the fire, and we thoroughly enjoyed their hot, sweet taste; but being far from home meant that Christmas was inevitably tinged with sadness.

Over the past year a fine new school, called the Joseph Rowntree Secondary Modern, had been built. All those over twelve, or who were to become twelve in the present school year, were to go there, and it meant that our Harry and thirty-five other children from Haxby and Wigginton would be amongst its first intake. Their departure meant there would be room for the older infants of the two villages, including me, to move up to the 'big' school.

11

'An Hour-glass on the Run'

The new school was a mile and a half from the village centre south of the Hilbra railway crossing and it became known locally as the 'Joe Row' (pronounced Joe-Roe) school. The opening ceremony took place on 12 January which marked the start of the new spring term, as the holiday had been extended to save on fuel.

Harry was surprised at the size of the school and felt a bit lost in the long corridors that were lined with modern classrooms. They now had a different teacher for each subject, whereas at Haxby they had just the one teacher. The school had a well-stocked library, a separate assembly hall and a dining room. The emphasis was on practical skills and there were large rooms and laboratories for science subjects. The girls, who all wore black gymslips, had practical cookery classes using modern ovens and the older girls even cooked the joints for the school dinners. In those days it was accepted that a woman's place was in the kitchen.

The pair of gentle spinsters had bought Harry a good second-hand three-speed bicycle with a Sturmey Archer hub gear that ticked over quietly when he freewheeled. It was his pride and joy and he oiled it and cleaned it till it gleamed. I would often see him with the bike nonchalantly propped up against his thighs, as he stood with a crowd of girls around him.

As the sharp frosts and snowy weather persisted, I was delighted at the prospect of starting life in the big school with the others. As we trooped along the snow-covered roads, the bushes and the gossamer-like spiders' webs were white with hoarfrost. By the time we got there our fingers were blue and our noses were red but even in the classroom it was bitterly cold with ice on the inside of the windowpanes. Our fingers hurt as the blood gradually flowed back into them and it took a long time for the coke-fired boilers to feed hot water through the pipes to the green, cast-iron radiators. I was pleased to learn that I would still be in Miss Francis's class; she was a teacher whose smiling demeanour and friendly tone of voice brought a touch of warmth and sunshine to those wintry days. Several teachers had stayed for only short spells and being with her for another year ensured some continuity.

The tall windows of the high-roofed Victorian classroom looked out onto the snow-covered playground and the crumbling bricks of the bike shed. The wooden sills, which were about four feet from the ground, had been designed to prevent schoolchildren, like me, from seeing out and thus being distracted. The small glass windowpanes were, of course, criss-crossed with the ubiquitous brown anti-blast tape and their upper parts were opened by means of the long white cords that hung down from them. We sat on the bench part of the old wooden desks that had been made shiny by generations of shuffling bottoms. The lids were covered with scratches, graffiti and ink blotches left by countless village children; many of them now parents and grandparents themselves.

There had been an influx of new children into our class as the formidable Miss Curry told us that Singapore had fallen to the Japanese on Christmas Day. Most of them had been attending the tiny school in Wigginton, but due to increasing numbers of evacuees, a few had been having their lessons in the minister's vestry or in the old Wesleyan Methodist Chapel. One of them was John Wade, who was a month older than me, and he had been among the first evacuees sent here.

He was a cheerful lad with a round, red, moon-like face and he now sat next to me and we became good pals. I showed him how to do pencil sketches of Spitfires and soldiers in uniform, as drawing was one of the few things that I was good at – apart from chattering and laughing, which tended to land us in trouble. As we crouched over our ink-splotched, penknife-etched desks, John said, 'I were billeted with a family in Wigginton when ah first came 'ere yer know. We walked t' t'house from t'railway station when we came 'ere at start o' t'war. The people 'ad t'choice of billeting RAF lads or us evacuees and Mr and Mrs Allinson kindly took me in. They were a 'appy and 'ard working family with two kids. That were eight-year-old Bernard, and baby Pauline, who were only about ten months old.'

I was green with envy when he had told me, 'Bernard had a real Meccano set and an electric, model-train set an' all. It 'ad two engines, carriages, goods wagons, stations, tunnels and tracks. One o' t' engines were a glossy green "Flying Scotsman" and it were all laid out on t'floor of his big bedroom.' How lucky could you get? I thought. 'Mr Allinson worked at gas works on t'outskirts of York an 'e pedalled to work every day on an old push-bike. When he were not at work, 'e spent a lot of 'is spare time working in 'is garden. 'E were allus busy so I didn't see him all that much.

'Through a gate at t'bottom o' their back garden, after passing t'outside toilet, was a big field that 'ad a pond an' a small brick building in it,' he continued. 'Next door, in t'first house, were t'Fletchers and they 'ad a fair amount o' land an' all. Mr Fletcher were just a little fella. 'E were a butcher and a farmer and 'is parents 'ave lived and farmed there since before t'turn o' t'century. They 'ad a butcher's shop and a barn that were full of straw and hay bales. Me and t'lads from next door used ter make dens in it. They 'ad a cow byre where they milked t'cows by 'and an' we played in t'fields for 'ours an 'ours.'

He was a right chatterbox and I couldn't get a word in edgeways. He told me that the Fletchers' two sons, who were young men at the time, worked on the farm. John said he enjoyed helping them out by putting the beet and turnips into the opening at the top of the shredder while one of them turned the handle. The Fletchers had two young evacuees from Middlesbrough. At a later date one of them was taken seriously ill and was taken into York County Hospital, but when his mother was informed she refused to come, stating that she 'did not wish to know'. John told me that during the snowy days of early 1940, he and Bernard had built a real igloo in the corner of the yard and had sat snugly inside in the glow of a lighted candle.

John was moved another three times before he came to Haxby School and was now living with the Dixons at Holme Farm. This was a smallholding just west of the Co-op store and his sister and six other evacuees, one of whom was Dot Sirman's brother Ray, were billeted there. He said that Mrs Dixon was very kind to him and he often helped Mr Dixon to 'muck out t'osses'. John said, 'Mrs Dixon treats me really well. A nicer person yer couldn't wish ter meet. She works five days a week as a domestic servant and cleaner for Mr Butterfield. One of my regular chores is ter collect three copies o' t'evening newspaper from Torville's shop and tek 'em t' t'Butterfields, Dixons and their friend Mrs Lee. Ah do odd jobs for Mrs Butterfield from time ter time, such as sorting out logs for t'fire.'

I was delighted when, at the end of the month, Mam and Dad came to see me. Mam told me that she had replaced Dinner Lady who had given up her post as cook. Dad had managed to get a forty-eight hour leave pass and they wrapped Jimmy and me in newly knitted woollen scarves and balaclavas and, holding our woollen-mitted hands, they took us through the snow-covered village. They spoiled us rotten, buying us cakes, small toys, sweets and comics from the local shops. Dad was wearing his khaki gloves and had his thick army greatcoat on and I felt so proud to be his eldest son and to be seen out in the village with him. I was tender and very sensitive around the ribs and Dad, knowing this, tickled me mercilessly. He repeatedly threw me up into the air and caught me in his strong arms after Jimmy and I had bombarded him with snowballs. When he laughed his whole face lit up.

Dad was proud of his regiment, and its badge – a side view of a large-wheeled cannon – was tattooed on the bulging bicep of his right arm. I thought that Mam, although her cheeks were lightly rouged, looked rather tense and pale, but the strain of the war left many people feeling run-down and anxious and children are quick to pick up on these things. Whenever they came to see us – even when Mrs Harris knew in advance – they were never offered a meal and were unable to stay overnight. We had so much to say and the time fled, and all too soon it was time for them to leave, as they had to catch the bus back to York station. I turned away with my heart breaking after yet another touching farewell. My lip started to tremble and the tears rose unbidden and I tried to take my mind off them by taking my newly bought *Beano* comic up to our cold bedroom. I tried to immerse myself in the adventures of Big Eggo the ostrich, Pansy Potter the strong man's daughter, Lord Snooty, Tommy the tin can boy, and Herman the German (the latter, of course, was a caricature of Goering), but it didn't work! As someone once said, 'happiness unalloyed is not for sentient beings' and I could not get the thoughts of Mam and Dad out of my head. I huddled under the bedclothes with my knees up to my chin shaking and crying my eyes out. I felt so alone and homesick and the snow falling from the leaden sky reflected my feelings.

After my tears were spent I looked out of the window to see that the back garden was thickly blanketed in pure virgin snow, and large, fluffy flakes were coming straight down before twisting and swirling around close to the ground. The falling snow, which looked like smoke being blown about on eddies of cold air, fascinated me. It settled softly on the skeletal twigs and branches of every tree and shrub and heaped itself up on top of the trelliswork and the garden fences. It piled up on the clothesline making it look like a thick white rope or a ship's hawser. It formed large white pompons on the withered remains of the hydrangea flowerheads so that they looked like white lollipops or white woollen balls on long sticks. Composing myself, I dried my eyes and rushed downstairs eager to play in it. Such is the resilience of childhood! Great clods of soft fresh snow clung to the soles of my shoes making them seem like deep-sea divers' boots. The sky was the colour of slate and we played out in it till teatime – and it was dark before six o'clock.

In early February the cold was so intense that, much to our delight, the school was closed for two weeks. The antiquated heating and water pipes had frozen solid and when a thaw came they burst causing floods. On those bitterly cold and frosty days the thickly lying snow became ice-encrusted and in some places the wind had formed it into weird shapes. The top layer froze and overhung looking like waves about to break and the dormant stems of the cow parsley were snow-capped. The ploughed fields were like corrugated iron under their blanket of snow and there was a thick layer of ice on Mr Harris's rain butt. We spent a good deal of our time enjoying the unexpected extra holiday up on the icy slopes by the windmill pond, where the rusty metal vanes of the old irrigation pump groaned and creaked forlornly as they swung to and fro in the icy wind. We sat on old tin trays and slid down the steep inclines keeping our feet raised off the ground. As our giggles and screams of pleasure were carried through the thin icy air we were completely lost to everything. Nothing else mattered and we wished that it would never end.

In that silent frosted world the little birds suffered; but they weren't the only ones. Our cold noses, nipping fingers and frozen mittens eventually drove us back indoors and, once inside, we got a clout round the lugs for getting our clothes wet. At other times we got lashed on the legs with the thin cane that Mrs Harris selected from her growing collection of punishment tools, which she appeared to enjoy wielding. The canes and belts that hung on the wooden strut supporting the kitchen cabinet were a constant visual threat. If we did not settle down quickly at bedtime she would shout up the stairs, 'Get to sleep or you'll feel the belt around your backsides!' There seemed to be no warmth or affection in her and we were being thrashed more and more often.

On going back to school our sleep was often disturbed by the deep, throbbing sounds of low-flying British bombers, while at other times it was the wailing of the air-raid siren that shattered our rest. It often startled us into full wakefulness in the middle of the night but, fortunately, most of the warnings turned out to be false alarms or the enemy planes were nowhere near us. The small bedroom fires were never lit and on bitterly cold mornings we often got dressed under the bedclothes with our teeth chattering. We had learned by experience not to put our bare feet on the cold brown lino. The lack of sleep left us lethargic in school, which did not make for much progress. With the teachers overstrained, harassed and numbed by anxiety, it was not exactly an ideal situation but, after being up half the night, we tended to be quieter and less boisterous. Even so, the village school with its rigid and stultifying syllabus appeared to Jimmy and me to be the most stable part of our tottering world. We felt safe there surrounded by the other children and our teachers.

The newspapers reported that things were not going well for the Allied forces in North Africa and 'the Med'. It was nice to have a new friend at school and John Wade told me that in the autumn of 1940 he had contracted impetigo and had been put in an isolation unit in a bungalow near the Hilbra railway crossing. 'It all started when I got blisters round me mouth and behind me ears,' he said. 'They 'ad 'orrible, yeller scabs on 'em. I 'ad ter 'ave loads of 'ot baths and they put green and violet stuff on me. They dabbed me blisters with mercury ointment until t'ard crusts went. When I got better I went ter live with Mrs Longhurst in North Lane.' Her bungalow was behind the Haxby Co-op, which had a wooden post high up on its rear wall from which a rope and pulley system hung. It was used to lift the traditional ten-stone sacks of flour and sugar up to a door on the upper floor. John said, 'I were well treated but I weren't there long. I were taken in by t'Smith family who 'ad come 'ere from Middlesbrough.'

Next door to the Smiths was another brick building called Prospect House that belonged to a quiet and very private middle-aged couple called Wilson. Behind it there were barns, outbuildings and extensive fields, and John told me that Mr Fred Wilson, the owner, had befriended him. He often took him into York on the high front seat of his old horse-drawn stagecoach, which made him the envy of every child in

Haxby. We often saw him perched on the driver's bench and my imaginations ran riot as I pictured it being chased across the Nevada Desert
by Red Indians led by Cochise, the chief of the tribe, who wore a magnificent, feathered head-dress and rode bareback as he fired arrows into
it. The coach had curtains at the windows, gracefully curving shafts
and wooden-spoked wheels, with the front ones smaller than the back.
Sometimes we played at being masked and caped highwaymen with
pistols like Dick Turpin, who Miss Francis said had been kept in a cell
at York Prison while waiting to be hanged. Mr Wilson, a man of very
few words, used the coach to deliver goods to York and to collect tubs
of pigswill on the way back.

It may well have been the coach once driven by Tom Holtby, an
enterprising and colourful character of old Haxby, whose house
still stood. He had been a driver on the York to Doncaster leg of the
London to Edinburgh stagecoach until the coming of the railways put
the coaches out of business and he became a horse-breaker in York.
John said, 'In the autumn I 'elped Mr Wilson to pick and bag spuds.
'E'd turn out a few rows with 'is fork on t'land at back of 'is 'ouse or
in t'field 'e owned at back o' t'owld chapel. He gave me a thrupenny
bit or a silver tanner each time.' It seems Mr Wilson had taken a liking
to him and John enjoyed doing jobs like helping to pick and store his
apples and pears on sacking in the loft of his barn. By a strange coinci-
dence, Nancy and Sylvia Robson, two of the little girls who had been
at The Settlement, Sutherland Lodge and Grove House with George
and me, were also billeted with the Smiths.

I loved to hear Vera Lynn singing and when her programme,
'Sincerely Yours', was on the BBC Forces Service we were allowed to
listen as long as we stayed quiet. Between her poignant songs she read
out messages of love and affection from the wives, husbands, sweet-
hearts and boyfriends of people in the forces. When war broke out
she had been a vocalist with the Ambrose Orchestra and her lovely
voice and sincerity of delivery helped to link those far away with their
loved ones at home. Her moving rendition of *Yours* was the signature
tune of the show that had first come on the air in November 1941
and it became an instant hit. She was affectionately known as 'The
Forces Sweetheart'. Entertaining the troops with ENSA counted as
war service, but with so many to entertain the talent was stretched
pretty thin. Some wags said ENSA stood for 'Every Night Something
Awful'.

Jimmy and I were quite pleased to hear that the government was urging people to bathe less often. People were not to use more than five inches of warm water and to share. This suited us; like most kids, we would not get washed if we could get away with it. It annoyed us when Mrs Harris roughly rubbed our faces and knees with a wet flannel before we went to bed, calling our efforts cat-licks. She used to line us up and say, 'Hold your hands out', before inspecting the backs and the palms. We never had toothpaste, we used powdered stuff that came in a small round tin, but most of the time we just rubbed salt or soot on our teeth and gums with our fingers.

Every Saturday after tea we were put in the bath in pairs for a soap-all-over job, using a block of green carbolic soap and the same water as the two before us, thus ensuring that we were clean for church the next day. As I stripped off, Jimmy often got me mad by calling me 'tin ribs' or 'skinny-banana-legs'. More hot water was added when the next pair climbed in and the water became blacker and blacker. Soap was now rationed to a three-ounce bar a month and soap powder was in short supply. Before bed on school days we were given a rub – including our legs – and in the morning a wash, excluding legs. More often than not, during the daytime, we were given a quick rub here and there with a bit of spit on the corner of Mrs Harris's faded pinny, the pattern of which had almost disappeared due to the number of times it had been washed. Quite often we deliberately avoided a wash by getting sent to bed early for squabbling or being cheeky.

The news of the Allies' efforts in the war continued to be disappointing and people were tired of hearing reports of defeats and failures. At the half-term break I was over the moon when Mam visited me again, and I was so excited when she came towards me along the ice-covered garden path. Picking her way carefully past the dead, blackened stalks and the frosted seed heads of last summer's flowers, her shy smile on seeing me warmed me through, reaffirming that special bond that exists between a mother and son. Whenever I set eyes on her my heart sang and my unhappiness was forgotten for a while. Mam was reserved and shy in nature and inclined to blush easily, and it appears that she had no suspicions concerning Mrs Harris's sly and nasty ways. She was so trusting of people and, believing in the nobility of the human spirit, was convinced that there was goodness in everyone. She said, 'We must learn to take the rough with the smooth. Life is full of ups and downs and you must know the bitter to appreciate the sweet.' We had been told never to say that anything was wrong and we were too frightened to tell the truth as Mrs Harris always seemed to be hovering close by when relatives visited. I didn't get the chance to tell Mam about the beltings or about the way she treated us. I wanted to tell her of how we often lay in bed covering our ears to shut out her angry raised voice as she shouted at and belittled her long-suffering husband.

By mid-March, when a thaw set in, the snow turned to slush and the tyres of Harry, Brian and Peter's bikes swish-swished through the puddles on their way to school. There were very few motor cars for them to worry about as most people went about on bikes at that time. Cycling to and from school the boys often saw Italian prisoners-of-war at work in the now piebald fields.

On a chilly, blustery Saturday afternoon, Harry met up with his young pal Peter, and with him was his lively eleven-year-old friend Derek Robinson, who lived only three doors from him. They cycled the eight miles to the large airfield at Linton-on-Ouse. They had come in the hope of seeing one of the mighty new Halifax bombers at close range. They caught a whiff of high-octane aviation fuel as a petrol bowser chugged past on the concrete of the perimeter track heading towards one of the Whitley bombers that had served so valiantly since the start of the war.

As slate-grey clouds scurried by above the control tower and the five large hangars, the station windsock was fully extended. Nearby were flat-roofed, brick buildings and the boys got quite excited on seeing a cigar-shaped bomb on a long trolley being pulled along by a tractor. It was heading towards a huge Halifax bomber that stood on its dispersal pad not far from where they peered through the wire of the perimeter fence. An RAF truck pulled up with a squeal of brakes and a sergeant pilot and his crew of six climbed down.

The airmen clambered up a metal ladder into the fuselage of the waiting bomber and, from the cockpit, the pilot gave a 'thumbs-up' signal to the aircraft electricians who plugged in a starter trolley just as heavy drops of rain began to plop onto the ground. The engines seemed to hesitate before spluttering, then bursting into life one after the other. The spinning airscrews looked like shimmering, silver discs as the deep-throated roar was torn away on the slipstream. Great puffs of smoke and blue flashes of flame from the exhaust cowlings showed up clear and bright in the gathering gloom. As the pilot opened the throttle a little the great aircraft seemed to tremble. Rainwater streamed from the trailing edge of the wings and the expanse of deep lush grass behind it was blown flat. The ground crew then dragged away the wooden wheel chocks by heaving on the long ropes attached to them.

The Bristol Hercules engines settled and ran more smoothly as they warmed up and the great bomber moved out onto the shiny, rain-wet perimeter track. An RAF fire tender stood by with its headlights hooded as the plane taxied to the end of the runway that disappeared into the mist. As the pilot opened the throttle the engines juddered and gave out loud throaty growls as the power burst forth in a series of great surges. They waited for the green flash of light from the chequered caravan, which showed up brightly in the fading light. The ground trembled and the air reverberated as the harnessed energy was released and the mighty Halifax rumbled along the wet, rubber-streaked tarmac sending spray up from its tyres as it picked up speed. The three boys stood open-mouthed in awe as the thundering plane lifted off and slowly banked to port. The undercarriage was raised just before the black and sinister-looking clouds swallowed her up.

On their return journey the boys were glad to have the strong cold wind behind them as the rain lashed down on their inadequately clad bodies. The snow that had only recently melted had saturated the fields, and the lads pushed on through a dank, misty, rain-sodden landscape. The sky was alive with movement as low, slate-grey clouds chased each other across it. They were glad to get home out of the rain that came down in stair rods and Harry's flaxen hair, now darkened and soaking wet, lay flat to his scalp as the excess rainwater dribbled down his neck. They were chilled to the bone, utterly miserable and looked like drowned rats, but – eventually – they agreed that the trip had been well worthwhile and they talked excitedly about what they had seen for weeks.

Most of the women (out of necessity) now went about bare-legged but some used gravy browning in place of the hard-to-get stockings. Mrs Fisher got a friend to pencil in the seams, which was fine until it rained. They used the still readily obtainable Ladder Stop as nail varnish, as by that time the real thing had disappeared from the shops. Increasing shortages of cosmetics led them to use beetroot juice in place of lipstick and rouge and soot was used as eye make-up. There were more unshaven and bearded men around as razor blades were in very short supply and Mr Harris resharpened his old blades by rubbing them round the inside of a glass tumbler. Some of the older men resorted to the old cutthroat razors still around from their parents' time, sharpening them on a leather strop. Rose-hip syrup went on sale nationwide – under fives were to get it free – and two million more children became eligible for free cod liver oil.

Mr Harris read in his *Daily Express* that his namesake, Air Marshal Arthur Harris, had been appointed by Winston Churchill as the new Chief of Bomber Command. Brusque and bluff, Harris was of a similar nature to Churchill; the man whose determination and doggedness had united and galvanised the nation. Vigorous and decisive, the new AOC (Air Officer Commanding) aimed to carry the war, by day and night, deep into the heart of Germany. They had been relatively untroubled up to that point, but things were about to change as he planned to send large numbers of bombers into The Fatherland and the occupied territories. Many, including Churchill, believed that this appointment could herald a turning point in the war.

For two and a half years we had battled alone against the might and aggression of Nazi Germany and the morale of the nation was low. Far better armed, the enemy was now in control of the entire western coastline of Europe and, with Britain's fortunes looking dismal, the only real hope of survival lay in a successful switch from defence to offence. By March the news bulletins stated that RAF Bomber Command had begun to mount mass, round-the-clock bombing raids. The RAF had learned from the eleven-hour-long immolation of Coventry, but the new policy of saturation 'area' bombing was to cause some controversy. It led to the AOC being given the sobriquets 'Bomber' or 'Butcher' Harris but, to our delight, Germany was now getting back some of the treatment that it had dished out.

The sight of the great bombers going out was awe-inspiring and it raised the morale of the people of Haxby no end, giving them fresh hope. The loud drone of the planes disturbed the ragged-trousered rooks in the smooth-barked beech trees making them take to the air just as they were starting to roost for the night. The raucous cawing of the large black scavengers assaulted our ears, and Mr Harris said, 'It's worse than t'Women's Institute in their tea break; and that's saying summat!' The cruciform shapes could be seen as black silhouettes against the fading light of the evening sky. The bomb-laden aircraft went out at dusk night after night, juddering our sash windows in their wooden frames and, sadly, some never returned.

In the madness of war food and clothes were in short supply but tears were always plentiful. The pubs echoed to the sounds of drunken airmen and locals singing songs like *Whispering Grass* and *Java, Java*, made popular by 'The Ink Spots', round the upright piano. Incidentally, the only black man we ever saw was an American Air Force sergeant who was billeted nearby. Even though the beer was watered down to make the limited supplies last out, the publicans often topped up the airmen's glasses on the house. They usually got on well with the locals but occasionally arguments would spill over into fistfights. Drinking hours were from eleven in the morning till two in the afternoon, and from six to ten o'clock at night, but the aircrews were sometimes treated to free beer after hours. We hero-worshipped the aircrew and, when they attended the dances at the Wiggie Rec, they were also exceedingly popular with the young ladies of the two villages.

On my seventh birthday, which fell on Easter Sunday that year, Mam paid a short surprise visit. I vaguely remember her wearing her best thick Lisle stockings and low-heeled shoes with a strap that buttoned across the insoles. It was a warm spring morning with a haze of fresh green on the hedgerows and, on seeing her, my sadness was lifted by the unconcealed love and happiness that emanated from her. The bond between us didn't need to be put into words. She said that Dad could not get leave but he sent his love and he had recently told her that women were to begin working on the gun battery and searchlights. With their nimble fingers they were good at adjusting the height finders and the predictor mechanisms.

Mam was no beauty in the conventional sense of the word but beauty is in the eye of the beholder – so to Dad and me she was. Neither plain nor beautiful but pleasing to look at, her presence could turn the darkness into light. There was an inner beauty and her lovely pale blue eyes and warm gaze radiated love and serenity. She had a soft and sensuous oval face and her fine, light-brown hair was parted on the left and combed across the top of her forehead. Unfortunately she, and her younger sister Hilda, had a muscular defect (medically known as strabismus) that prevented parallel focusing causing a slight squint in their left eye. It was what Gran called 'a lazy eye'. She also had her mother's rather heavy facial features with high cheekbones and a certain puffiness around the nose and eyebrows.

She was a stargazer with an almost childlike innocence about her and she was never far from either laughter or tears. There was a tactile impulsiveness in her and she liked to hug, kiss and touch me as often and whenever possible. She had visions and great hopes for the future when we would all be together again after the war. Fatalistic in her outlook, she believed that those who were good and generous of spirit would be rewarded with everlasting peace and rest in the afterlife. She truly believed that some mysterious force shaped our destiny. When the time came for her to leave she said, 'Keep your chin up, darling. The next time I see you I'll have George with me. He'll be coming to stay here quite soon.'

Her eyes were misty, her lower lip trembled and a tear hovered on the verge of falling as she hugged me close and kissed me, before – ever so reluctantly – dragging herself away. It was George's birthday the next day and she had to be with him, so, after giving me one last sweet haunting smile that pierced my soul, she quickly turned away. She waved as she hurried round the corner to catch the number ten into York. I was not to know that my memories of her and Dad would have to last me for a long, long time to come.

That day it was light until nearly 9 p.m. as double summertime was in operation again and the clocks had been put forward an hour early that morning. This meant that it was just getting light as Mr Harris left the house to go to work. We were not even up for our breakfast of lumpy porridge and the sun was well up by the time we set off on our walk to school.

On a night in mid-April, young Alan Clark, Peter Pallier's young cousin at Hilbra Avenue, was woken by the wailing of the nearby siren. On peeping around the blackout curtain he noticed a red glow in the night sky above the distant hills to the north, and the Misses Law and Barker saw the same eerie glow from their bedroom window. A couple of days later Alan's mam said to Harry, 'I've been told there's been a heavy air raid on Middlesbrough and the East Cleveland coast. They say a lot of people have been killed and made homeless.' In Middlesbrough itself a gas main had fractured and caught fire lighting up the sky, and it was that and the glow from burning houses that Alan had seen.

Our bedroom window faced west and though woken by the air-raid siren we couldn't see the lurid light in the night sky. We were up and swaddled in blankets under the table with Mr Harris and the girls were in the gas cupboard with his wife. Dot said afterwards, 'I couldn't get comfortable because the gas meter was sticking in me back.'

We went back to bed when the all-clear sounded and in the darkness and chill of that time just before dawn, when the human spirit is at its lowest ebb, I dreamt that I saw Mam in the bedroom. She seemed so real and looked as though she hadn't had time to comb her hair or put on any lipstick. She put her arms round me and quietly sang a soothing lullaby and her soft, radiant smile held the promise of infinite love and compassion. Then she faded away and I seemed to hear her tremulous voice, as if from a great distance, saying, 'Be strong, my son. Be strong!' I woke with a start to find that my face and pillow were wet with tears, and Jimmy said, 'You were crying in your sleep, John.' I was engulfed by an overwhelming sadness and at that point Mr Harris came into the room. Sitting me on his knee he lay my head on his shoulder and put his arms round me as deep sobs wracked my slender frame. 'There, there,' he said soothingly. 'It were only a bad dream. Go back to sleep now, son.' He was an exceptionally kind, sensitive and caring man.

12

Blitzed

The nights of the 23–26 April were cloudless with the waxing moon near to the full. From the wireless broadcasts, which always started with 'Last night Bomber Command ...', the Harrises knew that there had been bombing raids on the Baltic coast port of Rostock and Hitler vowed that he would lay waste the cities of Britain in return. The story goes that he had picked up a pre-war Baedeker guidebook to historic British towns and cities and ordered that all the places with three-star ratings were to be razed. The cathedral cities of Norwich and Exeter, along with Bath, were bombed soon afterwards.

On the evening of Tuesday, 28 April, our Harry sat in his room reading the *Yorkshire Evening Post*, which had been reduced to only four pages with fewer and smaller advertisements. The editorial was headed 'REPRISALS', which referred to the recent raid on Norwich, and it commented on York's run of good luck thus far.

That evening, as Mr Harris had tuned in to the short-wave channels, there was much whistling and crackling as he turned the dial. He often searched the overseas channels eager for uncensored war news and that night, during Lord Haw-Haw's English-speaking propaganda broadcast, his nasal voice had kept fading in and out, but he thought he heard him warn of bombers coming to York. Mr Harris took no particular notice as 'Haw-Haw' was always ranting on in that way and many people now looked on him as a bit of a joke. They settled down to listen to 'Sandy's Half Hour' of organ music on the Forces Service. We had been sent to bed just before eight o'clock and all was quiet as the adults went up to their bedroom at half past ten. Mrs Harris had her glass soda water syphon with her as usual and Mr Harris had to be up to start his long working day at the farm by 7.30 a.m. In York soldiers and airmen from the local camps and airfields caught their buses in Exhibition Square after a good night out and all was quiet and still.

It was a beautiful, clear night with a 'bombers' moon' and it was about half past two in the morning when we were woken by the loud, unsynchronised drone peculiar to German aeroplanes. They sounded very close and seemed to be almost on top of the house as Jimmy, Ducky and I shot out of bed and peered round the edges of the blackout curtain. With our bare feet on the cold lino, we saw that the sky in the direction of York was lit by the eerie flickering lights of Chandelier parachute flares that looked like white Christmas trees. In their silver light we could clearly see the dark-grey shapes of twin-engined Heinkels – the largest of the German bombers. As they roared over at around 200 miles per hour, we could see the black crosses on their wings and the swastikas on their tail fins. We heard explosions and felt the floor vibrating under our bare feet as clusters of incendiary bombs whooshed and crumped into the ground. At that point, Mr Harris rushed into the room and hurried us down the stairs into our allotted places, and Mrs Harris already had the girls in the gas cupboard with their blankets round them. The siren, which was supposed to warn of raiders approaching was not heard, and the chilling, pulsing wail was not sounded until after the first bombs had dropped. Something had gone wrong!

On hearing the roar of more German planes outside, being too young (or too stupid) to realise the danger, we rushed to the front window and were shocked to see in the baleful white light several green and light-grey planes with long thin fuselages. Jimmy, being an expert, said they were Dorniers and they seemed to be following the railway lines at the far side of the fields. Mr Harris angrily bawled out, 'You silly little buggers. Get away from that window!' and grabbing hold of us, he roughly shoved us under the table where we crouched crying and shaking with fear. We were scared, but also shocked by his anger and unusually raised voice. Angry shouting and physical punishment by Mrs Harris was the norm but it was most unusual for the generally quiet and placid Mr Harris to act that way. The terrible crumping sounds and the earth-shaking vibrations went on for nearly an hour and a half, during which Mr Harris apologised for his angry outburst. He said, 'Ah'm sorry to 'ave been so rough lads, but yer could've been killed by flying glass if a bomb 'ad dropped nearby.' He tried to make amends by hugging and comforting us and by giving us a toffee to chew on. As bombs landed the lights flickered and dimmed.

It was a long and terrifying night as York was badly bombed. At about four o'clock in the morning we were still cowering under the table wrapped in blankets, listening to the not-so-distant bombing that seemed to go on and on. After a time we heard and felt two very loud explosions that seemed very near and the house jumped on its foundations. They were too close for comfort, making us realise that even our little village was vulnerable. The windows rattled violently, soot was dislodged from the chimney and, as it billowed out in choking black clouds from the empty fireplace onto the hearthrug right next to us, we were petrified with fear. We found out later that a high explosive bomb had landed in a field between Towthorpe and Old Earswick village at the other side of the Foss, killing several cows and badly damaging some farm buildings. Mr Harris said, 'Mebbe t'plane 'ad bin aiming for t'Army camp at Strensall, or mebbe it'd jettisoned its bombs before fleeing t' t'coast and 'ome.'

And after a while we were pleased to hear the sound of British fighter planes attacking the fleeing German bombers. The short bursts of tinny sounding cannon fire seemed to be right above our heads. After that it went quiet except for the muffled voice of Mrs Harris telling poor Dot off for shuffling in the gas cupboard. We stayed where we were for a further half-hour until we heard the all-clear siren wail at 4.36 a.m., then we went back to bed, but it was hard to sleep after the fear and excitement. Harry, whose billet was a good half-mile closer to Clifton airfield than ours, said later, 'I saw a couple of small, single-engine Lysanders in the air just as the raids started. They were practising night landing and taking off.' After the war it was learned that the bombers had followed radio beams transmitted from France. The first wave of about twenty-odd aircraft had attacked completely unopposed, dropping eighty-five high explosive bombs that went 'whump, whump' as they hit the ground.

The new day dawned windy but dry at Haxby and we could see the pall of grey smoke that still hung over York. That day we did not have to go to school until the afternoon when Miss Curry addressed the assembled children. She looked tired and her eyes were sore as she said, 'I'm sure you are all aware of the dreadful air raid on York. I was on standby in my capacity as a part-time ARP warden and I was in bed at my parents' home on Gillygate when the first bombs exploded. I got my mother and our dog to the shelter as another five bombs exploded nearby. The noise was deafening and the poor dog was terrified.' Putting on her steel helmet, warm slacks and a thick jersey, Miss Curry went out to care for the homeless and the injured. It was a tough few hours for the resolute volunteers, the policemen and the emergency services, which were hard at it all night regardless of the risk of personal injury. The steep pitch of the roofs and the narrowness of the ancient streets made the job even more hazardous for the firemen who had to deal with flying glass, escaping gas and flames. Several were injured or affected in some way and the local people willingly opened their homes to offer kindness and comfort to those in distress. The Civil Defence workers performed heroically and the firewatchers put out many of the incendiary devices that rattled down on the rooftops before they could cause too much damage. As the all-clear was not sounded until half past four, it meant that Miss Curry could only snatch a little sleep before coming to school that afternoon. Mr Fox said, 'I'm sure we all very much admire Miss Curry's courage, compassion and dedication to duty. She has been through a gruelling and hazardous experience and I hope that you will all respond by being on your best behaviour today. Finally, let's put our hands together to show our appreciation of her sterling efforts on behalf of others. She is a shining example to us all and has done the school proud!'

The Harrises learned the details of the raid from a rushed-out edition of the *Evening Press*, who had managed to get the paper out even though their offices had been badly bombed. The headlines declared: 'York dive-bombed and gunned in reprisal raid', before adding, 'Coolness and courage under fire characterised the citizens of York last night, when the city underwent the ordeal of what was described by the Germans as a reprisal for the attacks on Cologne, Lubeck and Rostock'. It stated that more than seventy enemy bombers dropped around 200 bombs causing widespread devastation. Out of a total of 28,000 houses 9,500 were destroyed or damaged. The WVS posted grim lists of the ninety-two people killed, the injured, and those left homeless.

The following day was Harry's fourteenth birthday but Gran was not able to come due to the damage at York station. That night we were woken again by the wailing of the local siren and we quickly took up our air-raid positions. But it was not long before we were back in bed as no enemy planes arrived and the all-clear was sounded. It was reported the following day that another small raid had been attempted but the coastal defences had kept the raiders at bay. A day or so later Mr Harris sat at home reading the *Evening Press* editorial that was headed: 'THE HUN CAME TO YORK THE OTHER NIGHT.' In it there was a picture of a German bomb casing now being used as a charity collecting box. In the *Picture Post* magazine we saw dramatic coloured photographs of the Guildhall in flames; the ruins of the Bar Convent and the badly damaged offices of the *Yorkshire Press* in Coney Street. It was sad to see striking pictures of the wrecked railway station that made us realise how lucky the village had been to escape unscathed. The raid brought the terror of war that much closer. Until now York, with its narrow, winding medieval streets, had been a sleepy backwater for close on 300 years. It had been relatively undisturbed by war or violence since Cromwell's Roundheads had laid siege to the city in 1644.

Soon afterwards the Princess Royal toured the area, and four days later 3,000 people packed York Minster for a service of commemoration. In a broadcast by Lord Haw-Haw just after the air raid he claimed that the Minster had been left deliberately untouched as Hitler wanted to save it for the day when he would enter York in triumph after the invasion that was soon to come. It took many months to get back to normal and at least one of the deep bomb craters was not filled in until 1945.

Sunday was still looked on as a day of rest and was known as 'The Lord's Day'. Early every Sunday morning it was one of my jobs to walk down to Torville's shop. It was lovely to see the masses of purple aubretia hanging over the garden walls but some of the early daffodils were becoming wrinkled and brown. It felt strange to 'hear' the utter silence as I passed the empty school playground. On Saturdays the Home Guard unit used it for rifle drill. Once at the newsagents I got the *Sunday Express* newspaper for Mr Harris and cigarettes for his wife, as nobody bothered about selling cigarettes to kids in those days. Unfortunately for her, her favourite brand, Craven 'A', had become unobtainable by this time and she would have to make do with Player's Weights or full-strength Capstan's. She could not abide the Turkish cigarettes that were now on sale in the shops. I quite enjoyed this job, as Mr Harris often slipped me a penny that I spent in Bryant's shop where the sweets were scooped up from a square jar and poured into a paper bag. The quiet calm that lay over the slumbering village suited my mood. With very few people about and no noise or hurry I had time to think and I enjoyed what Wordsworth called 'the bliss of soli-tude'. I could reflect on my confused feelings and the sense of unease and deep disquiet that I felt.

Gran came to see Harry, Jimmy and me that afternoon and I thought she looked unusually pale, old and drawn. Trying to maintain a sem-blance of normality, she said, 'My word! How you have grown since I saw you last.' Standing Jimmy and then me against her, she measured our height against the buttons on her coat. This became a ritual that was repeated every time she visited and to this day I remember those large, round buttons that were domed and covered in leather.

She then explained why Hilda could not come to see Jimmy. 'Your Mam has joined the ATS and has been posted away.' She went on to say, 'A couple of weeks back we had a really bad air raid and the house was badly damaged along with a lot more round our way. We didn't have time to get to the shelters before a lone aircraft dropped its bombs. There was a roar and a whoosh and we heard a sound like hailstones as rubble and debris landed on the roof. Archie was slightly concussed and cut on the chest by flying glass, but don't worry, he's okay! He had just gone to bed when the window was blown in by the blast and Renee ran upstairs just in time to stop him from stepping out of the big hole where the window had been thinking it was the doorway. The air was full of dust particles and soot and there was blood on the jacket of his pyjamas where the flying glass had cut his chest. The skylight window – which I'd painted black because of the blackout – crashed in on the stairs right in front of me and there was wood and broken glass every-where and Archie cut his foot on a jagged piece. He has been off work for a few days and has not been able to go to his Air Training Corps sessions, which he loves.

'Next door was badly damaged an' all,' she added, 'and because their front door wouldn't open, Mrs Irvine passed her little girl Shirley out to us through the shattered front window. She is only four and she was really good and never cried at all, but mebbe that was because she was in shock. Renee, who is now working shifts as a trainee overhead crane driver at the Cargo Fleet steelworks, was having her supper after working a two till ten shift when the raid started and they were late sounding the siren. We've had to move into rented accommodation while the house is being repaired and our curtains, carpets, bedding and clothes will have to be replaced as they are impregnated with glass. We're now living in rooms in a big Victorian house on Linthorpe Road next to our family doctor. We've got the downstairs rooms, and Granny Knights and your Great Aunt Maud and her three kids have the upstairs rooms – they were bombed out like us. We share the kitchen and we have electricity now but I don't trust that new fangled stuff. There's even an inside toilet and a bathroom, and we're not used to such luxuries. Our houses are all boarded up now and quite a few of the houses on Laws Street were completely wrecked.' I thought to myself, 'I'm glad Mam's at Grove House with our George.'

By late spring most of the trees had put forth fresh green foliage, but the ash buds were still clenched black and tight. Vigorous green shoots of young wheat had sprung up to hide the brown ridges and Mr Harris's boss had said to him, 'I must have the barley sown and the swedes and mangolds drilled by early May.' The clover and hayseed had been broadcast soon after the harrowing was done and it gave them a feeling of satisfaction to accomplish these annual tasks. Scents of wild flowers and fruit blossom assailed their nostrils and Mr Harris was glad to be working long hours, as the destructive bickering with his wife was getting him down. The incessant nagging had done its damage; unhappiness and frustration had gradually taken root and had grown between them like some malignant flower. He always experienced a deep feeling of contentment when with his fellow farmhands. He found their slow, deep-toned and broad-vowelled banter comforting as they worked in the fields talking happily of simple things like pigmeal, mash rollers and fertiliser. The unhurried farming year had scarcely altered over the years but things were starting to change more rapidly now. Nearby Italian prisoners jabbered away in their excitable fashion while an armed soldier stood guard, and there were increasing numbers of Land Army girls in khaki jodhpurs.

It felt good to be out in the warm, fresh air away from the constrained atmosphere of home. Mrs Harris seemed to be permanently bad-tempered these days and he suspected that she was taking it out on us kids when he wasn't there. She certainly took it out on the locals, playing hell with the nurse, the policeman, the postman and anyone else that crossed her path. Most people tried to keep out of her way. 'The war affects different people in different ways,' he thought, 'and me and 'er seem ter 'ave little in common these days.' He comforted himself with the thought of how relaxing it would be to plod on with the tilling and planting and he found that grinding up the mangolds for the steers helped him to unwind. He tried to put his wife, and the bloody war that seemed to be dragging on forever, out of his mind. At the end of each day he knew that pleasant feeling that often follows a spell of hard physical labour, but she always spoiled it for him when he got home.

Harry only had a few more weeks at school before he left for good. Recently he had started a Saturday morning job at the butcher's shop on Front Street delivering the orders on a sit-up-and-beg bike that had a large wicker basket on the front. In between the deliveries he gave the neat and dapper Mr Atkinson a hand in the shop.

On reflection, the evacuation scheme seems to have been a rather hit-and-miss affair dependent on luck or the lack of it. George and I had been lucky at first, but that luck seemed to have run out since coming here. I was frightened by Mrs Harris's loud voice and intimidating manner as she seemed to have a stone where her heart should have been. Her eyes were cold and she knew how to hurt us. Public Information Leaflet number three proved to be far from correct in our case as it stated that, '… clearly the children will be much happier away from the big cities where the danger will be greatest … They will be well looked after.' It was only Jimmy's friendship and caring presence, along with Mr Harris's kindly nature, that had made being here just about tolerable. He was an undemonstrative and exceptionally nice man, but he worked long hours and was not always there to mediate on our behalf. When he was at home he bore the brunt of her anger but he tried his best to protect us from her increasingly angry and volatile behaviour.

Wartime anxieties and separations changed everybody to some degree and emotions tended to be heightened and intensified with nerves often stretched to breaking point. We found out the hard way that the choleric Mrs Harris had a cruel and nasty streak. We were now being punished more and more severely for minor misdemeanours or infringements of *her* rules. For example, I had recently been larruped with the belt for tearing my trousers on some barbed wire with the L-shaped tear being a sure give-away. On another occasion I was clouted round the ear for smirking and looking away while being told off. It was all down to nervousness and fear when she shouted straight into my face. 'I will not have it. Do you hear?' (Silence.) 'I said do you *hear*?' she screamed. 'Yes, Mrs Harris,' I whimpered in reply. I hated it when she exploded into action and grabbed hold of me. It was so humiliating to be held by the shoulders and shaken like a rag doll in front of the others and I often felt that my head would fall off.

Where does punishment end and abuse begin? Children should be trained not beaten. We had been separated from our loved ones at an early age and that was traumatic enough. We were old enough to know it was wrong to be naughty or to tell lies; especially to adults. But did we deserve this verbal and physical maltreatment just for being mischievous? We reasoned that she was an adult, therefore she must know best, as we had been taught to respect our 'elders and betters'. We were no angels but we were being whacked on the legs or rapped on the head for what seemed trivial offences. Our shortcomings were many, it seems. She was losing her temper and resorting to violence more and more often. When she took down one of the belts hanging on the kitchen cabinet, I would flinch in anticipation of the first blow. As we shielded our heads with our arms, or hid under the coats hanging on the kitchen door, she lashed at the bare part of our legs below our baggy short trousers and showed no mercy. We were often left with red, stinging, raised weals.

It took a long time to shake off the image of her red, rage-distorted, moon-like face, and I shut my eyes as the belt whipped down on me over and over again. I can still picture her wobbling jowls and the gingery hairs that grew out of her flared nostrils as she lashed at me. Tight-lipped and scowling, she seemed to enjoy watching us cringe and whimper as we slunk away like puppies with our tails between our legs. It was not the bruises but the wounds inside that would take the longest to heal. She had created a deep dread and uncertainty in us. I vowed that one day I would write it all down, but for the time being I had to put up with it – but I would never forget. To make matters worse, the obsequious 'Ducky' Barrett, who was an out-and-out creep, hardly ever got hit.

Poor Dot, who was as thin as a rake, was cruelly punished for the slightest transgression. She was clipped round the ear or caned on the palms of her hands causing them to become red, puffed up and sore. I still remember the whooshing sound of the thin cane as it sliced through the air. When she had stopped crying she sat there in shocked silence, keeping her eyes averted so as not to anger Mrs Harris again. Maybe it was because she was not 'the full shilling' – as they said – that she was picked on the most. When this happened, Jimmy and I looked at each other with our teeth and our fists clenched. We felt bad and tears came to our eyes, as her hurting hurt us. We felt guilty at saying nothing but at the same time we were glad that it was not our turn to get it. Mrs Harris could wield sarcasm with deadly effect and she constantly told Dot that she needed her head looking at but, in my eyes, by trying to degrade her she only degraded herself.

We were told that we were stupid, worthless and useless so often that we came to believe that it must be true and started to display symptoms of insecurity. The repeated beatings and the constant telling off lowered our self-esteem and we withdrew into ourselves more and more. It reduced our trust and faith in the adults around us and we felt that we had nobody to turn to for help and support. Even though school afforded some respite, we were too intimidated to confide in the teachers. Our reserves of resilience were almost used up and we instinctively said and did nothing in order to cope. We longed to be reassured but didn't know how to tell them what was happening as we thought they would think we were making it all up. When Gran visited again we tried to tell her but Mrs Harris was always there. She was all smiles, hugging us and putting on a big act of kindness.

The more we were punished the more we came to expect it. We started to believe that we must be bad children and deserved everything we got. It is a strange quirk of human nature to feel guilt on being badly treated. Jimmy and I became introverted and withdrawn and began to lose hope, and I longed for Mam to hug and cuddle me and soothe my fears, but she hadn't been to see me for some time. It seems that I subconsciously started to employ basic survival mechanisms. I learned to 'switch off' my mind and pretend that I wasn't there when Mrs Harris beat me. I believe that the psychologist's term for such a reaction is *disassociation*.

School provided a structure to our day and Jimmy and I felt safe among the crowds of children. For a time, Miss Francis, with her striking blue eyes and gentle, smiling presence, shamed me into making an effort. There was something about her that made you want to please her; an implicit trust that led to a certain restraint. After a lesson with her I felt better able to cope; she was like a second mother to me and her influence was more potent and lasting than if she had been a strict disciplinarian. Shouting and threatening are barren means of instruction. She taught me to read for pleasure, which enabled me to escape into another world, and was sympathetic when I desperately needed some kindness and understanding. The formerly mind-numbing class routine became a sanctuary in which I didn't have to expend too much time thinking. I put up a defensive screen, joking and clowning to mask the emotional hurt that was holding me back. I became like the vulnerable, soft-bodied caddis fly larva in the pond; a little creature that protects itself inside an armoured covering composed of bits of hard stone that it glues together. I hid inside my own mind and learned to build barriers so that no one would hurt me again.

Miss Francis had said, 'Don't be afraid to ask if you get stuck on anything.' But due to feelings of worthlessness and failure, I was not prepared to risk appearing silly in front of my peers. I would not ask when I did not fully understand something and never put my hand up to offer answers. I was so unhappy and I felt that I was not as clever as the other children in the class. A feeling of hopelessness was dragging me down and my schoolwork began to suffer. I got into trouble due to my increased lethargy and withdrawn churlish state. My emotions were kept bottled up until they came out in aggressive outbursts and I got into fights. I didn't like hurting people but I found that a good fight helped to get rid of some of my pent-up anxiety for a time. At home in Middlesbrough we had been materially deprived, but here we were being emotionally deprived and the effects were to last a long, long time.

There appeared to be two sides to my nature. I was quiet, subdued and deep thinking, and needed solitude from time to time. Solitude is not the same as loneliness. Lingering in the silence of the countryside gave me a warm pleasant feeling and I became a watcher of people and things. Still painfully shy and inhibited in company, I dared not reveal my unspoken dreams. At other times I became a more primitive, rowdy boy who ran wild with Jimmy and the others. Recently we had started to take heart-stopping risks, as traumatised children tend to do. We dared each other to do dangerous things and often ended up in even deeper trouble. Those early Sunday morning walks to Torville's shop were my brief periods of enjoyable peace and quiescence. These traits are apparently the two sides of the same coin: the yin and the yang of Oriental philosophy.

Life had become a fear and a mystery, and Jimmy and I were emotionally wounded and left with scars that would take many years to heal – and some never did. I had bad dreams and Mrs Harris, in trying to curb our exuberance and love of life, came very close to breaking our spirit. The human spirit can only take so much before it crumbles to dust, so we tried to avoid her, as she would give us a smack round the head for the slightest infringement of her rules. We even got a clout for getting in her way, but it was hard not to with so many of us in that small house. I cannot speak for the others, who also had their share of beatings, as I do not know how they turned out in later life, but Jimmy and I were being shaped by circumstances over which we had no control. It was time to do something about it. Jimmy and I started to think of running away.

The long-suffering and undemonstrative Mr Harris seemed to sense our unhappiness and tried to show us more affection to make up for his wife's increasing carping and cruel ways. We appreciated his many small kindnesses but it was not enough. Children have indelible memories and our minds were made up. We waited for a suitable time to make our getaway but, in the meantime, we escaped into the great airy spaces of the countryside as often as possible. Our hearts were heavy and the lightness had disappeared from our step as we trudged to school day after day. We were content if we scraped through the day without further hurt, and indoors we moped and said nothing or stayed out of the way in our bedrooms. We had long discussions and we asked the others if they wanted to come with us. Dot and Thelma willingly agreed and Ducky, who was a wimp and a sucker up, reluctantly agreed but only after much persuading. He said, 'It's all right for you lot, but Newcastle is a lot further away than Middlesbrough. Ah'd be on me own from there on.' We thought we had better keep a close eye on him in case he gave the game away. We decided to go on the morning of Whit Monday, the first weekday of our half-term break.

Jimmy went into Mr Harris's cluttered shed and found an old battered saucepan that he kept rusty nails and screws in and we washed it out in the pond. I stole a bottle of Camp coffee and chicory from the Co-op store that had an Indian prince and a kilted Scottish soldier on the label, which reminded me of what Dad had told us about his time in India. Consequently I suffered feelings of guilt and remember thinking, what if PC Manging found out? Would I be charged with larceny and put in a cell in York Jail? A picture of Dick Turpin in his cramped cell came into my mind. What would Mam think of me? The song *It's a Sin to tell a Lie* kept going round in my head. Dot pinched some broken biscuits from Bryant's and we hid them in a tin under the railway sleepers that formed the little bridge over the drainage ditch up Usher Lane. Thelma stole a teaspoon and a tin of Libby's evaporated milk and we bought a few ha'penny Oxo cubes with our few coppers. The thought of going home lifted our spirits no end and we couldn't wait for the big day to come. We thought that Middlesbrough and Grove House lay just over the ridge to the north of Strensall and that was the way we planned to go.

Whit Sunday was a day of changing cloud and sunshine as we put on our 'Sunday Best' ready for church. Mr Harris had built an arch of rustic trelliswork over the path that ran down the back garden and had trained climbing roses to twine around it. The young, almond-shaped leaves were reddish-tinted and, due to the warm weather, they were just coming into flower. The girls were wearing light-coloured dresses in honour of Whitsun and Mr Harris snipped off a few of the minia-ture, partly open buds and pinned one on each of the girls. He then put the stems of others through the buttonholes of our jackets. In church I usually tried to avoid being next to Ducky who always stood next to Mrs Harris. Creeps and unctuous people like him made my flesh crawl, and Jimmy whispered, 'I 'ope he don't say 'owt.' So this time I made a point of standing on the other side of her so that I could hear what he said. I barely remember the service that day as my mind was on more important things.

That day the hands of the kitchen clock seemed to crawl round and, on going to bed, we were quiet for a change. Usually we argued and tiptoed in and out of each other's bedrooms and Mrs Harris often had to shout up the stairs, 'Get into bed or you'll feel the belt around you! I won't tell you again.' Due to an excess of excitement, I lay awake listen-ing to the sound of the rafters creaking as they cooled and slept only for short spells. Ducky was snoring and letting off as usual and the night seemed to drag on interminably, but finally the first faint signs of dawn began to filter around the blackout curtains. It was only six o'clock and too early to get up but eventually a chorus of birdsong greeted the start of the new day. Mr Harris was out and on his way to work as the rising sun bathed the houses in its warm gold-tinted light. It was a glorious morning and I thought to myself that by the time it set I would be back with Mam. This was the day we had longed for and we could scarcely believe it was here. We put on our old threadbare clothes to give the impression that today was nothing out of the ordinary, and I had on my ragged pullover that had holes at the elbows as if I was just going out to play.

How we contained our excitement I'll never know. We ate as much porridge and toast and margarine as we could cram into our stomachs, and we kept back two of our mugs after Dot had done the washing up of the breakfast things. We hid them away in Thelma's canvas knapsack while Mrs Harris was outside in the back garden hanging out items of threadbare underwear that had seen too many washes. Thelma was then sent on an errand to the shops. We were ready and eager to be off and tried to hide our excitement as we waited impatiently for her to come back. At the last minute Ducky chickened out, saying, 'It's a barmy idea and ah'm not coming with yer.' We prayed that the oily creep wouldn't give the game away. 'Right,' said Thelma when she got back. 'Let's be off.' As we stepped outside the sun was well up but the air wasn't too fresh, at which Jimmy exclaimed, 'Phew! What a pong!'

The cattle had been taken in for milking at Abel's dairy and there was cow splatter all the way up Usher Lane. Taking care where we put our feet, we collected our supplies from our hidden cache and set off on our desperate bid for freedom, hoping we would never see the horrible Mrs Harris again. We were delighted at the thought of going back to our parents. We would go by way of Grove House where I would be reunited with my Mam and the others would then go on to Middlesbrough. It seemed that our dreams were coming true at last.

As we hurried past the house, in case Mrs Harris saw us and called us in to go on another message or something, there was a new spring in our step. On reaching Station Road, we went wild with released excitement before we crossed the wooden sleepers of the railway crossing. There were a number of large Victorian houses with ornately carved wooden porches, and long, pendulous bunches of light yellow flowers dripped from the laburnum shrubs in some of their gardens. Hopping and skipping up the twisting road, we left the houses on the eastern edge of the village behind. Thelma said, 'The lane goes north 'ere before it turns t' t'east and crosses Foss Bridge. Ah've been up 'ere before on me friend's bike.'

At this point a tall metal pylon towered above us and as we passed under the wires we could hear them humming and buzzing loudly. I was a bit frightened and was glad to get past and away from them – electricity was a scary mystery to me. We followed the lane, which was empty except for the odd military vehicle. A little way up the road a local farmhand rode past on his old sit-up-and-beg bike but he took no notice of us, as he knew that the school was closed for the Whitsun break. To our left was the high, grass-covered slope of the railway embankment, some parts of which had been dug over to grow vegetables, so we had a roll down that for a while. Patches of it had been turned black where the sparks from the fireboxes of the passing trains had set it alight. I selected a long, juicy grass stem to chew on, at which point a ladybird flared its wings and flew away home. We were doing the same thing but I hoped our houses wouldn't be on fire.

It was a glorious day and verdant, sun-drenched pastures stretched away into the hazy distance. When a freak breeze stirred the grass in a field beside the road, Thelma said, 'It's only t'fairies passing through. They say that if yer sit under a 'awthorn tree at this time o' t'year they can gain power over yer.'

We then heard the unmistakable harsh, croaking call of a secretive corncrake from the long grass at the far side of a field. Its 'crek-crek; crek-crek' call made me think of a creaking farm gate. When we reached the concrete pillbox we ran in and out of it pretending we were soldiers firing our machine guns through its outward sloping slits. Nearby a windhover, with a black band along the edge of its tail, hung perfectly still in the sky before swooping down on some tiny creature in the long grass. After much dallying and playing about we reached the low-walled, stone bridge that crossed the Golland Dyke. The grass verges and some of the fields were covered in golden buttercups. Here we made a drink with our oxo cubes and water from the stream but, with the water being cold, they were only partly dissolved and bits floated about in it. We sat on the parapet of the bridge basking in the hot sunshine and rested for a while.

The road swung sharply to the right just before it reached Towthorpe and Thelma said, 'I heard that a local man crashed his motorbike and was killed on this bend a few years back.' The day was becoming exceptionally hot for the time of year and we took turns at carrying the knapsack. Thelma, who was brisk and businesslike, had taken charge, as, at the age of nearly eleven, she was the oldest and had her head screwed on properly, whereas Dot tended to stand and gawp. As the sun beat down on the tyre-polished tarmac we were so happy and elated and hadn't a care in the world. Jimmy suggested thumbing a lift but nothing came along and Thelma said, 'We'll probably get a lift when we get on t'main road. Don't worry, just think what it'll be like back 'ome with our parents.' I tried to picture their surprise on seeing us on the doorstep.

Jimmy and I were busting for a 'Jimmy Riddle', so we went behind a bush, but Dot didn't seem bothered about us being there; she just crouched down for a pee in the long grass like a little partridge. Back on the road, we larked about popping the odd tar bubble that had started to form in the sun-softened asphalt, and as we skipped along we could hear tiny squeaks and the soft plopping sounds of voles dropping from the banks into the drainage ditches. We stopped to investigate things on the grass verges so often that the time just melted away and it was near noon by the time we arrived at Towthorpe Bridge.

As we stood by the low, stone parapet of the bridge we could hear the distant wasp buzz of a motorbike, which gradually grew louder, and we had to get out of the way as an army despatch rider suddenly appeared. He was wearing white gauntlet gloves and his motorbike purred as he coaxed it along the quiet by-road. We dropped sticks into the water and dashed to the other side of the bridge to see them float out. By this time the sun was scorching and there was a heat haze over the countryside. Beyond the small, irregular-shaped fields the trees in the distance looked blurred and quivery, and above them peewits rolled and tumbled in the clear blue sky. Getting hot and sweaty, we flapped our shirts about trying to cool ourselves down a bit as sweat ran into our eyes making them sting.

We slid down the embankment and sat on the grassy banks of the Foss where Jimmy punctured the tin of condensed milk by bashing a nail (which he had taken from Mr Harris's shed) into it with a rock. We made coffee with cold water scooped from the narrow river that ran clear and cool beneath the old stone bridge. We were in heaven, enjoying our bread and biscuits, and it was so still and peaceful with the river gently slapping against the banks, and purling quietly as it meandered along. The water sparkled and the sun beat down and we were glad to be in the shade for a while. As we sat huddled together, Thelma started to sing the Flanagan and Allen song *Underneath the Arches* and we all joined in. We sipped our mugs of cold, horrible-tasting coffee and tried to convince ourselves that it tasted delicious, but who cared anyway? The sweetness of the biscuits disguised the taste and nothing was going to spoil our day. We were so delighted and euphoric at the thought of getting away from the nasty Mrs Harris for good. We were going back to our loved ones at last!

13

The Old Order Changeth

It was well after midday on Monday 25 May 1942 and there was barely a breath of wind as we sat on the grassy banks of the purling river which sang its quiet song to the sun. Thelma, who had a great deal of nous, said, 'We'll have to be moving, and when we get to the main road we should be able to thumb a lift.' Quite happy at that we rinsed the pan and the mugs in the water. 'Right then,' said Jimmy, shouldering the knapsack. 'Lets get on.'

Rounding a right-hand bend we came to the collection of old, brick farm buildings. A little further on to our right stood Manor Farm and a small cottage and there was not a soul to be seen. It was only four weeks since that German plane had dropped a bomb hereabouts injuring one of the horses.

Cattle were grazing languidly on the lush grass and flicking their tails to keep away the clegs that constantly plagued them and, having recently suffered a nasty bite from one, I was wary of them myself. The heat of the afternoon was starting to get to us and the landrail, desperate to attract a mate after his long flight from Africa, was still making his raucous croaking calls from his hiding place in the tall grasses. We, like him, were also crying out for a little love and attention.

We kept stopping to lark about or to investigate things of interest and, getting annoyed, Jimmy shouted, 'I'll thump yer John if you don't stop chucking them Claggy Jacks on me back.' Claggy Jacks (Galium, also known as cleavers or goose grass) were plants that have tiny hooks on their stems, seed cases and the underside of the leaves, allowing them to adhere readily to any hair, fur or cloth that they come into contact with, therefore we were inadvertently helping to spread their seeds. The roadside hedges were white with mayblossom and the afternoon was slipping away by the time we reached the junction. As we turned left onto the main road that ran north through Strensall, we could see the extensive army firing ranges. Lots of army vehicles were passing to and fro but not one stopped to pick us up even though we thumbed them. There was a ramshackle wooden hut with a verandah by the side of the road that was a kind of cafeteria and it had a sign proclaiming that it was 'Mae West's Place'. Thelma said, 'It must've been named after that big busty blonde in the Hollywood fillums.'

As we trudged wearily on we saw a number of soldiers coming and going and we wished we had the money to buy a cold drink and something tasty to eat, as our biscuits had all gone by this time. Nearby we could see long regimented rows of wooden huts and bell tents, and on the right a little further north we passed the guardroom that stood beside the entrance to the vast army barracks.

Strensall Road became Flaxton Road as we reached the wide-open spaces of Strensall Common where thickets of trees almost met above our heads. Near the road there were stands of silver birch but a little further back was a small forest of pine trees. The common was a tiny remnant of the vast Forest of Galtres that had once covered this area. Mr Harris had told us that the Haxby Home Guard used to come here to train with the regular soldiers from time to time. We could hear an army sergeant using choice language, not really suitable for the ears of delicate young ladies like Thelma and Dot, as he bawled out and berated his sweating underlings. Fortunately, it did not seem to bother the girls who were enjoying the refreshing shade of the luxuriant growth. The foliage was thick and freshly green and the occasional chestnut tree that we passed was covered in a mass of red 'candles'.

The birds were quietly twittering and singing and the grass verges were full of dazzling white cow parsley, Jack-by-the-hedge and other tall wild flowers. Seeing a fallen log, we rested for a while and, as we came back into the open, it took a few seconds for our eyes to adjust to the sun's relentless glare. We plodded on placing one weary foot in front of the other trying to thumb a lift from the odd lorry or car that passed. As time passed, the shadows grew longer and the air began to cool. Jimmy and I were feeling hungry and tired and our lightheartedness had evaporated. We began to get worried and asked Thelma, 'How far away are we now?'

'Don't worry,' she replied. 'We'll be there soon enough.'

Niggling doubts began to enter our minds. 'What if we are still out on the road when it gets dark?' I whispered nervously to Jimmy.

'Don't be such a cowardy custard,' he replied, but I think he was just trying to appear brave in front of the girls.

We had heard stories about various ghosts in this neck of the woods. A phantom on horseback was said to gallop around the area on moonless nights; and it was said that an old clergyman had been seen out in the rain one dark and stormy night, but when a van driver had stopped to pick him up he suddenly vanished. We began to have second thoughts about this running away lark.

At that point Thelma thumbed a black car, which pulled in to the roadside a little way in front of us. Thelma shouted, 'This is it!' and we excitedly ran towards it, but, as we reached it, a black uniformed policeman got out and waited for us by the car door. He knew who we were as it seems that Mrs Harris had wheedled the information out of Ducky. The oily creep had split on us after we failed to turn up for our dinner. It seems she had hurried round to PC Manging's house and the village policeman had telephoned headquarters to inform them of the situation.

The police constable gave us a stern ticking off and said, 'Right you lot, into the car.' To Thelma he said, 'You are old enough to know better', before pointing out some of the dangers that we could have put ourselves in. Thelma hung her head in shame; Dot looked bemused and we were just relieved that it was all over. On the way back he asked us, 'What made you want to run away like that?' and we told him how much we had missed our mams and dads and how unhappy we were at being belted so often for nothing, at which he seemed kindlier towards us. It was the first time I had been in a car but I didn't enjoy it because of the guilt I felt. We were taken back to the house on Usher Lane and in a way I was glad to be back safely, despite the likelihood of more beatings to come.

When Mrs Harris came out of the house, she hugged us – a hitherto unheard of occurrence – and thanked the bobby profusely. She then took us inside and we thought we would get a real good belting, but I think she was too relieved to scold us and instead she was quite nice, saying, 'Get yourselves cleaned up and I'll warm up your dinners.' And, surprisingly, that was the end of the matter. For a time things improved and we were not hit or belted at all; instead we were sent up to our bedroom and missed a meal whenever we misbehaved. Maybe she was worried that she might end up in trouble with the authorities if it got out that she was belting us again. Possibly she had already had a warning. I don't know what she told Gran about us running away but nothing was said about it.

As the green of spring warmed into the gold of early summer, there was a very cloudy spell and it turned wet and thundery. By the late evening of the 30th it began to clear up and conditions were ideal as the first of Bomber Harris's thousand-bomber raids took to the air. It was said to be the greatest concentration of air power that the world had ever seen, with the force made up of Wellingtons, Whitleys, Stirlings, Manchesters, Hampdens, Mosquitoes, Halifaxes and the new Lancaster bombers. It was reported that the target was the city of Cologne with its heavy industry and its ancient Rhenish cathedral. In Haxby we became aware of the gradually increasing drone of approaching aircraft, which eventually filled the sky drowning out every other sound. Many of them were from Linton and the other airfields, such as Leeming and Dishforth, just to the north of us. In fact, Harry told us later that 400 of the total force had taken off from airfields in Yorkshire. The very air and the whole house vibrated as the throaty roar of the massed aircraft reached a crescendo before it slowly faded as they streamed south.

The newspapers used the term 'saturation bombing' for the first time, reporting that the massive raid had been an outstanding success describing epic feats of arms. They called it a turning point in the war and it was said that 1,046 aircraft from fifty-two airfields had taken part, with forty being lost.

The news bulletins said that Cologne had been set ablaze from end to end but the cathedral was left standing. The area of devastation in the city was six times larger than that at Coventry six months earlier. On 31 May Mrs Harris allowed us to stay up to listen to the news, which was now something of a national institution which folk endeavoured not to miss. As the chimes of Big Ben came to an end, John Snagge read out a glowing report on the raid, which provided a badly needed boost to the flagging morale of Bomber Command and the people of war-torn Britain. Afterwards, Churchill was to say, 'This is only a herald of what Germany will receive, city by city, from now on ... We are going to scourge the Third Reich from end to end.'

On 1 June a red-backed ration book for clothing was issued – not that I remember Mrs Harris ever buying us new clothes. Ours had been washed, patched and repaired so many times that they were now threadbare and almost unwearable. We ran around like young ragamuffins – even though Gran swore that she had been sending new clothes quite regularly. What happened to them remains a mystery to this day. Our ragged pullovers were unravelled and Thelma and Dot knitted them up again, and in this way our old clothes became 'new' jumpers.

The bulk of the nation's poultry feed had to be imported, leading to fewer poultry and, therefore, a shortage of eggs. Powdered egg was being imported from America, thus saving on shipping space. We were allowed a packet (the equivalent of twelve eggs) each four-weekly rationing period, which cost one shilling and ninepence at Haxby Co-op. The powder was reconstituted by adding water; but to me it never tasted the same as real eggs and in time we forgot what they tasted like. I must admit that I liked the bacon and egg pies that Mrs Harris baked and we had mashed potatoes made from packets of powdered potato called Pom. Mrs Harris would remark, 'Beggars can't be choosers.' But Harry was getting real eggs regularly supplied by Miss Barker's brother, and they swapped some of their excess farm produce for other items that they needed.

That month a new bomber airfield called RAF East Moor came into service. By the end of June it was fully operational and, as it was only two miles from us, this meant that the number of Halifax bombers flying over Haxby increased.

On a bright Sunday afternoon, I was in the kitchen when there was a knock on the door, and Mrs Harris said, 'Well, don't stand there like one o'clock half struck, go and answer it lad.'

Gran stood on the back step, and she said, 'I've got a little surprise for you.' At which my five-year-old brother George, who I had not seen for almost eighteen months, appeared from behind her. He was going to live here with us. Gran said, 'Your Mam won't be able to come for a while as she has left Grove House and is back home being kept very busy working as a cleaner for Ethel Gaunt again.' Mrs Gaunt did a lot to help the poorer people of Middlesbrough and was well liked and respected by all. She was a very kind, caring person who the family could depend on in times of trouble. Gran told me that she was the head of the nearby first aid centre and Mam was also working there as a voluntary helper looking after the casualties brought in after bombing raids. I thought Gran seemed sad and eager to be away, and she left as soon as she had handed over my brother's papers, his blue ration book and his belongings. This sudden change of living circumstances meant that our sleeping arrangements would have to be revised and Mrs Harris said, 'George will have to sleep in the bed with you, Ducky and Jimmy.'

We were arranged with Ducky and Jimmy at the head of the bed, while George and I had to sleep with our heads on pillows at the foot of it – with the sheet and blanket turned back. We often had the sweaty feet of the bigger boys up near our faces and cold draughts around our feet, and Ducky often pulled the blankets off us altogether. We soon got used to it and fortunately it was a warm summer.

Two weeks later, Renee, my auntie – by now eighteen years old, petite and attractive – came to visit us by herself. She took George and me along to Bryant's shop and bought us some stretchy jelly babies before taking us down to Harry's lodgings. She seemed quite pleased on getting a few wolf whistles from the local lads. Just before we got there she said to Jimmy, 'By the way, you know when you ran away?'

'Yes,' he replied.

'Well, you were heading the wrong way. If you had gone through Wigginton and up on to the A19 it would have taken you straight up to Middlesbrough.'

'I know, but we were planning to go to Grove House first to leave John with his Mam.'

On our arrival, the Misses Barker and Law couldn't have made us more welcome and they were delighted on seeing George. They seemed to have a weakness for blonde-haired children and they cuddled and fussed him and he loved every minute of it. He had now started school and was in Miss Curry's baby class in St Mary's hall. While we were out in their lovely back garden, I overheard Renee say to Harry, 'I'm a bit worried about Mam. She sits at home holding her head in her hands and staring into the fire for ages. There seems to be no life in her and she takes no interest in things around her since she got that telegram. Her mind seems to be a complete blank.'

It seems she had received a telegram from the War Office that said, 'I regret to inform you that your son, Acting Sergeant John Bradford, is missing. Believed killed', and she was devastated. She had lost so many children in her life without this on top of everything else, and a deep melancholy had descended on her like a dark cloud. However, on an evening a few days later, her younger brother Albert and his wife knocked on her front door. As soon as she opened it Albert, who could not contain his excitement, blurted out, 'John's not dead! We've just found out he's a prisoner of war!'

Gran was barely able to take in what was being said, and Renee was to say later that her mind went from initial disbelief, to doubt and finally to acceptance, relief and intense happiness. Tears of joy began to flow and she could not hold them back. Her shoulders shook as she sobbed. It seems that Uncle Albert and his wife had been listening to a Lord Haw-Haw broadcast on their wireless. In it he had listed the names of several recently captured prisoners of war. One of those mentioned was a certain John Bradford, the son of Mrs A. Knight of 15 Forcass Road, Dormaster, Redcar, Yorkshire. It seems that Uncle John had had on him a crumpled letter from his Aunt Hannah and it was assumed that this was his mother. Albert and Hannah *Knights* actually lived in Dormans*town*, which was between Middlesbrough and Redcar.

Gran had to find out if the news was true or not. When her initial excitement had abated a little she went in search of advice, but at least she now had hope to cling on to. The depression that had descended on her was suddenly lifted. Mrs Gaunt, who had sound connections, advised her to write to the Red Cross Society and eventually she received a reply from their London headquarters. It was signed in person by the Dowager Lady Ampthill, the chairwoman, and it stated, 'As broadcasts from foreign stations are not always reliable we fear that this news cannot be taken as official', before adding, 'We sincerely hope that you will soon receive an official notification confirming that your son is indeed a prisoner of war.' It was some time before she learned that John, along with 3,000 others, had indeed been taken prisoner.

When Gran visited in late July she was back to her cheerful self, and she told Harry that she had had a letter from the Borough Council stating that the bomb damage to her house had now been repaired and she could move back in when she was ready. As it was a nice day she took us for a walk up Usher Lane and we showed her Widd's field where we usually played. We dared not tell her about the soldier who had exposed himself to us. We didn't fully understand what had happened but we had sensed that it was wrong and were relieved when the soldier moved on, but we didn't know how to tell the grown-ups about it.

Gran took us down to see Harry who had now left school and had been offered the opportunity to train as a butcher at W.H. Atkinson's shop on Front Street. We heard Gran saying to him, 'It's lovely to be back in our own house but we've had some really bad bombing raids recently. Archie, Renee and me have had to lay awake half the night in the underground shelters on The Common. Some nights the sky is lit up by searchlights and the roar of the German bombers goes on for ages as they drop their high explosives, oil bombs and incendiaries. Archie hasn't been at the Britannia Works long and it was lucky that he wasn't on the night shift the other day. The railway line not far from us was hit and damaged and it's not long since the petrol tanks at ICI were bombed and set on fire. The raids seem to be happening more and more often and we're worn out through worry and lack of sleep. You should think yourself lucky that you're here and well out of it.'

One day as the skipping rope went slap-slap on the playground and the boys were chasing after the rosy-cheeked, lithe-limbed girls whose hair was tousled, tossed and blown about by the wind, we realised that the Home Guard were taking part in a mock battle with the regulars from Strensall Camp. They were practising street fighting and we rushed to the front wall to get a better view. Jimmy and I managed to find a ringside seat and all the kids were shouting out remarks such as, 'Watch out, he's behind you!' One of the Home Guard lads had hidden in a half-empty water barrel that stood across the road just before a group of army regulars appeared from the direction of Wigginton. As they crept along with their faces blackened they came up to the barrel, and we were all excitedly shouting, screaming, and pointing at it. One of the soldiers twigged and looked inside and the unfortunate youth was captured and escorted away. At that point Mr Fox appeared and he was fuming, as he shouted, 'You lot! Get back into school this instant!' and one or two of the regular troublemakers got a clout round the ear as they hurried by him.

The Shaws, who were the local domestic refuse collectors, were always at the school complaining about something or other and we often saw Mrs Shaw cycling round the village in her pinny. She rode so slowly that we thought that she must surely fall off, but she never did. We got on well with her and whenever she saw us around the village she would shout, 'Get yersel' 'ome! Yer Mam needs yer boots for bread tins.'

One morning, just before we broke up, a dark-green Civil Defence trailer was parked in the school playground. Mr Fox led our class outside and lined us up saying, 'You are here to make sure that your masks are still working properly and the civil defence men will tell you what you have to do.' The man in the blue overalls gathered us into groups of six and said, 'You will test your masks by going into the gas chamber with them on. Once inside you will be told to take them off for a second or two. You must then walk quickly out through the door. Don't worry, if your masks are ok and are properly fitted there should be no problems.' We reluctantly entered the trailer as instructed and ripped off our masks when ordered to do so by the ARP man inside. As soon as we got a whiff of tear gas there was a mad panic to get out of the trailer as quickly as possible and we tried to hold our breath as we made a dash for the door. As I staggered out into the playground gasping for air, my eyes stung like mad and tears were streaming down my face. It was not a pleasant experience to say the least.

It seems that the powers-that-be had noticed that our old cardboard gas mask boxes were now in a sorry state, or non-existent, and we were issued with long, round, lidded tins to keep them in. A large amount of cocoa powder mixed with sugar had been sent to Britain from Canada and we were told to bring a container to school. We used our gas mask tins and got them filled up, but by the time we got to the house the mixture had gone down a bit. We could not resist wetting our fingers with spittle and dipping them into it before licking them clean. This was a real godsend at a time of real shortages and for a while afterwards we were in Mrs Harris's good books.

Just after we broke up for the summer holiday, sweets – already in short supply – were put on ration and this was a real blow to us. Large chocolate bars became a thing of the past as we were only allowed two ounces of sweets per week and small ration-size bars began to appear in the shops. Shortages of milk meant that milk chocolate was very hard to come by and Rowntrees had recently produced wafer fingers covered in plain chocolate called Kit Kat that came in blue wrappers. In August the ration was raised to three ounces, but syrup, treacle and biscuits were put on points. We decided to spend our few coppers on the smallest sweets we could find, as Jimmy had said, 'If we buy Nips, pear drops or Fishermen's Friends they'll last much longer,' and in this way we kidded ourselves that we had a lot. Nips were tiny black sweets with a strong liquorice flavour.

Harry had attended the Joe Row School for only six months before leaving at the end of the summer term. He was now fourteen years old and couldn't wait to start work full time at the small butcher's shop. It was here that Harry learned how to kill pigs and drain their blood off to make black pudding.

When we were in the school playground we could hear the doomed pigs squealing and smell the blood. The girls put their hands over their ears to block out the piercing, high-pitched cries and Eva Pulleyn said, 'They sound just like a baby crying.' Harold only killed them when there was an R in the month, explaining that, 'It's done in order to prevent the meat from going off in the hot summer months as we haven't got a refrigerator.' Nothing was wasted and Harry used to say, 'The only part of a pig that you can't eat is the squeal.'

Harold, a bespectacled, dapper man of medium height, was one of the few people in the village who had a telephone. His little butcher's shop had rows of hams hung up on meat hooks and it was kept immaculately clean and smelled of scrubbed wood and sawdust. Harold really looked the part in his blue-and-white, vertically striped apron that reached down to his shins, and he wore his straw boater at a rakish angle. One of our Harry's jobs was to wash down the white-tiled walls, the chopping block, the counter and the work surfaces. Harold was urbane, courteous and polite when serving customers but was deferential to the point of being obsequious as he said, 'And how may one help madam?'

Harry said, 'He has the typical shopkeeper's manner. He tends to be a bit smarmy and oily, especially with the lady customers, and it makes you cringe when he sucks up to them. All the same, most of them seem to like it and, if he likes them, he often slips an extra bit of meat, a bit of dripping or a couple of sausages into their shopping basket.' He was good to Harry and he gave the housewives as large a ration as the law would allow. These now included Mrs Harris, as she had switched her meat dealer after Harry started working there. Maybe she thought that as we were part of his family she might get preferential treatment.

14

The Turning Tide

So another long, hot, summer holiday started and the great outdoors beckoned. In the languorous summer heat we played in Widd's field and watched the farmhands bringing in the tassel-headed oats, followed soon after by the bearded barley. We now had our George to think about and Mrs Harris said, 'Now, you look after him or you'll have me to answer to. Do you hear?'

'Yes, Mrs Harris,' I meekly replied.

As he was only five we had to keep a close eye on him, especially when we were by the pond, which was shallow and quite safe as long as he didn't fall over in it. Fortunately for us, Thelma enjoyed holding his hand and taking him everywhere with her, and anyway, we didn't want a little kid hanging around with us all the time – we had more grown-up things to do. Jimmy and I missed our mothers, who had not been to see us for some time now, but we just had to accept it when Gran said they were too busy to come.

In August Renee came to visit us again and we were over the moon when she gave us three wooden rifles that Uncle Albert had made for us. We seldom got shop-bought toys. She had brought a friend called Francie who worked with her in the steelworks. We heard her say to Harry, 'Middlesbrough station was in a right state when we left as it was bombed by a Dornier 217 on the afternoon of Bank Holiday Monday. The plane flew in below the barrage balloons, somehow managing to miss the steel cables. There were two direct hits and the roof fell in and they haven't got everything cleared up yet. You've never seen such a mess! There were great buckled roof girders and glass all over the place. Luckily there was only slight damage to the railway lines or we wouldn't be here now.'

Jimmy and I got very excited when she told us they were going to take us to the pictures as neither of us had been to see a film before. They took us into York on the bus, which was the first time I had been to the city, and the narrow crowded streets were a bit scary and over-powering at first. I held tightly on to Renee's hand as she took us along Coney Street where repairs to the bomb-damaged buildings were still in progress.

They took us to The Picture House for the afternoon showing of a Hollywood film called *The Black Swan*, starring the handsome, swash-buckling Tyrone Power. Before the lights were lowered we gazed at the grandeur and opulence of the place. We had never experienced anything like it and could hardly believe how comfortable the seats were. The brightly coloured cartoons took our breath away and we had a good laugh at Tom and Jerry.

At the start of the Pathé news, a big black and white crowing cockerel filled the large silver screen. We had seen pictures of Winston Churchill in the newspaper but here he was walking and talking, larger than life. Carrying his silver-topped walking stick and wearing his famous Homburg hat, he made the Victory-V sign with one hand whilst smok-ing a fat Havana cigar. As he visited a bomb-damaged area wearing a siren suit that bulged at the waist, the people cheered and shouted, 'Good old Winnie!' He was a symbol of hope, epitomising the bulldog spirit of our beleaguered nation. Renee said, 'Everyone admires him for stand-ing up to Hitler and his rotten cronies.' Because of him it never entered people's heads that we would lose the war and he had recently given their hopes a boost by declaring that, 'The tide of war is starting to turn!'

We sat transfixed when the main feature film came on and it made a great impression on our young minds. At the end of the film we stood silently to attention while the National Anthem was played. The feature film fuelled our imagination for weeks to come and during our games in Widd's field we became dashing pirates attacking treasure ships as we sailed the seven seas. We fashioned cutlasses from bits of wood and tied bits of cloth round our heads as bandanas. Jimmy played the baddie who had a hook in place of a hand. In reality it was the hook off a coat hanger but he said he was Captain Hook from the *Peter Pan* story. I said, 'Yer look more like Fred Potter', as Harry had told me, 'He's the signal-man at the York-Hull railway crossing and he has a hook where his left hand should be having lost it fighting in the Great War.' 'I didn't know they 'ad pirates in the last war,' I said, and got a swift clip round the ear for my trouble. Inside our heads we sailed the ocean blue and shouted things like, 'Avast me 'earties! Stand by to repel boarders!' and suchlike. The war games took a back seat for a little while.

When we started back at school in September there were a number of changes. The lovely Miss Rutter was now my teacher and Jimmy felt badly done to as he was now in Mr Fox's group. Miss Rutter was the unpaid deputy head, and although she was slender-waisted, sprightly and vivacious, she could be quite strict at times. I remember the faint waft of scent that followed her as she passed by and the touch of her soft wavy hair as she leaned over to check my work. Scent was a luxury by that time so I don't know where it came from. Maybe she got it on the black market. When she smiled her rosebud lips parted slightly to reveal a glimpse of sparkling white teeth, and Jimmy got jealous when I talked about her and gave me a thump in the ribs. He was eight and a half and was starting to change his mind about girls, deciding that maybe some of them had their good points.

There was growing concern over the increased number of road deaths caused by the blackout regulations. At Haxby there were very few cars but a fair number of military vehicles passed to and fro, and while the weather held, we were taken out onto Front Street to prac-tise the recently introduced kerb drill. It was drummed into us, 'Look right, look left and look right again and, if the road is clear, walk briskly across. Do not run!' We repeated this routine *ad nauseum* until it became a lifetime habit.

During potato-picking week Jimmy and I got a job at Haxby Lodge Farm but the girls had to stay in to help Mrs Harris with her cooking, preserving and pickling. They had been taught domestic skills from an early age. We were picked up outside the house early in the mornings and we climbed into a farm cart pulled by a huge chestnut Shire horse. It was nice to hear the jingling of the chains and harness of the sturdy animal as we clip-clopped up Usher Lane, and up a track that led off the Strensall road. The hedges were hung with black clusters of ripe, juicy blackberries and festooned with flimsy gossamer webs on which the frozen dew drops sparkled like diamonds.

As the horse calmly plodded along the furrow, dragging the whirl-ing wire-tined spinners of the potato lifter – which threw out potatoes caked in mud – the work was back-breaking. Luckily, we weren't expected to work as hard as the older ones and we thought of it as a bit of fun, glad to be earning a bit of extra pocket money. We were glad of the short break at mid-morning and again in the afternoon, during which an attractive, well-endowed Land Army girl would bring a huge steaming can full of tea. Wearing khaki-coloured dungarees and wellies, she was one of two new arrivals who were later to be seen in the village wearing green jerseys, fawn knee breeches, thick khaki socks and felt pork pie hats or a headsquare that was tied under the chin. They had been among the first to respond to the appeal for female labour as it was either that or be called up into the forces or do a factory job.

One of the farmhands lifted Jimmy up onto the back of the horse and led it a few yards up the field. Jimmy sat there with his legs sticking out, as they were too short to go round the horse's flanks, and he was terrified as he hung on to the mane for grim death. He shouted, 'I don't like! I don't like! Get me down! Get me down!' When asked if I would like a go, I said, 'Not on your nelly!' Being too little to work a full day we walked back to the house in time for our frugal dinner each day. Mrs Harris put George to bed at seven; I went at eight, and I tried to get to sleep before Jimmy and Ducky got into bed at the other end and let the cold air in.

Soon afterwards, a frisson of excitement ran through the two villages when a Halifax Mk II bomber on an air test from RAF East Moor crashed behind *The Black Horse* in Wigginton. It came down near Crow Lane, which was an ancient snickleway that came out by the old Vicarage up on Moor Lane. Derek Robinson was there like a shot of course, determined to add to his collection of military treasures. He had been potato picking for the Midgeleys at nearby Manor Farm when the crash happened. He had to keep a sharp lookout in case his old enemy PC Manging was already there on his bike, as he called regularly at the farms to check shotgun permits and the like. We saw and heard ever more aircraft flying out at dusk as the gallant crews set off on their hazardous bombing missions, and we often heard them coming back in the early hours of the morning.

The nights had started to draw in and the leaves on the chestnut trees were turning brown and curling up at the edges. It was a time for the closing of doors and the pulling down of blinds but there was still a bit of light after tea due to the double summertime. As we went for walks, there was a feeling of wistful melancholy in the air that was congenial to my spirit. The hedgerows along Usher Lane, which had become

ragged and overgrown, were silhouetted starkly against the crimson sky
to the west. The evening light tinged the fields and trees a ruddy, rosy
hue, and as we reached Jubilee Farm the upper windows of the old
stone-built farmhouse reflected the orange orb of the setting sun. Birds,
their feathers ruffled by the breeze, sat in long rows on the telegraph
wires preparing for the long journey south. As we came closer they
took flight and the sky was turned black by their rolling and wheeling movements. I could hear the wind soughing softly along the wires
and the countryside was peaceful and still. I missed Mam and Dad so
much and wished that I could fly north, and, if they didn't come soon, I
feared that I might start to forget what they looked like.

When Gran came again she said to Mrs Harris, 'I'm glad to say that
I've had word from the Red Cross that John is definitely a prisoner of
war. The Italians 'ave got 'im.'

'Well, that's a relief for you,' replied Mrs Harris, pretending to care as
she always did when Gran came to visit. 'They say that the Italians treat
them better than the Germans, and much better than the cruel Japs.'

Around that time the tide of war had begun to turn in our favour
and Mr Harris learned from his newspaper that Churchill had
sacked General Auchinleck and replaced him with General Bernard
Montgomery. He felt that the small, sharp-featured Montgomery, who
had total confidence in himself, was the right man for the job and so
it proved. Very decisive and thorough in his preparations, the men ral-
lied behind him, and by now the Eighth Army had the most powerful
armoured force that had ever been seen in the desert. Its strength lay
in its American Sherman and Grant tanks and it now outnumbered
the Axis troops in men and weapons. Montgomery set about making a
stand with the aim of defeating Rommel once and for all. The Luftwaffe
had been weakened due to their supplies not getting through and the
Allies had regained air superiority.

At a little place called El Alamein the Allies attacked while Rommel
was ill at home. On Friday evening, 23 October, Mr Harris sat listening to the wireless and he shouted up the stairs, 'The Germans and
Italians are copping it at El Alamein! Come and listen to this, kids!' On
coming downstairs, we could hear the tremendous din of the big guns,
the whoosh of mortars and exploding mines that was being broadcast. It was said to be the heaviest artillery barrage ever carried out.
In early November they attacked again, with Montgomery's 'Desert
Rats' carrying out relentless tank and infantry assaults until they finally

broke through. For the first time one of Hitler's field marshals was being thoroughly thrashed in battle. Rommel's troops retreated 1,000 miles back through Libya and the Allies retook Tobruk on the way. On 15 November, as mouldering leaves littered the gutters, Winston Churchill gave the order for church bells all across the country to be rung in celebration of the great victory in Egypt. The people of Usher Lane poured out into their gardens to hear the joyful sound of the external bells of St Mary's that had been silent for two and a half years. Churchill spoke to the nation with the now immortal words: 'We have a victory, a remarkable and definite victory ... Now, this is not the end. It is not even the beginning of the end. But it is, perhaps, the end of the beginning.'

That month the first of the new Canadian squadrons took over at East Moor airfield equipped with well-used Wellington Mk III bombers. This meant that we saw a different type of aeroplane flying over the village and many Canadian airmen came over to Haxby on their blue RAF issue bikes as their airfield was only three miles away. The Americans had arrived in this country earlier in the year and at first we thought that the Canadians were Yanks. Whenever we saw them we would say, 'Got any gum chum?' and they gave us packs of small white sugar-coated pieces of chewing gum called Chiclets that were wrapped in shiny red paper. Some of the cheeky lads would ask them for cigarettes and they usually gave them Passing Cloud or Sweet Caporal's. The Canadians seemed to be well liked by both the RAF lads and the locals – especially the ladies, some of whom were now wearing the aluminium rings that they had made for them. Their smart uniforms with the Canada shoulder flashes became a familiar sight as they came and went between the three pubs.

The day before we broke up for Christmas, Anthony Eden stood up in a hushed House of Commons and condemned the Germans for going along with Hitler's plan to exterminate every Jew in Europe. He said, 'Those responsible for these crimes shall not escape retribution.' This was evil on a gigantic scale and it was anything but a happy Christmas for thousands of people across Europe. The terrible plight of the Jews – men, women and children – was often reported in the newspapers.

At school we got swallowed up in the mounting excitement as we were kept busy preparing for the forthcoming Christmas events, and time passed quickly. I had a walk-on part in the Nativity play but was far too shy for any speaking parts. We got stuck into the eats and enjoyed the fun and games at the school Christmas party. Women were allowed to attend church without a hat for the first time, as their old ones were becoming too tatty and new ones were hard to come by. Gran came through on Boxing Day and brought a few sweets, nuts, lead soldiers and a wooden fort made by one of her brothers, which I thought was great, and Mrs Harris even let me play with it in the front parlour.

On New Year's Eve Mrs Harris let us come downstairs just before midnight to see the annual first-footing ritual: an ancient custom thought to have been brought to these parts by the Norsemen. There must have been a temporary cease-fire in the long-term bickering between Mrs Harris and her husband; their relationship seemed to have been one long series of storms and calms – with more storms than calms. Mr Harris stood outside in the snow like most of the other men of Wold View Terrace, the majority of whom had dark hair as that was considered lucky. They were all shivering from the cold with their hands deep in their pockets and each of them clutched a piece of coal and a silver sixpence ready to herald in the New Year. Inside the house Mrs Harris had a small whisky and a piece of cake ready, and as the midnight chimes of Big Ben were heard on the wireless Mr Harris knocked on the front door. His wife let him in and he said, "Appy New Yeer every-one. I 'ope t'war will soon be over and that this yeer will be t'best for a long time.' He handed over the coal and silver saying, "Ere's 'oping we 'ave warmth, wealth and good 'ealth in t'yeer ter come.' Mrs Harris handed him the whisky and cake along with a perfunctory peck on the cheek. This routine was carried out in all of the houses in the village.

It was to be another long, hard, snow-covered winter. One night early in the year we were woken by the unsynchronised sound of a German plane overhead, and as we peeped around the edge of the blind, snow was creeping up the windowpanes and the underside of the snow-filled clouds could be seen lit up by the searchlight. In the powerful beam, we could clearly see the black crosses on the wings of a low-flying Dornier, but it flew off and the night passed quietly. For some reason the siren had not been sounded and we were not being woken by it quite as often now. Throughout January there was snow and cloud so there was not so much flying. However, there were spo-radic attacks on the area.

On those crisp, wintry days we sat shivering in our classroom with the old, wrought-iron radiators working overtime in an attempt to combat the bitter cold, but the warmth did not reach far into the large, high-ceilinged rooms. One playtime, I went to talk to Jimmy and found him very upset and I could see that he had been crying. 'What's the matter, Jim?' I enquired. 'Well, there was this sixpenny National Savings stamp on t'corner of a desk. It was just laid there doin' nothin', so I picked it up, and before I 'ad time to 'and it in I was accused of nicking it. The locals always blame us if anything goes wrong and Miss Curry grabbed 'old of me ear and marched me off to be caned by t'headmaster. I told 'er I'd found it but she didn't believe me. Luckily, Miss Rutter came along and spoke up for me, saying I was an honest lad and she knew I wouldn't do such a thing. Luckily, Mr Fox believed 'er and she got me off.'

There was a school Savings Club and most of the kids usually bought a sixpenny stamp every Monday, which they stuck on a card until they had filled it and then they exchanged it for a fifteen-shilling certificate. We could not afford sixpence a week but we were given one occasionally as a reward for good attendance. The register was marked in the morning and afternoon, which counted as two attendances.

Just three weeks into the year we had just gone to bed when the siren sounded, and Mr Harris dashed into our room shouting, 'Come on lads, tek cover, quick as yer can!' We dashed downstairs with our blankets and scrambled under the front-room table, while the girls got into the gas cupboard. We heard the sound of a low-flying Jerry plane screaming by directly over the house and there was heavy fire from the local anti-aircraft gun. The noise was tremendous and we were terrified when a second or so later there were two loud explosions nearby that made the floor jump. We learned later that a Dornier had jettisoned two bombs. We clung on to Mr Harris as the glass in the front window caved in, but the blast tape held most of it together. My ears hurt a bit and the front door frame was loosened by the blast making it difficult to close thereafter. On York Road the windows of Harry's billet were cracked.

The next day – being a Saturday – we went up Towthorpe Road to see what damage had been done. Nearly the whole village and lots of people from Strensall were there. We had not been up that way since we had tried to run away. One bomb had just missed the railway line, making a huge crater in the railway embankment near the Golland Dyke, and the other had exploded in front of Manor Farm. Derek Robinson was there of course and he told us, 'The bomb blast killed a cow outright and t'flying, razor-edged shrapnel injured an 'osses tail so badly that it 'ad to be cut off by t'vet.' The regular soldiers and Home

Guard men were keeping people away but we still managed to get some bits of shrapnel for our collections.

At school during morning assembly Miss Curry regularly kept us informed on the progress of the war and she told us that the German army at Stalingrad had surrendered. The German offensive, that had started so brilliantly, had come unstuck in the terrible Russian winter and this defeat, on top of the victory at El Alamein, gave lie to the myth of Germany's invincibility. She said that the British were pushing back the Japs in Burma and that we should all be very proud of our brave fighting men. 'It looks like the tide might be turning at last.' We didn't know what a myth was and we didn't think much of them telling lies about being invisible. What the tide had to do with it we weren't too sure, but we thought it must be good news.

So the long winter dragged on and, as Thelma held George's hand and took him to the infant school, she had trouble in keeping his shoes dry as he tried to jump in every puddle with both feet. When we had the money, Jimmy and I called at Bryant's shop before school to buy a ha'penny Oxo cube or a small packet of powdered soup to suck on. We wished we had plenty of money like those at Harry's end of the village and the posh people who lived on The Avenue. We wondered whether the toffs really deserved all the privileges they had, and I remember saying to Jimmy, 'When I grow up I'm going to have a house full of monkeys and loads of red double-decker buses to play with.'

'I'm going to be either a tramp walking all over the countryside or else a train driver,' he replied.

Some days flew and others seemed to crawl by and it made a nice change when Renee came and took Jimmy and me into York on the bus. George, being too young to go to the pictures, stayed in the house with Thelma who loved looking after him. It was February and, as Renee took us round by the Minster with its graceful gothic arches, the snow and frost had relented a little. Words fail to do justice to its awesome splendour and Renee pointed out the ugly stone gargoyles that had melting snow dripping from their twisted, slavering mouths which frightened me. She bought us a lovely red-green toffee apple on a stick that had a nice crunchy flat bit on top where it had been stood upside down to dry.

There was an afternoon matinee with Bing Crosby and Fred Astaire starring in the film *Holiday Inn*, in which the hit song was *White Christmas* and we loved every minute of it. Renee bought us a packet of

Smith's crisps and warned us, 'Don't rattle the packets when the film's on and don't eat the blue one because it's a small packet of salt.' We were warm and comfortable in the picture house but I was a bit worried in case a bomb dropped on it when we were inside. Renee said, 'Don't worry. If the siren goes they'll put a message up on the screen to tell us to go to the nearest air-raid shelter.'

The bus was crowded on the journey back to Haxby but Renee let us have the only seat while she stood hanging on one of the straphangers. We had to walk back to Usher Lane on our own, as she had to stay on the bus in order to be at York station in time to catch her train home.

In March the weather turned treacherously cold again and more snow fell and settled, but it turned to sleet and rain later in the month. Some days it teemed down all day and we came in from school sodden. Because of the wet weather we had to stay in at the weekend and make our own entertainment. We played cards, ludo, tiddly-winks and draughts up in our bedroom but the fire up there was never lit and the house was always cold. On other days we had thick white blankets of dripping, clinging mist or fog and our skin became chapped and sore. After dark, when the fog made landing the planes difficult, the searchlights in the area were switched on for a time and their beams would cross directly above the East Moor runway. We could see them clearly from our bedroom window. As the Wellington bombers with their Canadian crews returned from bombing or mine-laying sorties, the lights guided them in.

Just before Jimmy's ninth birthday Mr Winterburn the postman, who did a bit of boot and shoe repairing part time, brought him birthday cards, but again there was nothing from his dad. Mr Winterburn had a wooden right leg which he swung round as he walked and his bike had been specially adapted for him. It had a fixed wheel and he used his left foot to turn the pedal while the other pedal remained still. Aunt Hilda came to see Jimmy on his birthday wearing her ATS uniform and she looked slim, petite and attractive in it. One of his presents was a brand new leather belt with a metal buckle. Jimmy really treasured it as very few boys had belts in those days; most wore braces to keep their trousers up. Aunt Hilda told him that she was now a nursing auxiliary at Fenham Barracks in Newcastle and was on leave. She took him into York on the bus so that they could spend some time together. After giving the three of us a kiss before she left, she seemed more upset and tearful than usual.

A few days later, Jimmy was with Dot in the kitchen when she asked in her slow dilatory manner, 'Can I have a look at your new belt?' He passed it over but the next thing he knew she had the belt in one hand and the buckle in the other. Jimmy flew into a rage, grabbed the buckle and threw it at her as he burst into tears shouting, 'Now look what you've done you dozy article!' On catching sight of the white-enamelled pail next to the wash tub in the corner, he grabbed hold of it and 'hoyed' (threw) it at her causing a small cut on her hand as she raised it to protect herself.

On hearing the commotion, Mrs Harris rushed in and wrapped her arms tightly round him to prevent him causing any more damage. 'Get up them stairs and stay there!' she shouted at Dot, before taking Jimmy up to his bedroom to calm him down. She fixed the detachable buckle back on to his belt and he was happy again, but he was also very surprised, as he had expected a good hiding at the very least. Instead she had taken his side and had given him a glass of milk and a biscuit.

Finally spring, with its promise of warm days, arrived. The snowdrops and crocuses went over and primroses, daffodils, cowslips and forget-me-nots appeared in their due time. Masses of white blackthorn blossom adorned the hedgerows and flowering bluebells carpeted the ground under the fresh green foliage of the trees in the woods. My eighth and George's sixth birthday arrived but only Gran and Renee came to pamper us and take us out for special treats. Gran said, 'I know you miss your Mam and Dad but they send their love and they asked me to give you your present and a big kiss from them. They couldn't come themselves because of their war commitments.' At that she gave us big wet kisses on the cheek which I immediately rubbed off with my jumper sleeve. I whispered to Jimmy, 'I hate all that sloppy stuff. It's alright on the pictures but that's not for real.'

Ten days later, as we were coming out of school, we heard a terrific explosion over towards Huntington village which was about a mile away. A cloud of thick black smoke was rising into the air and we learned later that a Wellington bomber from the RCAF (Royal Canadian Air Force) East Moor airfield had lost power in both engines causing it to stall and crash into a pair of semi-detached houses, killing the crew of five and two civilians. One of the dead was an old lady who had lived in the village for years. Several people – including Derek Robinson – tried to get to the prang, but it was too horrific and the soldiers would not let anyone near.

At school Miss Curry informed us that the Battle of the Ruhr had started and that Bomber Command aircraft were pounding Germany's industrial heartland night after night. There was a noticeable increase in aerial activity over the village and we saw lots of Wellington bombers, plus the new Lancaster bombers for the first time.

One afternoon, after a wet morning, we were playing on the grass verges up Usher Lane when Jimmy, who was a deviser of dares, said, 'I dare yer to jump over t'ditch.' It was deep and the sides were muddy and wet and I refused to do it. 'Cowardy, cowardy custard!' he retorted, 'Look, I'll show yer 'ow it's done.' At that he took a running jump but his take-off foot slipped on the muddy bank and he landed with a splash in the dirty water at the bottom. We were creased with laughing until our stomachs hurt. His clothes were clarted in mud and we suddenly thought, 'What will Mrs Harris say when she finds out?' In all probability he would be in for another belting. Thelma said, 'We'd better try and get 'im cleaned up and quick.'

The girls' sandals and our boots were in a bit of a mess as well, so we climbed the gate into the field and took them off and it was nice to feel the cool, soft grass under our bare feet. By then the weather had cleared up and the sun was shining as we headed for Widd's pond so that Jimmy could wash his socks in it. We wore woollen socks that had bands of blue and red at the top that always seemed to end up round our ankles. He rubbed the mud off his trousers and his jumper with a wet rag and whirled his jumper round and round to throw off the excess pond water. He then lay his socks and jumper on the top of the hedge to dry. Luckily it was now warm and sunny and they dried enough for him to put on. The rest of us washed the mud from our footwear.

On going back to the house at teatime we thought we had got away with it, as Mrs Harris didn't seem to notice anything wrong, and we sat and had our tea as usual. We had thick 'doorsteps' of bread spread with beef dripping sprinkled with salt and I loved it. Our Harry saw to it that we were kept well supplied with it. We then filled up with plum jam sandwiches without margarine and all seemed well until Mrs Harris suddenly came storming into the room in one of her rages. Grabbing Jimmy by the scruff of the neck, she hauled him off the bench shouting, 'Let me see your boots you sly little devil!'

He took them off and she closely examined the lace holes and found traces of mud in them. That creep Ducky had split on us yet again. Out came the belt and Jimmy was marched up the stairs and given another good thrashing on his backside as he lay face down on the bed. He wouldn't give her the satisfaction of seeing him cry, although he cried later when she had gone. She was red in the face with anger and the exertion when she came downstairs. 'Thought you could fool me did you? Now get up to your rooms and don't come down. There'll be no cocoa and biscuit for you lot tonight.' Ducky was allowed to stay up, as he had been a 'good' boy.

In school the days seemed to drag. The gardens were aglow with spring blooms, the lush green fields beckoned and we couldn't wait to get out to play soldiers in Widd's field. We would put mud on our faces and crawl along in the long grass on our elbows holding a thick stick in our hands to represent a rifle as we had seen the soldiers doing. We spent hours playing at being Desert Rats like our Uncle John and it never entered our heads that there was no long grass in the desert. Our imaginations ran riot and our 'battlefield' was stained red with the blood of fallen Germans. In our imaginations we heard the crackle of small arms fire as shells whistled past and machine guns rattled. As we charged at the enemy, we would fall down with a sharp cry and writhe around in agony. I suppose this was our way of coping with the horrors of the war. When Mrs Harris saw the grass stains on our clothes we got yet another belting. She didn't seem to understand that we were wounded war heroes.

Later that month as we came out of school we couldn't believe our eyes. 'Tek a look at that! It's a real spitty. What a beaut!' shouted Jimmy in great excitement. On the green there was a Vickers Supermarine Spitfire with the RAF roundels on its fuselage standing out clear and bright in the spring sunshine. Flaxton District Council had acquired it as the centrepiece of their 'Wings for Victory' fund-raising week. The war effort was costing Britain millions of pounds every day, and funds were desperately needed, so they charged a few pence for people to go and sit in it. Six RAF officers and ten erks were lined up in front of it to have their photograph taken by the local pressman. 'What's the difference between a Spitfire and an 'urricane?' we asked Mr Harris.

'Well, a Spitfire's got a metallic coating, it only 'as three propeller blades and it's a bit smaller than an 'urricane. That's canvas covered but t' spitty's faster and more manoeuvrable in t'air.' We were thrilled to bits when he gave us a few coppers saying, 'Go and 'ave a sit in it for thissen.'

As we walked up Front Street I took in the aircraft's beautiful proportions and its flowing lines. The thin legs supporting it looked so delicate that we thought the wind might blow it over and when we got close up it looked huge to us. We had only seen them up in the sky before now but to me it was a thing of grace and beauty. It seemed to be all curves with not a straight line anywhere. A wooden platform with steps and handrails had been placed alongside it so that people could get up to the cockpit, and as I climbed the steps I was trembling with excitement and anticipation. An airman helped me onto the walkway of the wing where it joined the fuselage and handed me a helmet saying, 'Here, put this on, son.' The little door below the Perspex canopy had been dropped down and I stepped through it into the cramped cockpit. The airman on duty pulled the canopy forward and once I was closed in my imagination took flight.

In my head I am now a Battle of Britain fighter ace going into action. I am wearing my Mae West inflatable life jacket in case I end up in 'the drink'. I sit down on my parachute, test the joystick and strap myself in. I adjust my silk polka dot scarf; pull on my leather gloves with the pure silk inners and adjust my close-fitting leather helmet. Then, after adjusting the facemask, I plug in the radio transmitter lead and check the flow from the oxygen tube. I have it all off pat. Then it is just a matter of checking the fuel gauge and the brake pressure and putting the magneto switch to 'on'. I press the starter button and the engine engages with a metallic 'clung'; the three-bladed Merlin airscrew turns slowly then the engine fires and runs evenly. I check that the door is closed and signal 'Chocks away' to my ground crew.

In my imagination, my 'Spitty' waddles across the grass, picking up speed and away we go sailing smoothly up into the wide blue yonder and I bank to port. I'm up to 400 miles per hour in no time and, as I float over the countryside, I glance to my right to see the others in Vic formation alongside me. My headphones crackle and a voice says: 'Come in blue leader. Dorniers at two o'clock high! Out.'

'Understood: am engaging: Roger, wilco [will comply] and out,' I reply.

I look through my gunsight, press the button and there is a terrific clattering noise. Tracer bullets stream out and the nose of the Dornier shatters as bullets rip into it. Thick black smoke, glycol and high octane fuel stream out of her port engine and she goes into a spiralling dive. I stop firing and pull the stick hard over. My machine judders and stalls then fires again and I swing clear. I see the Dornier's wing break off as she plunges earthwards. 'Got her!' I shout. 'That's one less Jerry bomber to worry about.' My Spitfire soars and wheels until I come back down to earth with a bump (literally and figuratively). Sliding back the canopy I lever myself up and out of the cockpit. 'That was great!' I shout to Jimmy. ' Come on, it's your turn now.'

One night after we had gone to bed, we were running in and out of the girls' bedroom and having pillow fights when Mrs Harris shouted up the stairs, 'If you don't get into bed and settle down this minute there will be serious trouble.' For a time we kept quiet but then we started messing about again. 'I won't tell you again. If there's another peep out of you I'll send Mr Harris up!' she shouted from the foot of the stairs. However, as we were in a silly mood, the running about and giggling soon resumed and the next minute there was the sound of heavy footsteps on the stairs. We shot into our own rooms and Jimmy was just going to shut the door when the belt clattered round the edge of it. The brass buckle caught him above the eye and cut his eyebrow, which started to bleed profusely. Mr Harris became really upset. He said 'Ah'm so sorry, lad. Ah don't like belting yer but Ellen meks me do it. Ah only meant it as a warning and didn't expect anyone to be be'ind t' door.' He dressed Jimmy's eyebrow and gave us all a sweet to suck on but Mrs Harris said, 'It serves him right. They had plenty of warnings!' The next day Jimmy had a black eye but at school he told Mr Fox that he had walked into a door without looking. He liked Mr Harris and didn't want to get him into any trouble.

Not long afterwards the good hidings and belittling comments started again. Mrs Harris, a real martinet, was forever finding fault with us and she was becoming more touchy and irritable by the day. She would fly into terrifying rages and lay into us. We were not her children and our noise and high-spirited behaviour seemed to get on her nerves. Maybe that was the reason why she would not let us bring our school pals to the house. I don't think she disliked them but if they were in the house she wouldn't be able to hit us.

Later that month Ducky went home to Newcastle and we never saw him again. We were not sorry to see him go. I had never liked him or he me as he was slimy and lazy (and crafty with it) and the dislike was mutual. He had an oily, sly nature, he sucked up to Mrs Harris no end and we had learned not to trust him or to let him in on our little secrets as he was forever telling tales. Tommy Robson, a scruffy ten-year-old lad with a ratlike face who came from Gateshead, took his place. He had sweaty feet and wore strange-looking boots, which he said were fancy American boots that his Mam had got from a charity sale. He became known as Geordie Robson at school and I don't remember much about him except that he was a tough lad with a good pair of fists who knew how to use them. He had no problem in dealing with the school bullies and it didn't take him long to sort out a lad called Harris who was always in trouble for fighting. After being belted by Mrs Harris he didn't stay long.

On Easter Sunday the bells of St Mary's pealed out joyfully on the warm spring air as white blackthorn blossom adorned the hedgerows. The same day the twelve great bells of York Minster rang out and were broadcast to the nation. It was 25 April and only that week Winston Churchill had proclaimed to the House of Commons that, 'The church bells can now be rung on Sundays and on other special days to summon worshippers to church.'

Harry, and several other local boys and girls of about the same age – who had all been baptised – gathered at the parish church where the petals of the daffodils in the graveyard were now brown and papery. Over the past few weeks they had been attending the Confirmation classes conducted by the vicar. Having 'come to years of discretion', the Reverend Donald now considered them fit to be brought before the bishop. Before they entered, little knots of mothers and guardians straightened ties, combed hair and fussed with the girls' dresses. Harry, who was to celebrate his fifteenth birthday four days later, felt a little self-conscious in his smart new suit.

The group was expected to have learnt the Creed, the Ten Commandments and great chunks of the Book of Common Prayer by heart. Harry gave his responses in a cracked voice that revealed the onset of puberty. Our little gang went along to see him confirmed and we watched as he knelt at the altar rail to take the bread and the wine at his first Holy Communion. I thought all that God-eating stuff seemed a bit vampirish and weird. The Misses Law and Barker, inordinately proud of their saintly-looking boy with the golden-halo, were beaming from ear to ear. Gran and Renee had come down from Middlesbrough, but they seemed to be rather quiet and sad. Neither my Mam or Aunt Hilda had come and Gran said, 'Your Mam is still working at the Red Cross Centre and Aunt Hilda is still in the ATS where she is a medical orderly and can't get leave very easily.'

15

Comings and Goings

In May, Mrs Harris complained to the parish council – mind you, she complained about everything from the postman to the state of the roads – stating that she could not tolerate poor Dot's slow wits and dilatory ways any longer, adding, 'I want her removed from the house. She is neither use nor ornament and is the instigator of much of the trouble with the others.'

When Renee visited again I overheard her saying to Harry, 'What children need is stability, not punishment and rejection. Sometimes the problem is not the child but the family that they are put with. They should not be made to feel unloved and unwanted. Not that I can find fault with Mr Harris; he is a really nice man but he should stand up to his wife more. She gets her own way far too much and I think her nasty, spiteful ways really upset him.' So, Mrs Horn made arrangements for Dot to be billeted with Mrs Brown, the school dinner lady, who lived on North Lane. She was a very reserved and quiet 'Grandma' type of lady who wore her hair flat to her head and tied in a bun at the back, and she always seemed to be wearing a crossover pinny whenever we saw her. Dot was delighted on learning that she was getting away from Mrs Harris at last and she gladly made the move into her new billet.

We were becoming more adventurous and roaming further afield. At that time of the year the white curds of the elderflowers were just starting to form and tall white candles of blossom stood on the horse chestnut trees. Down by the river the weeping willows dipped their green fronds in the water and the cloying smell of wild garlic was overpowering. The white-flowered plants were growing in profusion under the alder trees as I slashed at the stinging nettles with a stick, making sure that I always had some dock leaves handy to neutralise any stings. We searched for the little green bugs that made the frothy cuckoo spit on the plants. Apparently it had a foul taste, so the birds left them alone. We squashed the crawling grubs between our thumb and forefinger and called the large, green adult bugs 'froghoppers'. The Home Guard had fastened a rope round a thick overhanging branch of a willow tree to enable them to swing across to the far bank during their exercises, and we made good use of it. We played down there for hours on end, occasionally seeing a flash of red and blue as a kingfisher skimmed along above the surface of the water.

In school assembly Miss Curry informed us that in North Africa the last of the Axis forces had surrendered and that the 'Dambusters' raid had taken place. The bravery and stirring deeds of the bomber crews captured the public's imagination and their story was told in a major film.

In perfumed June, when Jimmy's Mam came to visit him, there was a right to-do. It seems that Aunt Hilda had saved up her leave entitlement from the army so that she could spend some time with her son and, knowing that she could not be put up at the Harris household, she said, 'I would like to take Jimmy back to Middlesbrough with me for a few days holiday. It will be a nice change for him.' But the words were scarcely out of her mouth before Mrs Harris flew into a rage, showing her true colours to her for the first time. She shouted, 'Yes you can take him, but if you do, don't bother to bring him back!'

Hilda, determined to have Jimmy with her, stuck to her guns, and going upstairs she packed his case and brought it down to the kitchen. Mrs Harris did not want him to go as Jimmy had been with her from the start and the argument became violent. She threw his case out onto the lawn by the back door and bundled Jimmy and his Mam down the steps and slammed the door shut in their faces. We were in tears as we peered through the kitchen window watching the furore. Poor Jimmy was scrabbling around on his hands and knees gathering up his things and putting them back into the small case; luckily the weather was good and the lawn was dry. Hilda, taken aback at first, became very angry, unable to believe that 'the old dragon' had been so intransigent. We ran out onto Usher Lane and watched them until they reached the end of the road where Jimmy had a last look back and waved goodbye. They then had to catch the bus into York and the train home. I was very upset and cried; Jimmy and I were very close and had not been apart for over two years. We had gone everywhere together.

In the days that followed it felt strange going to school without Jimmy and Dot, and shortly afterwards two of the little girls that had been with us at Sutherland Lodge and Grove House came to stay in their stead. Sylvia and Nancy Robson were sisters and they had been at The Settlement in 1939. Sylvia was my age and was in Miss Rutter's group with me, but Nancy was only six and was in the same group as George at the infant school.

The gangly Mr Fox wore grey slacks and a tweed jacket with leather patches on the elbows when he took us for cricket practice in the summer months. Seeing scratches on a boy's hands he accused him of robbing birds' nests and, when he admitted it, he gave him a good thrashing with the cane. This reminded me of what Mr Harris had told Jimmy, 'If yer gonna get caned, rub a bit of raw onion on yer 'ands and it'll deaden t'pain.' Anybody who larked about got a crack on the neck from Mr Fox's swagger stick and the persistent troublemakers and bullies were made to clean out the pavilion. The pretty, slender-waisted and nubile Miss Rutter took the girls on to another part of the field to play rounders, and as she ran around in her short, pleated skirt several of the older lads seemed to suddenly lose concentration and got themselves bowled out.

As the green of late spring became the gold of high summer, cow parsley grew tall on the verges and we saw ever more Lancaster bombers flying low over the village after taking off from East Moor, where the Canadians were being trained in their use. Gran came through again saying, 'I have had another letter from your Uncle John.' He was now in Campo 73 at Carpi, a small town in northern Italy not far from Modena.

'I'm glad to hear the Red Cross parcels are getting through to the boys,' Mrs Harris said, pretending to be concerned. 'Don't you have something to do with raising money for them?'

'Yes, I go round the houses collecting the contributions to the Red Cross Penny-a-Week Fund every week in all weathers. They are doing a grand job for the boys in the prison camps who really look forward to receiving them.'

Just before we broke up for the summer holidays Miss Curry updated us on the war situation: Allied forces had invaded Sicily; 150,000 men had landed on 10 July and were moving steadily forward; General Montgomery was leading the Eighth Army, known as the 'Desert Rats' after the long-legged rodent called the Jerboa, and the American General Patton was in command of the US 7th Army.

I missed Jimmy very much and when Gran came again I cried and pleaded with her to take me home. When Mrs Harris left the room I said to her, 'I hate it here and Mrs Harris is always hitting us. Can't I come home with you?' 'Don't be silly now. I'm sure it's not that bad,' she replied, just as Mrs Harris came back into the room and we were sent upstairs to play while they talked. When we came down nothing more was said. Mrs Harris must have convinced Gran that she did not hit us and we noticed that the belts and cane were missing from their usual prominent place.

Gran then turned to me and said, 'Jimmy is staying with Aunt Ruby while his Mam sorts out her discharge. He sends you his love as do your Mam and Dad. Keep your chin up and be good boys.' She did not stay long as she had to catch the Darlington train, and on arrival there she would have to hope that she was not too late to catch the connecting train to Middlesbrough. It would be a long tedious journey for her with the windows painted over and the blinds down, and she would not arrive home until well after midnight. Luckily she enjoyed knitting, which helped to pass the time. She told us that, 'Sometimes the trains are so packed with servicemen that they lay on the luggage racks.'

During the summer break we heard on the news that Mussolini had fallen out of favour and had been dismissed from office by the king of Italy bringing an end to the Italian fascist government. We knew it was good news but it did not really affect us and, as it was another lovely summer, we roamed far and wide in the local countryside. Pink-flowered spikes of rosebay willowherb grew tall on the grass verges as large white trumpets of bindweed were fully open in the hedgerows. The days were hot, and golden sunlight danced on the surface of Widd's pond as we tried to catch the newts, the silvery-looking diving beetles, the pond-skaters and the waterboatmen that skittered across the surface. On leaving the field we always jumped the drainage ditch and Nancy Robson, who had bobbed, mousy hair, and wore wire-rimmed glasses, thought she could do the same and fell in. She was covered in mud and when we got back Mrs Harris dumped her unceremoniously in a bath of cold water with all her clothes on. She got a good slap on the legs and was sent to bed for the rest of the day and we got an earful for letting her do it.

The summers seemed to last forever in those days. When Gran came to visit us again, she told us that, 'Aunt Hilda is out of the army and has got herself a job in the steelworks. Renee is still driving the overhead crane at Cargo Fleet Steel Rolling Mill and Archie is serving his apprenticeship as a steel plater in the Britannia Bridgeyard.' The steelworks were now involved in the manufacture of landing craft and amphibious vessels for the planned invasion of Europe, but the workers had been sworn to secrecy.

Sometimes I would see the little curly-haired figure of Maud Fisher tottering around in her mother's high-heeled shoes and wearing her jewellery and strings of beads. She was only four years old and I felt that she should not be out on the road on her own. Taking her tiny hand in mine made me feel more grown up as I took her back to her front garden and told her to play in there. Luckily very few cars came along Usher Lane in those days. One day I noticed Nurse Lealman's bike propped up by the Fisher's front door and I found out later that Maud had pushed a clay marble up her nose and her mother, being unable to get it out, had sent her older brother to fetch her.

As day succeeded day, I found the blazing sun tedious and irksome and I missed Jimmy who had always come up with good ideas for things to do. Flies and biting insects plagued us and dust settled on the leaves of the hedgerows turning them a greyish green in colour. After finding that Nancy had warts on the back of her hand, we thought we would try out an old country cure. Mr Harris had told us that rubbing a black slug on them before impaling it on a hawthorn spike usually did the trick. So we did this and waited, as it was said that when the slug died the warts would be charmed away. We examined her hand every day and, to our astonishment, the warts became smaller and gradually disappeared. It was pure magic! On the verges of the lane beside the tall, straggly hedges, goldfinches fluttered and pecked at the thistledown causing the tufted seed heads to float away on the wind. Mr Harris often worked until ten at night getting in the harvest; then our summer holiday came to an end and we went back to school.

I was pleased to learn that my group teacher was to be Miss Francis again and I always felt secure in her comforting and smiling presence. Miss Curry – in comparison – was rather prim and proper as she informed us that the Allies had taken Sicily in August. This meant that Allied shipping was now able to sail through the Mediterranean Sea to Egypt virtually free from enemy attack and things were starting to look up on the war front. She pointed out to us where these places were on the large world map before proudly announcing that, 'The invasion of Italy is now under way. General Bernard Montgomery's Eighth Army is steadily advancing northwards from the toe of Italy.'

At playtimes, Billy Pyecroft, whose dad was a member of the local AFS, could usually be found standing on a box peering over the school wall. He was a scruffy kid who always seemed to have a snotty nose and when it ran down onto the upper lip of his loose, floppy mouth he would lick it off. He was a bit simple and too young for school, but we didn't mind him being there as he was a likeable lad. The family tended to keep themselves to themselves. Young Billy would have loved to play football with us but he was too awkward and uncoordinated in his movements. His older brother, who was a good pal of Bernard Fisher, had been born with two thumbs on one hand. I heard Mrs Harris say that these birth defects were the result of years of inbreeding, which was quite a common thing in the old days. The wireless was helping to break down the isolation of these small rural communities and, as travel became easier, fresh blood was coming in, but there still seemed to be at least one idiot in every village.

I was glad I was not in the headmaster's group at school. It was bad enough having Miss Curry for singing lessons in which we sang mostly traditional songs like *D'ye Ken John Peel*, *Lavender Green* and *Greensleeves*, which I have hated ever since. The older lads said Mr Fox could be quite sarcastic and he sometimes humiliated the quieter, shy children in front of his 'chosen few'. He also forced children who were left-handed to write with their right hands saying it was an unnatural practice and against God's will. We called left-handed people cuddy-wifters. By this time the lanes were lined with sodden piles of fallen leaves and it was starting to get chilly in the big, high-ceilinged class-rooms. Cold draughts crept in and wrapped themselves round our bare legs like a cat and we stood with our behinds pressed to the big, green, cast-iron radiators at every opportunity.

When our nineteen-year-old aunt Renee came to see us, I could smell the cheap perfume on her neck. Harry was with her and she was saying to him, 'Think yourself lucky that you're with Miss Law and Miss Barker who only give you the best. They seem able to get anything they want. Money definitely talks round here.' The cracked timbre of Harry's voice had disappeared now and he spoke in deep manly tones as they took us down to see his foster parents in their comfortable home.

A dish of dried lavender scented the air and the homely couple seemed like a throw back to a more mannered age. Harry had nicknamed my little brother Podge as he still had a fair amount of baby fat on him. We were offered a choice of delicious cakes from a gold-rimmed bone china cake stand and drank our pop from real crystal glasses. Renee told Harry that their elder brother John had sent Gran a letter, and it seems he had been taken to Germany when the Italians surrendered. The journey of around 300 miles had taken eight long days.

In Haxby, violent October winds hurled the boughs of the tall elms around threatening to throw down the large nests of the ragged and ungainly rooks. Gran visited us again and told us that Jimmy was living with his mam and dad again and they were sharing with her friend. They had got back together after he had turned up in uniform saying he was on leave from the Duke of Wellington's Regiment and he swore that he was now a good Catholic and had seen the error of his ways. He promised her that things would be different this time round, and she believed him. Aunt Ruby had talked her into going back with him after seven years apart.

The ice formed early in the gutters that winter as tragedy struck the Bradford family yet again! We were told that Jimmy's mother was dead. The days in school dragged and I spent much of my time in a trance thinking about poor Jimmy as I gazed out at the dim November light filtering through the tall sash windows. As if the family hadn't suffered enough already. Poor Gran had now lost six of her eleven children with another one a prisoner of war in Germany, and she was worried to death about his safety. In December we had squalls of pelting rain and thick fog and we heard that two Canadian Thunderbirds had crashed on their return to Linton airfield from raids on Berlin.

That year it was clear and frosty at Christmas and the celebrations were somewhat muted and toned down but we made the best of it. Gran and Renee brought us the odd home-made toys and a few sweets, and Sylvia and Nancy's parents came to see them, which made me feel sad, as mine didn't. Nancy got a doll with a pot head and a cloth body that she loved and took everywhere with her, and Sylvia got a doll's house made of thick cardboard. We didn't get so much to eat but we enjoyed what we had and Mr Harris had acquired a few chestnuts, which he roasted for us. He put them on a shovel, and held it over the fire, and we laughed when they split open and jumped about. They were steaming hot and had a lovely sweet taste. We had collected lots of hazelnuts from the hedgerows in the autumn and we cracked and ate them, as nuts were very hard to come by in the shops at that time. We wore paper hats and pulled the crackers that we had made at school from crêpe paper and in each of them we found a boiled sweet.

So another year turned and we had snow and frost and had to endure one of the coldest winters on record. There was thick, low cloud for most of January which made flying conditions difficult and there was less aircraft noise as a result. The ice on Mr Harris's rain butt was four inches thick at times and the driving snow froze on the windward side of the trees and stayed there for days on end. The air-raid siren was seldom heard in Haxby these days so we slept well, but in school the days dragged.

Our history lessons seemed to involve long boring lists of English kings and queens who always seemed to have been good or bad, i.e. 'Good Queen Bees' and 'Bad King John'. The dates when they reigned and died had to be memorised and it all seemed to be a confused hotchpotch of things that had no connection with each other. History seemed to have nothing to do with the present day and us and I tended to fidget, switch off and daydream. I enjoyed learning about the Roman Empire, the Viking raids and the Norman Conquest, which fed my imagination that ran away with me at times. I also loved the Robin Hood legends, the siege of Norman castles and the stories of Richard the Lionheart and his crusades against the Saracens.

Geography lessons seemed to be used as a means of infusing us with patriotic fervour. We were told that we were the children and heirs of a proud and mighty Empire and a large, brightly coloured world map accompanied each lesson. It was printed on the outer waxy coating of a rolled-up oilcloth, which was slung over the top of the blackboard. Large parts of it were pink in colour and it was proudly pointed out that these represented the British Dominions. Our great British Empire spanned most of the globe and we were told that belonging to it gave us many advantages in life. It provided us with true and lasting values and we should be proud at being British, as we were a great race. Empire Day was celebrated every year at the end of May with parades and a special church service. We were, of course, unaware that the balance of world power was rapidly changing. Great Britain was no longer the power it had once been and this early brain-washing took many years to be unlearned.

Mnemonics were often used as aids to memory and these tried and tested methods were to stand us in good stead for the rest of our lives. We didn't have electronic calculators; we had to work things out for ourselves.

When we saw the Canadians in the village we knew which were aircrew by the wings or other brevets on their breasts, and by the white lanyard round their left shoulder that was attached to a whistle in their breast pocket.

On a snowy day in February I was sent home from school feeling unwell with a very sore throat and a high temperature. Mrs Harris was unsympathetic, as usual, saying, 'There's no need to make such a song and dance about it. Stop snivelling every time I speak to you, it's probably just a bit of a cold.' I developed a blinding headache and she put me on the settee in the front room and drew the curtains to shut out the weak winter sunlight. When I started to vomit, she put a white-enamelled pail on the floor beside me and I was sick in it several times. She thought it best that I should not sleep in the bed with the others and I spent a restless night on the settee where I slept fitfully and had nightmares. As I seemed worse the next day, she sent for Nurse Lealman and I was somewhat apprehensive, as the last time she came I had a painful septic spot on my thumb and, without warning, she had jabbed her scissors into it making the pus spurt out. However, it worked and the spot soon healed up, but it left a scar to remember her by.

When she arrived she said to Mrs Harris, 'His face is very flushed, except round his mouth, and his pulse is rather fast. I think you should let the doctor have a look at him.' She then cycled to the surgery to ask him to call and, in the meantime, Mrs Harris rushed about like a maniac dusting, tidying up the house and putting her best soap and clean towels out in the bathroom.

Dr Riddolls had been the local GP for the last sixteen years but Mrs Harris had not put her name on his 'panel' when she moved into the house on Usher Lane. Like most general practitioners of that time, he performed small surgical operations in the patient's home and he often worked late into the night. The old, bald doctor with the grey beard and moustache eventually turned up at the house on his little autocycle, as his large black car had been put in storage to save on precious petrol. 'And what seems to be the problem, tuppence?' he said, without waiting for an answer. He always called the local children tuppence and after placing a glass thermometer under my tongue, he examined me. He placed the ivory ends of his stethoscope in his ears but, unfortunately for me, he hadn't bothered to warm the membrane at the other end before putting it on my chest, and as my skin was really hot and feeling as rough as sandpaper, I jumped.

Turning to Mrs Harris he said, 'The lad has a very red throat, a "strawberry" tongue and a rash everywhere – except on his face. The swollen glands in his neck; the redness of his skin and the pale area around his lips are typical of scarlet fever, which is highly infectious and we must get him to the Fever Hospital at Malton straight away. Nurse Lealman will make arrangements for the ambulance to come and she will see that your doors and windows are sealed with tape before the house is fully fumigated. She will have to burn the clothes he was wearing for school and, by the way, my fee for a home visit is five shillings.'

Mrs Harris was none too pleased at having to pay up on the spot but she could claim it back from the parish council. When the cream-coloured ambulance came the men knocked on the front door and I was granted the singular honour of being carried out of the house through it. I think that was the only time I ever used it. The canvas stretcher had a wooden pole through each side of the canvas and I remember that the ambulance had small oval windows in its back doors. The house was fumigated before the others came in from school and Thelma told me later that Podge and Nancy were quite upset, asking, 'Do you think he'll die, Mrs Harris?' Someone must have told them that the disease was still a killer.

On the fourteen-mile journey to Malton, I was 'burning up' but I felt chilly and shivery and don't remember much about it except for the loud clanging of the bell. I was isolated and barrier nursed behind screens; treated with penicillin and I stayed in the hospital for two weeks. My bedding, crockery and cutlery were kept separate from those of the other patients and the nurses in their white-starched caps and aprons had to wear white gowns and face masks when dealing with me. I was given bed baths and was not allowed visitors. The nurses were gentle and caring, which was something I had not experienced since leaving Grove House three years earlier. My tongue was sore and I found it hard to eat, so I was given lots of milky drinks and soft foods like porridge, soup and scrambled eggs. I particularly liked the jellies, custard and the macaroni, which I called 'pipes' and I loved it when I was given honey, syrup and chocolate; things which we never saw at Haxby. The rash turned scaly then peeled off and as I got better I enjoyed being mollycoddled by the nurses. I liked the quiet atmosphere and felt warm and cared for, except when Matron, who ruled the wards with a rod of iron and reminded me of Mrs Harris, did her rounds. On seeing a man sitting on the edge of his bed, she blew up, shouting, 'Get off that bed this instant! You are either in bed or out of it, never *on* it. Do you understand?'

I thought the nurses looked really nice as they prepared to go off duty. The staff nurses proudly wore a large, ornate, silver filigree buckle on their belts and the red bands of their navy-blue cloaks were crossed over the white bibs that protected their royal-blue dresses. The colours seemed so bright and very patriotic and I felt happy and secure in their tender care and didn't want to leave.

After being discharged I was still weak and had to stay off school for some time to recuperate. During the day Mrs Harris allowed me to lie on the settee in the parlour and, as the snow lay deep on the ground outside, I felt snug and warm under a couple of blankets. She kept the curtains drawn as the light still hurt my eyes and I quite enjoyed being the centre of attention for a change. Gran came to see me and brought me sweets, comics and chocolate but I was disappointed that Mam was not with her. I thought she might have come to see how I was getting on. In fact, I was starting to forget what Mam and Dad looked like and their images were becoming as fleeting and as insubstantial as ghosts. When I started to wallow in self-pity, Gran shamed me by telling me what Uncle John was going through at that time. She said, 'He is a prisoner in Germany now and he and the others were taken 400 miles further east in cattle trucks at the end of October. So don't you go feeling so sorry for yourself. You don't know when you're well off.'

March continued in the same vein and as I braved the icy roads on my return to school the wind passed through my clothes like a flu shiver and I longed for the spring to come. The crocuses still managed to penetrate the soil's icy heart to burst into flower but, due to the long cold winter, they were late this year.

It didn't take long for the undeserved slaps and the beltings to start up again, but when it came to my turn I tried a different tactic. I had learned the hard way and as soon as Mrs Harris took down the leather belt, I would run full pelt into the bathroom and crouch down in the small space between the lavatory pan and the wall. At other times I would squeeze into the space between the end of the bath and the wall. Either way, when she lashed at me she hit the wall, the pan, the bath top or herself more often than she hit me. She would finally give up and go away fuming and mumbling. 'I'll see to you later, you crafty little devil!' she called over her shoulder. I would stay there until I heard her go upstairs then, I would dash outside and make myself scarce. When I came back she had usually cooled down a bit.

As the austere whiteness of winter gave way to the fresh leafy greenness of spring the days grew longer and lighter and we played out again after tea. We had the freedom to roam as long as we returned at the times set for our unappetising, frugal meals. By this time I had started to put a bit of everything on my fork in order to disguise the taste of the things I didn't like – a habit which persists to this day. The grass in Widd's field was lush and green again but we made a point of avoiding the fairy rings. The grass on their outer edges was darker than the grass inside the circles and Sylvia said, 'I read a book that told of children stepping inside these rings and not bein' seen agen. It seems that the fairies 'ad tekken 'em away.'

In April I was nine and Harry would soon be sixteen, when his apprenticeship would begin. He would then go to the abattoir in York once a week to learn the skills of the slaughterman and be taught how to kill and dress animals. Harold Atkinson was good to him in that way and he was to have a thorough grounding, which would stand him in good stead for the future.

I clearly remember the loud crunching of the gravel as the steamroller rumbled and hissed forward and back as it resurfaced Usher Lane. We all rushed outside to watch, taking care to avoid the flying chippings, as a man walked in front of it spreading the gravel with a rake. The roller had a big, whirring drive wheel and belt. The driver in his greasy flat cap had to turn the knob on the top of the tiny steering wheel many times to make the great roller alter direction by just one inch. I loved the smell of the hot tar fumes as the fire flamed and roared beneath the boiler. Unfortunately, I got a taste of a different kind of belt when Mrs Harris found spots of tar on my clothes afterwards.

One day we got a surprise when Renee ran up the side path and started hammering on the back door. When Mrs Harris opened it she was red in the face and trembling and almost fell into the house.

'What on earth's the matter?' Mrs Harris enquired.

'There's hundreds of cows charging down the lane,' she gasped.

'Is that all? You townies have no idea about life in the countryside, have you? A few cows can't hurt you. It happens every day. Have you not noticed the cow pats all down the road?'

'Well, I can't abide the big smelly things,' she replied, still shaking a bit. When she had settled down she gave us the latest news from home. On leaving the house to visit Harry she looked up and down the lane to make sure the cows had gone before venturing out.

Mrs Rust's two little girls had been billeted with Mrs Oliver in the big house on the corner of Usher Lane and Station Road for some time when their mother decided that it was safe enough to take them back home to London. There was a family wedding coming up and she wanted them to be there. Sally and Nancy were lovely, well-liked little girls who were never a ha'porth of trouble in school or out of it, and it wasn't long since they had stood beside us watching the house martins collecting mud to construct their nests under the eaves of the houses. They, like us, had been fascinated on seeing the graceful birds repeatedly swooping and gliding down to gather beakfuls of mud from the edges of a puddle. A few weeks later we heard that their house had been destroyed by one of the first German V1 flying bombs. Sally was killed and Nancy, the youngest, had to have both legs amputated.

At school we were kept busy rehearsing and helping to make scenery for a forthcoming pantomime. Miss Curry, who was in charge of the singing practices, had told us that it looked as if a 'second front' was going to begin quite soon. She said, 'It is vitally important that we in Haxby support the war effort by raising as much money as possible, hence the pantomime.' Mr Fox decided that the school should put on *Dick Whittington* as their contribution to the Salute the Soldier week.

The local committee had set a target for Haxby and Wigginton of £5,000. A huge board was erected under the school clock to show how much was being raised. We didn't know what a second front was but we got quite excited when Mr Harris told us, 'It means an Allied army is goin' ter go over to sort out t'Jerries in Europe.'

On Saturday 29 April, which was Harry's sixteenth birthday, the fund-raising began with a concert in the Wigginton recreation hall. In the evening, when it had cooled a little, Mr Harris took us to see the '25 pounders' – the main British field guns at that time – on the green. We were also allowed to stay up late to watch a PT demonstration by baton-twirling men in white vests and navy-blue shorts on the football field. It was the most excitement the village had experienced for some time.

On the Friday it was our turn. It was the day of the pantomime at the Wiggy Rec, which was well received, and Sylvia, Thelma and I were in the chorus. The hall was crammed to the doors and Mr Fox was as proud as Punch as he appealed to the people to contribute generously to the campaign. As a result £7,400 was raised that week, easily beating the target, and the people of the two villages felt proud at having done their bit. There was an air of expectancy as we waited impatiently for the day of the big invasion and the country seemed full of soldiers on the move. It was all very hush-hush and there was deliberately no mention of the increased activity in the newspapers. There were rumours that the east and south coast areas had been closed to the public and all leave was cancelled.

The Misses Law and Barker put up the money for Harry to buy a 1936 Norton motorcycle with a leather seat and springy suspension. Petrol was becoming a little more obtainable and Harold Atkinson had let him have some of his, and Harry thought he was the bee's knees as he cruised around the village on it. He had filled out and was a handsome, golden-haired youth by this time and several of the local girls had taken a fancy to him. He must have seemed very attractive to them as he sat astride his throbbing motor bike as it purred along like a big cat. He used it to get to the abattoir in York.

When Renee visited again, Harry said to her, 'I appreciate their kindness and generosity but I get very annoyed at Miss Law's obsessive behaviour with regard to so-called germs. She even puts sticking plasters on her fingertips and on the door handles. Miss Barker's brother, Arthur, and his nine-year-old daughter Sarah, came to see them recently in their pony and trap. He got really angry at the way she wraps her knife, fork and spoon in tissue paper and he told her what he thought of it, but it had no effect at all; she was as bad as ever after they'd gone. One day, when the washing was out on the line in the back lane, an old tramp came round to the back door begging. She flew outside in a panic and brought the washing into the house, terrified that he might have touched it and put germs on it, and she washed it all over again. I think she's a bit loopy and needs to see a "trick cyclist" [a psychiatrist].' At the end of Renee's visit Harry offered to take her back to York station on his motor bike, but she retorted, 'What? Are you kidding? No! Thank you very much indeed.'

At Whitsuntide, which was hot and sunny, the hues of the freshly burgeoning leaves ranged from light brown to bright green. The tiny new leaves of the oaks and sycamores were tawny brown and tiny lime-green leaflets were forming on the ash trees. The waxy leaves of the ivy, which clung to the tree trunks, were a shiny, pale green that contrasted sharply with the dark green of the previous year's growth. The seemingly infinite variety was a delight to the eye but later in the summer the shades would take on a darker, more uniform look. There were masses of pinkish apple blossom on the trees in the orchards and lilac and laburnum trees were in full flower. The hawthorns dripped with sweet, snowy blossom as birdsong filled the air. Unfortunately, the herd of Friesian cattle at Crompton Farm was decimated by an outbreak of foot-and-mouth disease and the brown-clad Italian POWs were brought in to assist with the culling and burying. Fresh soil lay in great heaps as they dug deep pits into which the diseased cattle were dumped and covered with lime before the soil was shovelled over them.

On 4 June high winds and heavy rain swept across the countryside bending the green wheat and blowing the crab apple blossom from the trees along the lane. Several Lancasters and Halifaxes flew over the village in the next day or two on their way to bomb the German defences on the French coast. Then on 6 June the long-awaited news came and we heard John Snagge report that the biggest invasion ever known had begun just before dawn. *Workers' Playtime* was interrupted just after ten o'clock in the morning with further reports on the troop landings and the people cheered and wept with joy. Nearly 200,000 men and 6,000 ships were taking part in the vast amphibious operation called Overlord that stretched for sixty miles along the Normandy coast. Some 5,000 planes supported the vast armada. There was a mood of euphoria throughout the village and we began to believe that we were winning the war at last and that we might soon be back home with our loved ones. In the days that followed the papers were full of reports and maps showing the progress of the Allied invasion and we followed every move forward from the beaches with great interest. The names of lots of little places in faraway Europe became familiar to us.

On a hot day in early summer the hazy light gave way to a glowering greyness and the air became humid and heavy. Black and purple clouds gathered and heaved up and before long we heard the deep rumble of thunder. Violent flashes of lightning crept ever nearer briefly lighting up the darkness of our classroom before Miss Francis turned on the lights. The clouds burst and the rain came down in stair rods and raced along the flooded gutters; it really pelted down. Apparently Mrs Fox was busy ironing clothes in her kitchen when she was violently flung across the room. A thunderbolt had struck the chimney blowing all the fuses in the electric box in the corridor. There was pandemonium and panic amongst the children, while in the classroom next to us, Margaret Mann — Harold's eight-year-old daughter — became hysterical. The normally stern Miss Curry, showing a great deal of compassion on this occasion, did well to calm everyone down. We were delighted when we were sent home for the rest of the day. Then, like a great lumbering beast, the storm moved on and the air felt clean, fresh and exhilarating.

Although it was cloudy on most days, summer was awakening, and as the runner beans sported their bright red flowers and the pea pods filled out in Mr Harris's allotment, he brought a bag of them back to the house. Mrs Harris gave me the job of hulling and putting them into a bowl. Nancy had just been given a clout round the ear for wetting her finger and dipping it in the sugar bowl, and to stop me eating any of the peas she told me to whistle as I worked so that she could hear me all the time. When she left the kitchen I got Sylvia to whistle for me while I ate a few of the lovely sweet-tasting peas. Unfortunately, Mrs Harris soon realised it wasn't me whistling and I got another smack round the head that made me see stars, and I was sent to bed and missed out on my tea — all for the sake of a couple of peas. She had said earlier, 'If you find a pod with nine peas in it, keep it separate from the rest. It is considered to be very lucky.' I didn't find one and it certainly wasn't lucky for me.

At school Miss Curry told us that the worst storm for forty years had halted all Allied troop movement from the beaches into France. It wrecked one of the huge Mulberry harbours being anchored offshore for landing troops, vehicles and weapons, and the Germans put up stiff resistance with many Allied soldiers having to pay the ultimate price. In the first month of the invasion progress was slow. There were set-backs and many casualties. In the middle of June Hitler sent over his new 'secret weapons' believing that they would win the war for him. The first of the V1 rockets fell on London causing terror and thousands of casualties. The jet-propelled, cigar-shaped, pilotless planes, which carried a ton of explosives, sputtered and fell silently to earth as they ran out of fuel. They were soon nicknamed 'doodlebugs' but the RAF fighter pilots quickly learned how to shoot them down before they could cause more havoc. It was said that they were now destroying eighty per cent of them in the air but 6,000 — mostly in London — had already been killed by them. Bombers with Canadian crews were flying out from the Linton and East Moor airfields to bomb the launch sites in France and Belgium.

For us in Haxby there was now a sense of time hanging in the balance, of waiting for something big to happen. Day succeeded day, each one much the same as the last, and we were still getting belted and clouted round the earhole. I had just endured a good hiding when Mrs Harris went off the deep end on finding that I had put my big toenail through one of the threadbare bed sheets and Sylvia was made to sew yet another patch over it. As the summer holidays drew near, school felt more like a holding pen than a place of education. When we were sent to do some hoeing on the school allotment, a stubby, wind-ruffled robin redbreast sat close by on the handle of a fork, cocking his head to one side and trilling away to his heart's content. A child's senses are wide open and I was filled with wonder and pleasure by the sweet song of the little bird. On another occasion, as we were out on one of our nature walks, we came across a German POW working in one of Outhwaite's fields. The fair-haired man greeted Miss Francis with the words 'Guten Morgen', before he asked her, 'How old are ze kinder?' 'Most of them are nine years old,' she replied, at which point he took out a small, dog-eared, black and white snapshot of a young blonde woman and a small boy. He became quite emotional as he caressed the faces on the photograph with his fingertips. There was a catch in his voice as he said, 'Zese are mein frau und kinder in Deutschland', before turning away to conceal the tears that were welling up in his eyes. Some of the POWs had started to carve wooden toys for the children of the village.

We were taken to the field to play rounders and cricket and Mr Fox bawled at me, 'Wake up, lad!' as I stood daydreaming in the outfield while the ball sped past me to the boundary. I was too busy watching the swallows, with their swept back wings, wheeling, gliding and fluttering to catch insects on the wing. My mind would often slip away when I wasn't looking and I would go into a kind of trance.

Gran started to visit more often and I sensed that something was afoot. Plans were being made for George and me to go back to Middlesbrough. I was excited and apprehensive at the same time at the thought of going home and seeing Mam, Dad and Jimmy again. Even though Mrs Harris, with her floppy body that spilled at random from her ill-fitting clothes, had made our lives a misery, it had not been all bad. We had been beaten, sent to bed early and regularly derided, and any praise had been very rare with the criticism oft repeated. However, we loved the countryside and I had shared many happy times with Jimmy and the others in spite of her.

16

The Return

George and I were so excited when Mrs Harris told us that Gran was coming to take us home, but when she arrived I sensed that something was troubling her. The RAF was bombing Germany day after day but I had no inkling of the devastating bombshell that was about to be dropped on me. Gran, normally so steadfast and controlled, took us into the front room, and as she sat us down on the settee there were tears in her eyes and a catch in her voice as she said, 'I'm very sorry to have to tell you that your Mam and Dad were killed in the bombing of Newport in 1942, so you will be coming to live with me.'

It was the hardest thing she had ever had to do. How do you tell young children such a devastating, life-changing thing as that? At first the words, which fell like hammer blows, failed to register and I sat there with trembling hands unable to speak, until grief overwhelmed me and the tears came. I don't know how long I cried for but it set George off and Gran, with her shoulders stooped, put her arms around us and held us to her capacious bosom. Nothing had prepared me for this bolt from the blue and the finality of death was just too hard to grasp. Mam and Dad had gone forever! In the space of just a few seconds my life had been irreversibly changed.

Mrs Harris had packed our cases beforehand, not that we had much to put in them, and, as far as I can remember, Mr Harris was out at work. The farewells were brief and perfunctory with no tears and no promise of any reunions. I can't honestly remember much of the bus ride into York and the train journey home except for a brief glimpse of the towers of the Minster soaring up above the rooftops. I must have been in a state of shock the whole way but I clearly remember us walking down King George Street to Gran's house in the hazy August sunshine. The long terraces of old, two-up, two-down street houses were brick-built and it all seemed so drab, grimy and grey, and there was a closed-in feel about everything after nearly five years of life in the wide, open spaces of the countryside. Gran had Archie and Renee at home, so the sleeping arrangements had to be changed to accommodate us. If Gran hadn't taken us in we would have been put into the grim Victorian orphanage at Nazareth House.

There was still no electricity in the house, which was lit by two swan-necked gaslights on the chimneybreast in the kitchen. On going to bed we had a candle in a holder, which was placed on a chair next to the bed, the only other furniture being a wardrobe and a small dressing table under the window. The coalhouse and toilet were at the bottom of the yard, so there were chamber pots under the bed for use during the night and there was no bathroom. The table took up most of the space in the tiny kitchen. Gran's wooden rocking chair stood by the side of the black-leaded fire range and an old, leather-covered chaise longue stood beneath the casement window. There was a cupboard under the stairs and a step led down into a pantry with a rectangular, white-glazed sink. The back door led into a small area under a closed-in lean-to, in the corner of which was a gas cooker.

As I climbed the steep stairs with their strip of threadbare carpet, I noticed that there was a quarter of an inch gap between them and the wall, and it dawned on me that it had been caused by the blast from the bomb that had killed Mam and Dad. The realisation caused a big black cloud to descend on me and I felt utterly bereft and alone. I sat on the stairs and sobbed my heart out for my dead parents and what might have been. Gran left me to get on with it and, when I had cried myself out, I crawled up the stairs on all fours and got into bed and snuggled up to George, who was sound asleep, and I must have eventually dropped off. The next day my emotions were in turmoil, life seemed wearisome and I did not want to go out or to meet anyone. I found refuge in the small space between the front door and the inner glass-paned door where I sat brooding for a long time – a sad, listless little boy striving hard to remember what his parents looked like. George couldn't remember them at all as he had been only five when they died, but I had fleeting and poignant memories of their deep and tender love. In my mind Mam and Dad would remain forever young and fair, but I began to cry at the thought that I would never again see their beloved faces. As another wave of grief hit me, I curled up with my arms around my bent knees and rocked back and forth.

In our society death is usually hidden from us as we grow up, which makes it all the more shocking when we have to confront it. The only other place in which I could grieve undisturbed was in the brick lavvy down the yard where I would sit feeling sorry for myself. Never again would Mam wake me in the morning with a kiss or take me on her knee and explain things. Never again would Dad dandle me; tickle me; throw me in the air to catch me in his strong arms or gallop and prance around with me on his broad shoulders. At these thoughts an unspeakable sadness welled up and my small frame was wracked by sobs that hurt inside and out. When the tears that coursed down my cheeks one after the other dried up, I went back into the house with my eyes red-rimmed and sore. I could see the pain and anguish reflected in poor Gran's eyes, for after all my Mam was her eldest daughter and who can ever know a mother's pain when their own flesh and blood is taken from them.

I seemed to see the world differently then and there was a void; a big black hole; a nothingness where there should have been a mother's love and the emptiness was unbearable. I had never felt more alone in my life and when Renee took me out to show me the bombed area, I became jealous of other kids when I saw them doing things with their parents. The roads had been cleared and the rubble of the broken houses had been made safe but the scene brought home to me the horror and the reality of that dreadful night. Powerful emotions kept bubbling up and in my utter distress I sobbed so much that Renee was obliged to take me back to the house. I was like a sleepwalker and found it hard to carry out even simple tasks. On the Sunday I went to St Cuthbert's church with Gran and Renee but it seemed as if it wasn't me walking around, the real me was locked inside. When the vicar spoke of Jesus Christ crying out, 'God, why hast thou forsaken me?' at his crucifixion, I knew the feeling, and I started to feel a sudden anger and bitterness towards Him for having dropped such a devastating bombshell on me when He was meant to protect us. How could He have let such a thing happen? What had I done to deserve it?

Later I sat behind the front door shouting at Him and the Germans, who I hated with a passion for taking Mam and Dad away from me. As I wallowed in self-pity, Gran must have heard me, for she took me into the front room and, sitting me down on the settee, cuddled me and tried to console me. But I got angry with her as well, as Renee had told me that everybody knew, except me and George, and they had said nothing. All the teachers and the nurses when I was in hospital must have known and they had kept quiet about it. Even Jimmy knew! I shouted out, 'Why did this have to happen to me? Why didn't you tell me? You lied to us and I'll never forgive you for it!'

The terrible hurt that Gran had endured at the time of the bombing and in telling us never entered my self-centred mind, but I was to feel guilt at the way I had treated her as I grew older. 'I was only trying to protect you. I thought that telling you when you seemed so happy would only upset you. I thought it best to wait until you were a bit older. I didn't want to hurt you when you were so young and far away from home,' she said in an apologetic tone. Feeling that God had let me down, I longed for someone to reassure me; to take away my deep sadness and to answer the thousand and one questions that filled my head. I became surly and diffident and suffered spells of melancholy with long silences as the 'whys of it all' gnawed away at me. Gran said, 'Still waters run deep', which I didn't understand. At other times I whinged and chuntered on and on, until Gran said in exasperation, 'Whisht now, you've got my head splitting. You'd better get that chip off your shoulder young man or nobody will want anything to do with you.' An enduring anger was to simmer inside me for many years and I told myself that I did not need anybody. I became reticent and found it difficult to show affection and just wanted to be left alone.

Gradually the debilitating grief gave way to a grudging acceptance and I locked the pain away in my heart where it could not be reached. My personal tragedy had eclipsed everything and the emotional pain lay there like a long, dull ache that never went away. Eventually there were no more tears. I had reached that stage of grieving when a strange sense of relief descends as the first wave of grief passes and I slowly emerged from my self-made cocoon. I needed some of that spirit that Mr Churchill had shown when he had said, 'We must fight or go under!' I had to buck up and get on with life. I decided that it was fate; you had no choice in the matter: what will be will be!

Shortly afterwards Jimmy called at the house and knocked on the front door as I was sitting behind it. Many years later he told me that he had heard a squeaky voice call out, 'Who is it?' It was great to see him again after fourteen long months apart, but luckily grief does not linger too long in the very young and by that time the blackness had lifted sufficiently for me to start taking an interest in the things around me again. Jimmy had known the same bitter taste of grief and loss as I had and had got over it, but it affected our outlook on things for the rest of our lives. We picked up where we had left off, as if we had never been apart, and he came round to play with me and the local lads nearly every day but, after our tragic loss and the cruel treatment at the hands of Mrs Harris, our self-esteem was low and we were lacking in confidence.

It took some time to get used to the miasma created by the steel and chemical works and the incessant metallic clanging from the nearby rail sidings. We played in the drab dusty streets and back alleys and got into all kinds of scrapes, but Jimmy's presence helped to lift me out of my sullen, withdrawn frame of mind. The resilience of childhood came to my aid again, and we climbed all over the mountains of rubble and the charred beams that were being colonised by weeds, and made dens in it so that I didn't have time to brood too much. It felt strange seeing the broken toilet pans, the empty fireplaces, the pictures and the wallpaper in bedrooms that were open to the sky. They looked like the insides of damaged dolls' houses and I felt a bit guilty, as though I was prying into people's private lives (or deaths).

Gran thought that we were out playing games in the street, which we were most of the time, but at other times we were clambering about on the rubble or in the bomb-damaged house on the corner of the block opposite. It had been boarded up but we forced the back gate and the door and climbed the rickety, creaking stairs, edging our way round the huge gaps in the bedroom floorboards and risking a drop of sixteen feet or so into the cellar below. It was scary but exciting and anyway Jimmy had dared me and I couldn't refuse a dare.

It was quite a while before Gran told me the details of that awful night. It seems that Dad had arranged to take some leave that weekend and Mam had come home to meet him, as they were to go to Grove House to collect George before bringing him to live with us in Haxby. They had packed a case with clothes, shoes and toys and had left it in the front room ready for first thing in the morning. They had just got into bed when the siren sounded at 10.37 p.m., as enemy aircraft were in the area. The warning was late and not many people had managed to make it to the underground shelters a hundred yards away on The

Common. They could hear the droning of a Dornier overhead as they stepped out of the front door. A bomb dropped right on the house and they were crushed under the falling masonry, never hearing the continuous note of the 'Raiders Passed' siren at 1.27 a.m. Renee had been eating her supper after a two till ten shift at the steelworks when the first of four bombs landed nearby, with four more falling into the river. She had dashed down Booth Street heading towards our house and was horrified on seeing the devastation. The wrecked and badly damaged houses were illuminated by a great column of flame from a gas main that had been fractured by the explosion. As searchlights and flashes from the anti-aircraft guns lit the sky, the steel-helmeted policemen would not let anyone near and Renee feared the worst as the area was quickly cordoned off. In her desperation to find Mam and Dad, who she loved so much, she dodged under the tape and an ARP warden shouted 'Looter!' She was grabbed hold of but her desperation gave her extra strength and she fought him, but eventually she had to give up and go home. It was Middlesbrough's worst night for fatalities with twenty-eight killed, including Mam and Dad and eleven children, and, as Gran said afterwards, 'If you hadn't been evacuated, you'd have been among 'em.'

It took the heavy rescue squads three days to dig the mangled bodies out of the rubble and Mam's light-brown hair had turned completely white, so that, when Renee went with Gran to the cold, white-tiled mortuary at the General Hospital, she did not recognise her at first. She told me many years later that, 'Your Mam's skirt was blown off by the blast and your Dad was identified by his tattoos, which included the badge of the Royal Artillery on his right arm, and by certain items in his pockets.' Gran said, 'Before the funeral service at St Cuthbert's church and the burial at Acklam Cemetery, Mrs Ethel Gaunt was really kind to us. She and your Mam had been very close and she loaned us clean white sheets to cover the mirrors and to put up at the windows.' It seems that in Suffolk, where Gran's ancestors originated, they held the belief that the reflection of a person in a mirror held that person's soul and it was customary to cover them to stop the devil gaining access to it. Gran then said, 'Mrs Gaunt kindly paid for the bodies to be laid out in our front room.'

At least I had not been there when the stillness of death had pervaded the house, and had been spared from hearing the hollow thud as soil was thrown down onto the coffins, which lay one above the other. I think my anger would have flared up if I had been present, when the vicar had proclaimed, 'Forasmuch as it hath *pleased* Almighty God to take to Himself Evelyn and Alf …' The Imperial War Graves Commission paid for a rose bush and headstone with their names and the badge of the Royal Artillery engraved upon it. In Haxby I had carried on blithely, completely unaware of these catastrophic, life-changing events, but I wouldn't say that my ignorance had been bliss.

As soon as she was able to get to the wreckage of our house, Renee had searched through the rubble for any trace of Mam and Dad's prized possessions but all she ever found was a bent spoon. She swore that Mam had a hundred pounds in a tin in the cupboard under the stairs but there was no trace of it. The rubble remained there until after the war ended, when it was used to fill in the underground air-raid shelters on The Common.

In early September I started at the local Junior School, the same school that Mam and all her brothers and sisters had attended over the years, and at which Jimmy had been a pupil for just over a year. The Victorian, brick-built school (founded in 1884) was tucked away behind a beetle-ridden pie factory (we called the shiny, hard-backed bugs 'blacklocks'), the flea-ridden Pavilion cinema and *The Acklam* public house on Newport Road. Half of the school buildings were being used by St Paul's, the school just up the road, which had been destroyed in a bombing raid in 1941. Miss Leng was the headmistress of the girls' school, the boys' head was Mr Hague and my teacher was Miss Trewitt, who was man-like and had a thin black moustache. It took some time to adjust to the smelly old classroom, that was crowded with so many strange people and things, but Jimmy was in the year above me and he protected me from the rough, uncouth lads in the playground. Being orphans George and I were now entitled to free dinners. Jimmy again showed me where the best sweets and lovely, creamy 'Dainty Dinah Toffees' and cinder toffee could be bought at 'Toffee' Turner's little shop on the corner.

At home we had baths in front of the fire in the zinc-coated tub that usually hung on a nail in the back yard, and we had to go to the outside lavvy in all weathers. Its brick walls were whitewashed and a supply of toilet paper (made by tearing the pages of the *Radio Times* into four small squares) hung on a nail beside the high cistern. To get to it we had to hurry past Gran's chickens – which were meant to provide us with fresh eggs but had turned out to be cockerels – that pecked at our bare legs. Archie, now twenty years old, went down Cannon Street to the slipper baths where he paid sixpence for a good bath every week.

Every day I carried the hurt of my loss with memories forever crowding in on me. I suffered morbid nightmares in which I saw my parents mangled in the rubble; their life-blood draining into the dust from the hideous wounds in their bodies, which had the waxy whiteness of alabaster. As the light – which had once shone with joy and love – left their eyes, they slipped away into the long, deep darkness of death and I would wake with a start to find that I had been crying. In my sleep-fuddled state it would slowly dawn on me once again that they were no more. They say that those whom the gods love die young, so may they sleep long and well in that silence beyond all suffering. In other dreams I would picture Mam coming through the door smiling with love shining in her eyes, and I knew that their spirits had gone to heaven and were watching over me and one day I would be with them again. I sensed their presence in the air that I breathed and in the wind that ruffled my hair. How sad to die in your thirties but, as they say, 'Time like an everlasting stream bears all its sons away.'

Gran was very friendly with the Reynolds family who lived next door but one to her. She had befriended the Nichol family when they first came to live in Middlesbrough from County Durham in the 1920s and Lily Reynolds was Mrs Nichol's sister. We called Lily Reynolds *The News of the World* as she was always gossiping and she knew everybody's business, and Gran used to say, 'If you want anything spreading around, just tell her.' One day, when I was in the back alley, her ten-year-old son Terry made some disparaging remark about my Mam – something about her being a do-gooder – and I saw red and laid into him. I beat the hell out of him and had to be dragged away as blood was pouring from his nose onto my hands. After that, instead of looking on me as a soft country bumpkin, the local lads showed me much more respect and Terry and I became good pals.

I also became friendly with the local lads. Day-to-day life took over and we played the usual street games of tee-ack, leapfrog, tip-tap and marbles (we called the glass ones 'alleys' and the big, much-sought-after metal ones 'bongies'). We tied ropes to the crosspieces at the top of the lampposts and swung round on them like Tarzan, and we played football and cricket in the street with a wicket or goal chalked on the wall of the gable end of the house opposite us. Most Saturday mornings we went to the matinees at 'The Pav', which we called 'the penny push', to see *The Adventures of Flash Gordon* or *The Perils of Pauline*, which always ended in a cliff-hanger with the hero or heroine in grave danger of death but always managing to escape unharmed in time for the next episode. On many occasions the film broke down and we shouted remarks like, 'Put a penny in the gas meter!' and stamped our feet until the film resumed. I even remember being taken by Renee to see Charlie Chaplin in the silent film *The Gold Rush*, in which he was so hungry that he boiled his boots and ate them putting the nails on the side of his plate as if they were small bones. A pianist played quickly or slowly to correspond with the action; the dialogue was printed out on the screen and the films were changed twice a week. Food rationing was still very rigorous and on returning to Gran's house we were often sent out again to stand for an hour or more in the long queue outside Meredith's bakery shop on nearby Union Street. After standing all that time, we got just one rice cake to share between the five of us, which was all that each customer was allowed.

In mid-September the blackout was lifted – after six long years – and the gas lamps in the street were lit each evening by a man carrying a long pole affair. We heard on Gran's accumulator-operated wireless, which stood on a shelf in the alcove next to the black-leaded fire range, that our hero, Group Captain Cheshire, had been awarded the Victoria Cross; Paris had been liberated; the Allied soldiers were sweeping through Belgium having broken through the Siegfried line, and that the Germans were on the run. Meanwhile, Hitler's new secret weapons, the terrifying long-range V2 rockets, had started to rain down on London. In October we heard that the first German city, Aachen, had fallen to the Allies. British troops retook Greece and landed on Crete again after an absence of three and a half years.

As the icy winter drew on, Gran sent us to buy a stone of coal whenever word got round that they had some in, and we brought it home on a rickety bogie made from bits of wood and old pram wheels. If we had a couple of coppers we walked down to the front room of Annie Storey's house to buy a bag of winkles in a paper bag and walked home eating them – pulling out the curled-up, snail-like molluscs with a pin. Still inclined to be moody and sullen I would sit moping for hours on the padded leather lid of one of the boxes on the end of the fender in which sticks for the fire were kept.

Gran would sit in her rocking chair in her pinny combing her long, greying hair that reached to below her waist, repeatedly singing, 'Come in to the garden Maud for the black bat night has flown.' It seemed to be the only bit of the song she knew. Before bed each day she had a bottle of stout that she swore 'kept her regular' and helped her to sleep. She was a good cook (maybe that's where Mam's cooking ability came from) and she kept our bellies filled with good wholesome food, despite her meagre income. We loved her home-baked fadgies that had a flavour all of their own, the like of which I haven't come across since, and her meat and potato pies that were very tasty and filling. We got jam (and margarine!) on thick, crusty, freshly baked bread and, if we were still hungry, we could always fill up with salted beef dripping on bread. Such a diet would be frowned on these days but at that time we loved it; we had a lot of catching up to do and were still quite skinny.

Gran went through to Haxby to visit Harry about once a month and Renee, now a pretty and petite twenty-one-year-old, looked after us while she was away. At school my drawing ability was finally recognised and put to use as the staff prepared to put on the Christmas pantomime *Aladdin*. I was asked to draw and paint a long frieze, portraying the genie of the lamp, on three long sheets of paper that were then stuck together and put up high on the wall around the school hall, and I was thrilled to bits. The recognition helped to boost my self-belief no end but I was still near the bottom end of the class when we were tested.

In December the Home Guard was stood down but it was not officially disbanded just yet. Gran told George and me that as we were officially war orphans we had been invited to a Christmas party at the Assembly Rooms on Linthorpe Road. There was ham and fish paste sandwiches, meat pies, jelly and custard and the like laid out on long trestle tables and I thoroughly enjoyed the eats; but I hated the silly paper hats and party games when children raced around giggling, squealing and dodging the adults. I got embarrassed and annoyed when the mayoress and the other ladies in their fur coats and posh dresses fussed and petted us and ruffled our hair.

It was nice to see the shop windows lit up and decorated on our first Christmas back home, not that we had much, but we enjoyed its never-failing magic just the same. We didn't get many toys or clothes and by now our shoes had holes in the thin soles and we put cardboard in them to try to keep out the wet. Gran made us tasty meals, with Archie – who was looked on as the man of the house – always getting the largest portion. He 'let the first foot in' at New Year when the house was open to any of our neighbours who cared to pop in for a wee tot and a piece of cake. Christmas was for the children and Hogmanay was for the adults and, as the year turned, the noise from the local works and the ships' hooters on the river was ear-splitting. The excitement was contagious and people's spirits were higher than ever this year following the good news from the Continent.

Enemy aircraft still appeared overhead from time to time (probably from Norway, which remained occupied) and when the siren sounded Gran hurried us into the nearest street shelter, but no more bombs fell on the area. We huddled in blankets while the adults made tea on methylated spirit stoves and had singsongs. Granny Knights sometimes had something stronger than tea, and when she sang and danced she showed her knee-length, elasticated, pink bloomers. Gran would say to her, 'Sit down yer silly old bugger and stop showing yerself up!' We kids thought it hilarious.

Gran was dismayed to learn that the Germans, who were putting up stiff resistance, had made a surprise breakthrough in mid-December. The Americans had neglected to defend the Ardennes region of Belgium strongly enough, as had the French four years earlier, and the Germans were sweeping forward again in the mist and snow. When the weather cleared the Allied bombers took a heavy toll of the enemy tanks, but it took till the end of January for Germany's crack troops to be overwhelmed by sheer force of numbers and the six-week offensive came to be known as the Battle of the Bulge. Meanwhile, the Allied forces were driving back the Japanese, who were a cruel enemy, and Soviet troops were advancing into Eastern Poland, and Gran's hopes of an early release for Uncle John rose.

So the long, bitterly cold winter passed and Jimmy and I played out in the streets, back alleys and on the Newport Bridge, where there was a steel sentry box in the shape of a policeman's helmet. We climbed all over the flat roof of the electric powerhouse that stood beneath the iron steps that led up to the top of the approach road of the bridge. Sometimes we swam in the filthy river with raw sewage floating past our noses, but we never came to any harm. At other times we went over the river bridge to a railway bridge on the far side, where Jimmy dared me to wriggle and weave in and out of the steel girders supporting the roadway until I emerged out the other side. Needless to say, I did it pretending that I was not scared of becoming stuck halfway along it, or of falling off the narrow concrete ledge onto the railway lines twenty feet below. On another occasion we were playing football in the back alley when the ball got kicked onto the lean-to roof at the back of someone's house, and Jimmy dared me to go and get it. So, of course, I climbed up and worked my way across the blackened top of what I thought was a solid roof, to find out – by falling through it – that it was made of glass, which had become thickly coated with grime over the years. How I survived to adulthood is a mystery, especially when Jimmy was around. George, who was now Gran's new 'baby-boy', was too young to play with us and he stayed at home being spoiled and pampered.

On a clear night in mid-February Bomber Command, with more than 1,000 aircraft, laid waste the city of Dresden. Over the next few weeks the Allied ground troops advanced and spread out along the west bank of the River Rhine in preparation for a massed crossing into the heartland of Germany, and it was now only a matter of time before Germany would admit defeat. In April Gran was shocked to learn that the advancing troops had found further proof of the rumoured Nazi death camps and crematoria. Thousands of bodies had been burned, after being stripped of their clothes, hair and valuables, with the ashes being bagged up and used as fertiliser on the land. She was worried about the safety of Uncle John, who was, as far as she knew, still a prisoner of war in Poland into which the Russians were rapidly advancing. We stared in disbelief at the horrific scenes of the skeletal survivors at Belsen on the cinema newsreels and never forgot. The shocking evidence of these Nazi atrocities only served to deepen my already bitter and intense hatred of the Germans.

Meanwhile, as spring crept on, we played cricket and football a little further afield on the area of tarmac known as the Linthorpe Recreation Ground, or the Rec. Occasionally we walked to Albert Park, where there were wide paths and grassy areas to play on. Beside its ornate wrought-iron gates were long lists of names of the World War I dead inscribed on brass panels on the white Portland stone walls. It was an exciting place to be, as well as a haven of peace and tranquillity when we were in a quieter frame of mind, which wasn't often. On going to the larger lake at the far end of the park, we were envious of those who could afford to hire a rowing boat. We played hide and seek in a wooded, hilly area known as Bell Hill, on top of which was the base of the old wooden post that had supported the bell. It was spooky and Jimmy scared us even more by telling us the tale of young Mary

Cooper who had been murdered here. I didn't like it up there on my own, even though the incident had happened many years back.

On the way to the park, opposite the large, impressive buildings of Forbes' Bakery, lay Linthorpe Old Cemetery. When you looked through the keyhole of the spooky old stone building in the centre, all you could see was blackness, but Jimmy put the wind up us by saying, 'If you look hard enough you can see daggers floating about in the air.' Close to the road there was a very old grave with a broken stone slab, and Jimmy said, 'If you walk round it three times and bend down and put your ear to it you can hear the spirits talking.' On doing so I received a swift boot up the backside.

The last of the deadly V2 rockets, which had killed and injured thousands, fell to earth in late March before the Allied troops overran the launch sites. In late April Gran was relieved and delighted when she received a telegram from Uncle John (prisoner number 220615 in Stalag 383 at Hohenfels at the foot of the Bavarian Alps near Munich). It stated that he had been liberated by the Americans and would be home on leave in mid-May. In it he wrote, 'I wish you could have seen the boys when the American tanks arrived here. We heard them firing over the hill, and about half an hour later one of the boys rushed into the barracks shouting, "They're here!" The poor bloke nearly got killed in the rush to get outside and see them.'

Gran was to learn later that because he and his mate Jock had problems with their knees – which were swollen making them unable to walk far – they had been taken across Germany in cattle trucks. Thereby, they avoided the Death Marches of up to 900 miles that many of their unfortunate colleagues had to endure, including his pal Joe. Most felt guilty about being captured and imprisoned and did not want to talk about it when they got home (including Uncle John). Their suffering had been overshadowed by the horrors of Auschwitz, Belsen, Dachau and the other concentration camps with their obscene gas chambers and ovens, therefore their plight was overlooked. In May, Uncle John and the others were brought home in converted Lancasters and Anson aircraft and, on landing, he knelt down and kissed the ground. Later he was to tell Renee that, while he was a prisoner at Lamsdorf, there was often a sickly sweet smell carried on the air whenever the wind was from the north-west. It was not until later that he realised what had caused it. Auschwitz concentration camp was only sixty miles away in that direction.

Hitler committed suicide on 30 April 1945 in his bunker in Berlin, and the Germans fought on for another seven days before the war in Europe finally came to an end on 8 May, with Germany being split into Russian, American and British sectors. In the divided city of Berlin the Russians built a huge wall to stop people from coming in or out. John Wade, Eric Ward and the rest of the evacuees came home from Haxby and returned to Newport Junior School, and we excitedly celebrated victory with a street party at which there was enough food and drink to last well into the night.

Before long Gran had the remnants of her family around her again, except for Harry, who remained in Haxby until he was eighteen years old, when he was called up to do his two years of national service in the Royal Navy. John was demobbed from the army, coming home after three years in captivity to a hero's welcome, with tears, hugs, fluttering bunting and Union flags. He returned to his old job in the Britannia Bridgeyard. Archie did his national service in the RAF and Renee, having given up her job in the steelworks when the men came out of the services, started work as a 'clippie' (conductress) on the hot and crowded local buses. Jimmy came to live with us at Granny Bradford's where we slept three to a bed and grew up as brothers before going our separate ways.

Appendix

The following poem was inspired by a visit to my parents' grave:

The Family Tree

The elder stood above the grave
her roots deep in the earth:
believed to aid, in days of yore,
fertility and birth.
A sudden blast of wind sprang up
from out a leaden sky
to set the branches thrashing
and cavorting up on high.
A pair of hearty leaves
came spiralling to the ground,
to settle very gently on
the grass clad burial mound.

As I gazed on the earthen plot
that stormy autumn day,
I thought of my loving parents
violently torn away.
On a moonlit night, as sirens wailed
in 1942,
they'd left their bed and quickly dressed,
planning to scurry to

the blacked-out street and the safety
of the shelters nearby;
as a single bomber (sounding close)
droned loudly in the sky.

Long, blanched beams of searchlights probed
the gleaming barrage wire.
There was bedlam from demented guns
and anti-aircraft fire.
Father, home on army leave, planned
to visit us next day.
Mother had the cases packed all
set for going away.
My brother, two, and me, aged four,
had long since gone to stay,
far away from the dangers
of such a fateful day.

They'd reached the door and turned the key
and quickly stepped outside.
A bomb came down; the walls collapsed:
in each other's arms they died!
The loving pair – still in their prime –
were buried in the rubble,
as rescue workers scrabbled near
with urgent pick and shovel.
Now they lie in their deep dark bed,
as in days gone by,
in cold embrace, with souls entwined,
eternally to lie.

Ashes to ashes: dust to dust …
We shall remember them.
Age will not weary them;
nor the passing years condemn …
The essence of their mortal lives
exuded through the ground;
taken up by the elder roots
and in its leaves is found.

Tears welled up unbidden, as I
pictured the awful sight;
the flames; the screams; the horrors
of that dread-filled April night.
So many were left homeless –
bereft, forlorn, and sad.
Twenty-six others lost their lives
as well as Mam and Dad.

I recalled the sobbing boy as he
sat upon the stair
and his shouts of accusation
at a God who didn't care.
As I stooped to kiss the headstone –
grey, lichened, cold and bare –
the aching void within my heart
was, oh, so hard to bear.
The icy rain was channelled down
the names etched in the stone,
salty tears streamed down my cheeks
as I stood there – so alone.

At that time of pain and anguish,
the loss within me burned,
for in my heart I knew my love
could never be returned.
I picked up the leaves and turned
and slowly walked away:
heart sad at living far from there
and travelling home that day.
Now many years have passed
and time has eased the pain.
Love of a wife and children have
restored my soul again.

The leaves were placed in the Holy book
on the shelf above –
a source of poignant memories
of lost parental love:

treasured mementoes till I die
and return to welcoming arms,
problems finally at an end,
and rid of all my qualms.
Our essences then will mingle;
our spirits shall be free,
borne upwards, incorruptible,
within the family tree.